five times lucky

A Novel

five times lucky

A Novel

P. David Temple

Cover Design by Allyson Paisley

Author Photo by Karen Temple

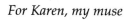

For Karen, my muse

"I greet you from the other side of sorrow and despair."
—Leonard Cohen

CHAPTER 1

THE AIRLINER GAINED and lost altitude with such astonishing force that a barefoot boy returning from the lavatory was thrown to the aisle carpet, then lifted momentarily weightless into BunnyLee's lap, crushing her in-flight magazine. The boy's forehead whacked against her shoulder and his dirty foot stirred the orange juice she was savoring.

"Oh my gosh! Are you okay?" BunnyLee asked.

Hands from every direction helped guide the frightened boy to his parents' row.

BunnyLee focused on steadying what remained of the trembling liquid. She wasn't going to drink it now.

The engines labored to recover lost altitude. Their hum turned giddy when the plane seesawed through another free-fall. The fuselage twisted and overhead luggage compartments popped open.

A pair of small antique drums she'd carefully stowed above slipped out of their yakskin bag and walloped her arm, splashed what was left of the juice onto her sarong, then bounced down the aisle toward the back of the plane in a topsy-turvy deeply resonant rhythm.

She exchanged worried looks with a half-dozen strangers.

Over the PA, the pilot apologized for the unforeseen turbulence. A flight attendant followed with an invitation to all who felt the need to avail themselves of one of the airline industry's few remaining cost-free amenities—the Air Sickness Bags or ASBs for short as he thereafter referred to them, "using both hands whenever possible! In the unlikely event of a water landing…" the steward continued.

None of this seemed like business as usual. The overnight flight originating in Bangkok was still an hour west of Los Angeles out over the mighty Pacific. The thought of relying on a seat cushion as a flotation device in that vast, storm-roiled, undulating ocean below seemed preposterous.

The girl in the seat next to BunnyLee, whose headphones leaked Goth heavy metal for the past sixteen hours and who was not shy about singing along loudly and off-key, spoke to BunnyLee for the first time.

"We are all going to die."

BunnyLee was not ready to die! She was still in her twenties. Her life was a harvest basket of ripe, juicy, un-tasted fruit. There were ten thousand dreams yet unrealized—wrongs she meant to right, places she intended to visit, career paths unexplored, people unmet, love untendered.

Notably, fame was no longer the top of that list. It had sunk near the bottom among other passing interests like conquering Everest and leech farming. She was older now, more sensible.

Religion was still the big unanswered question. BunnyLee was open to cosmic notions. She wanted to believe in something transcendent. Something she could hold on to in times of need. Like now!

She had no Higher Being to turn to.

Those antique drums packed as a wedding gift were artifacts from an era when cultures were lavish with religious ceremony. Bumming around Southeast Asia, BunnyLee admired what remained of those ancient traditions; they confirmed to the faithful that individuals were a part of something bigger. She sought out the pageantry and delighted in the ritualism. She was specifically drawn to the Hindu female deities. Their colorful wardrobe informed the way she was dressed today in a green and beige silk wrap-around and woven sandals—not exactly plane crash attire.

The unforeseen turbulence was getting worse. People were praying. A man was sobbing.

BunnyLee's mother would be saying the Twenty-Third Psalm, placing her fate in the hands of her Shepherd. BunnyLee had never felt that connection. Up until now BunnyLee had gotten through the rough patches in life simply by feeling lucky. In fact, a shaman priest at the Bayan Temple in Cambodia artfully measured her chakra with sticks and declared, "You are five times lucky!"

She cast a wide net in her reading, cherry-picking ideas. She knew she was not alone in her reasoned doubt. When she read that Kierkegaard, the earliest Existentialist, wrote: "I must find a truth that is true for me...the idea from which I can live or die," BunnyLee felt that this was what she was searching for, too.

The clock was ticking on eternal salvation.

"Do you think they recycle these Air Sickness Bags?" the girl next to her asked.

BunnyLee gave her a quick glance to see if she was kidding. Either way, she was impressed by the young teenager's environmentalist spunk. Traveling halfway around the world added significantly to one's lifetime carbon footprint. The fact that BunnyLee could embark on such a journey simply to be a bridesmaid at her friend Heather's wedding did portend ominous consequences for the future habitability of the planet. Today's turbulence was the foretold result of worldwide political dithering. And BunnyLee had neglected to factor the environmental impact of a world filling up with used nausea bags, one of which could possibly be hers. She clearly wasn't doing her part to save the world from global warming.

"It says here on the bottom that the bag's made of 100% recycled material," BunnyLee said, adding a measure of hope to the subject of salvation.

"Well, I doubt these were made out of used bags!" the Goth girl said. She either had the world's driest sense of humor or, more likely, the prospect of crashing had unhinged her.

BunnyLee dared not turn her head to check. The jarring motions of the plane could surely wrench her neck.

"The Buddhists believe in a form of metaphysical recycling," BunnyLee said to buck the girl up. "Something like the soul never dying, but rather, being forever recycled through different forms of existence." This struck BunnyLee as a comforting thought.

"Yeah, but if they don't actually recycle the used bags, then the cycle ends here!"

The plane took a sudden dip, straining their seat belts and then, just as gracelessly, regained altitude. The girl grabbed BunnyLee's arm and dug in.

"We're all going to die!"

"I know, you said that, but...that really hurts!"

Her seatmate wouldn't let go.

"I don't want to die alone!"

"Okay, just not the fingernails!"

BunnyLee placed her hand over the girl's. Together they waited for the flight to reach its unforeseeable end. There were people who would miss BunnyLee when she was gone and she sorrowfully bid them all a happy life.

The girl chose to use her Air Sickness Bag after all and BunnyLee noted how using only one hand instead of two contributed greatly to the sloppy results. She gave the girl a tissue to wipe her nose ring and black tunic.

"The Existentialists believe that life begins at the other side of despair," BunnyLee said, guessing that alienation was a subject more in line with a withdrawn teenager's angst-ridden outlook, "where nausea gives way to elation."

The girl didn't respond, so BunnyLee dropped it. Just as well. She too was experiencing the dizziness of nausea. She focused her mind on quelling the urge. She held the paper bag open with both hands just in case.

During a break in the action, the flight attendant came through with a giant trash bag to collect the used ASBs. He offered replacements for those spendthrifts onboard who weren't content with just one.

"Do they recycle these bags?" the Goth girl asked.

The man looked at BunnyLee for a reaction.

"What an interesting question! I'm going to go out on a limb here and say, doubtful. But if you'd like, I can bring you a suggestion form to fill out. Those I know are one hundred percent recycled."

"But does anyone read them before they're recycled?"

"Whoops, there you've got me again. I'm wanting to say yes, but..."

When the wheels finally hit the tarmac, there was a cheer from the passengers. BunnyLee was buoyed with collective relief. It was definitely a feeling of elation, too soon to tell whether the Dizziness of Nausea had changed her in any fundamental existential way. But her faith in luck was restored. She felt lucky to be alive. They were all lucky to be alive.

She heard her drums finding their way back to her. Beat by beat, people tapped the taut skins as they handed them forward—a makeshift ceremony in the celebration of living. She raised her hand to identify herself as their owner. Others raised their hands to point the way and it became a gesture of kinship. Intricate drum duos brought smiles to the faces of these fellow travelers, as did the rhythmless riffs. In this every-man-for-himself modern world, here was evidence that they were all in it together.

Once out of the plane, there was no time to dawdle. BunnyLee left the harrowing experience behind and joined an increasing number of people from a dozen jumbo jets disembarking simultaneously from all over the world. BunnyLee quickened her pace. She was anxious about getting to the hotel in time for a last-minute fitting before tonight's rehearsal dinner. Others no doubt had tight schedules, too. So much for unanimity. An unspoken race among the fit sprang up to outdistance the tired, hungry and huddled masses into America.

The immigration hall was teeming. She settled into the line of other returning citizens. She took a deep breath to slow her pulse. She was just so happy to be on firm ground! She balanced her shoulder bag on her rolling carry-on and relaxed her shoulders.

The line did not appear to be moving. The kiosks were down.

She checked her watch. Another deep breath. She had come so far and jumped over so many hurdles to get here in time. She didn't want to disappoint Heather by being late.

A man in a crisp dark suit with what looked like a security earpiece motioned to her in line.

"Me?" BunnyLee looked around to see if there was some mistake. "Did I do something wrong?"

"Courtesy Service."

He unhooked the rope for BunnyLee to step out of the queue and re-hooked it behind her.

"VIP Treatment," one of her fellow travelers whispered to a companion, "for celebrities."

BunnyLee was escorted to the front. She wondered who it was she was being mistaken for. She handed her passport to the immigration officer. Things were looking up.

"Love yer smile, Ms....Welles!" the officer said.

"Huh? Really? Thanks!"

Minutes later she handed her declaration form to the Customs Officer, who winked at her.

"Operators are standing by!" the woman said in a sultry tone.

It sounded like the punchline of a trending joke that BunnyLee clearly was not in on.

Through the sliding door and into the Southern California daylight with her checked bag in tow, BunnyLee felt invigorated. She waved off a porter.

"Nice teeth!' the man said as she passed.

"Thanks!"

She wondered again who it might be that everyone thought she was. She texted Heather, "Cleared customs in record time!" Obviously, fame had its perks.

She closed her eyes in the back seat of the Lyft. It was midnight back home. The physical stress of being squeezed on a plane for nineteen hours with its roller coaster finale, coupled with the financial squeeze to her pocketbook, took their toll on her normally sunny disposition. The cost of her bridesmaid dress was more than some of her students in Thailand earned in a year. She'd had to take a leave of absence for the duration of the summer term—another financial hit. She fought back a growing feeling of desperation with the sunnier realization that the hard part of the trip was now behind her. It was time to enjoy herself.

Heather had sweetened the deal by offering BunnyLee her apartment for two weeks while the newlyweds honeymooned in Mexico and she'd thrown in the use of her car while they were away. Heather was BunnyLee's roommate from college, and events like weddings were once-in-a-lifetime events. Presumably.

Anyway, she couldn't say no to being there for Heather.

BunnyLee looked forward to seeing a gang of friends from her acting days at UCLA. Even an old boyfriend, Ted, would be there and she was O.K. with that. He achieved a measure of success as a stand-up comedian and she was happy for him. In those college days BunnyLee was the one cast in the lead roles. She was the one everyone said had the best chance of making it big.

She felt a pang of regret for having walked away from it all.

She reassured herself she was a better person for all her

travels. Her journey was not just a journey to foreign lands; it was a philosophical journey, a journey of self-discovery. She wondered whether this might translate into her being a better actor. Not that she planned to tread the boards again.

"You could even go to some auditions while you're here," Heather had written. "You know, just for the fun of it!"

"Maybe," BunnyLee replied. She'd never found auditions to be fun.

The car was off the highway, headed up Wilshire Boulevard, inching along where the road merged with Santa Monica Boulevard. The driver, a Pakistani, his hair wrapped in a headscarf, studied her in his rearview mirror. He held up his phone for a selfie that included BunnyLee over his right shoulder.

"Smile!"

He pointed up at a billboard and he took a picture of that, too. BunnyLee slid across the seat and lowered her window for a better view as they crept along.

From her acute angle she could see a billboard promoting The Wrestling Jumbo Slam Pay-Per-View coming up next month in Las Vegas featuring a guy named the Dust Devil. Next, coming into view, was a billboard with a huge close-up of a woman's face, a blonde woman, young, one of those pretty faces that advertisers often chose for its fetching smile. There was a knowing look that belied a hidden secret, like the woman posing knew something that other people didn't know. Like she knew the way to a better smile because the name of the product was Love Your Smile!

BunnyLee didn't get what was so remarkable about either ad until the driver said in his precise style of English.

"Is you, right?"

BunnyLee looked again. It did look like her.

"Operators are standing by, right?" he said.

There was that single dimple in the poster woman's left cheek that gave her that uneven, enigmatic, crooked smile.

"Omigod!" It was definitely her.

"Over there, too. Big sign!"

A well-dressed man jaywalking through the slow-moving cars in front of the Beverly Wilshire Hotel gave BunnyLee a double-take. BunnyLee rolled her window back up.

She counted six more billboards before they turned onto Coldwater Canyon. And there she was on the sides of every city bus.

BunnyLee sent Heather a follow up text, "WTF?!!!"
Heather responded, "Love your smile!"

At the Sportsmen's Lodge the other bridesmaids, including two from her old improv class who hadn't exactly been pals, greeted her with squeals. Their boyfriends stood near the poolside bar and jockeyed to meet her. Out came the cameras for more selfies featuring BunnyLee. A Dial-a-Denture spot she'd done before she left was an internet phenomenon. It recently morphed into a billboard campaign for teeth whitening gel that went up seemingly overnight. Without knowing it and against all odds, she'd become famous.

"I didn't know how to tell you," Heather said. "The signs literally just happened. And besides, if I had, you probably wouldn't have come!"

Heather was right about that. BunnyLee loved acting, but she shied away from the attention that so many in her circle of schoolmates craved.

Four years ago, on a lark, BunnyLee answered an open call for non-union actors to play operators in an infomercial for a startup company that sold dentures online. They were debuting a low-budget promotion for late-night TV. BunnyLee was originally hired as an on-camera extra in a non-speaking role sitting at a phone bank in a room full of nice-looking young operators 'standing by to take your call!'

The union actress who was cast as the lead arrived that morning of the shoot with a huge boil on her forehead. Makeup could hide the red color, but the boil was growing into a full-scale beauty emergency. It was somewhere between humungous and ginormous depending upon whom you asked. The clients and agency were in panic mode. Another eligible actress was asked to read the copy and her performance was so dry BunnyLee had to laugh. She could tell by the pained reaction of the director that he wanted something else. An old acting teacher taught her a fallback auditioning technique: when all else fails, seduce. BunnyLee raised her hand and asked to read. The director shrugged and the agency gave their okay. She spoke the words in as seductive a way as their meaning would allow—akin to Marilyn Monroe in *Gentlemen Prefer Blondes*, "Operators are standing by!" And she winked. She was afraid she'd way overdone it, but the director was smiling. A couple of alternate takes just to be sure along with a series of still-shots and they had it in the can. At the last minute the director crafted a tagline for her to say—"Love your smile!" and it was a wrap. She got her Screen Actors Guild union card out of the deal, too. Yeah, and an agent. It was a slam-dunk.

The Dial-a-Denture campaign opened without fanfare. Some puny residual checks dribbled in, then nothing. Her short career was apparently in the dumps and money was in short supply. When the opportunity to teach English as a second language in Bangkok came along, BunnyLee thought about giving that a go. She called her new agent, Angelo, at Theatrical Management Inc. for his opinion.

"You're young. What people want today is experience," was what he told her. She wasn't sure that the man even remembered who she was. She felt invisible—just another pretty face in a city of pretty faces. She told him she would need to be out of the country for a year and he said, "It is what it is. You gotta do what you gotta do."

What she did do was get on a plane, and until now, hadn't looked back. One year had turned into four.

At tonight's dinner, BunnyLee found her place two empty chairs away from Ted.

"I see I'm at the celebrity table," BunnyLee said. She moved her name-card next to his and sat.

"How does it feel to be famous?" he asked.

"Me? I was referring to you. I hear your stand-up routine is really taking off."

"I have a following. Nothing like yours."

"I don't know whether that's a good thing or bad. I couldn't check into the hotel today without everyone in the lobby taking a picture with me first. I guess it was fun. The bellhop made a big show of getting down on one knee and proposing to me."

"Impressive! In the years we dated I never had the courage to do that. I wonder what your answer would have been if I had?"

"Good question! Our parting was amicable, though, wasn't it?"

"I remember you stopped laughing at my jokes."

"I remember you stopped writing new ones."

"I wrote a bunch of ex-girlfriend jokes after you left."

"Really? I've become your muse now, after the fact?"

"It's my most popular routine, part of an evening I call Ted Talks."

"Cute. Is the audience laughing with me or at me?"

"Mostly at you."

"Thanks a lot!"

She knew he was kidding in that deadpan manner of his, or at least she hoped he was. Their relationship had always tilted toward the competitive, but he'd never made her the butt of his jokes.

"This just keeps getting better and better," she said. "Because I am pretty certain that people are laughing at me rather than with me right now seeing my gargantuan image all over town."

"You're larger than life!"

"I'm Godzilla!"

"I love it! You're the monster that devoured L.A!"

BunnyLee pretended to slice her wrists with her butter knife and slumped back in her chair to die.

"What does it matter?" Ted asked. "Either way, you're famous."

"To me it matters. A lot. I care about how people see me."

"That's great to hear because I am feeling so much joy right now. Your new found celebrity adds a giant face to my club act!"

"So now, in addition to being famous, I get to be infamous, too? It's the gift that keeps on giving."

BunnyLee wasn't averse to attention. She liked people and she wanted people to like her. She knew that the kind of notice that fame brought could set you apart from your friends.

Ted was only half-listening. He held his phone and typed with both thumbs.

"How do you spell Godzilla?" he asked.

"You're shameless."

BunnyLee turned to greet the couple next to her.

"But people are still laughing with you, too," Ted said.

BunnyLee swung back around. "Right. And how does that work, again?"

Ted finished with his phone and turned his attention back to her.

"Everybody knows you from your line, 'Operators are standing by.'"

"I don't get it. Everywhere I go, people repeat that line."

"It's become a meme. Actually, that's how I open my act—with the words—I dated a meme."

"I'm not sure I even know what meme means."

"You've been away and out of the loop. Basically, meme means mimicry, but with a twist. Remember that old movie with Bogart and Bacall and she says, something like, 'if you need me just whistle. You do know how to whistle, don't you? Just put your lips together and blow!'"

"Okay, and?"

"You both are saying—in a very suggestive way—I'm waiting for you to make the next move. The only difference is that you say it in four words whereas it took Bacall three sentences! People quote you all the time. They post the GIF of you saying it at the end of their emails. You're famous for it. You're part of the language. And that shot of you saying, 'Love your smile?' That's coming into its own as a meme now too."

"Ugh. So what's the twist?"

"The twist is that a meme changes depending upon who says it and how it's said. Love your smile could mean I love your smile or it could be a command as in—you need to get to a place in life where you love your own smile! But that's just the beginning. The meanings of memes continue to change with the times."

BunnyLee sat very still. Her world was altered in ways she could not fully comprehend.

Heather's maid of honor, Rebekah, a local television news reporter whom BunnyLee barely remembered from school, tapped BunnyLee on the shoulder. She had a cameraman from the station with her who was moonlighting as the wedding videographer.

"Heather was hoping you might give a toast," Rebekah said.

"Sure. I mean, I guess." She had thought about what she might say if asked and had jotted down some notes. But things were different now.

"Great. Heather also said that you came a long way to get here today. So I'm going to mention that."

"I've been living in Bangkok."

"That is a long way. You wouldn't have happened to have been on that flight that hit all the turbulence this morning?"

"I sure was! It was scary, but I guess that happens all the time."

"Huh. Not really. Hey listen, I'm the MC for the evening, so I've got to move things along here. But later, could we talk?"

"Sure."

After the main course was served, Rebekah stepped onto a small platform and her cameraman flipped on some soft-lights. There was a TV monitor set up for people in the back to see. Guests helped her bring the evening into focus by ringing their wine glasses with their forks. Following the groom's father's toast, a corresponding toast by the bride's mother and a few words from the best man, Rebekah noted that people traveled from near and far to come here tonight.

"The award for the most loyal of friends who literally traveled half-way-around-the-world goes to BunnyLee Welles! BunnyLee, would you like to say a few words?"

"She also happens to be Hollywood's most recognizable person!" Heather called out from her table.

"You mean I have the most famous teeth," BunnyLee said taking the mic. The light was brighter than she expected and the camera a bit closer. "Wait a minute!" She faced the lens, "Do I have some food stuck here?" She pointed to where her incisors met her gums in an extreme close-up that brought a laugh.

"I want to read you a text Heather sent me just before I got on the plane." BunnyLee read from her phone, "btw u r going to find life here in LA very diff than b4." Okay, so that was a little cryptic. I was thinking that maybe the city of Los Angeles had finally outlawed smog or they'd somehow solved the traffic problem. No way did I suspect that Heather had arranged to have my picture plastered on billboards and buses all over town. What a nice homecoming gift, Heather. You thought of everything!"

The audience was really on her side. She shot Ted a cheeky look. He was too busy typing to notice.

"As some of you know, for the last few years I've been living in Asia, the land of Yin and Yang. It's been a kind of passion for me. I've studied Bodhisattvas and could name my favorite goddesses. Five thousand years of Taoist writings have given the world a treasure trove of truisms for women like me to quote in wedding toasts. They all boil down to this: The happiest people, the luckiest people, those most fortunate people, are the ones who have found balance in their lives. Man completes woman and woman completes man—it's a phenomenon that transcends time and place. In their special way Heather and Joe have found their balance, their shared love. And if there is one thing that all religions in the world can agree on, it is that love is divine.

"Heather and Joe, your kids and grandkids will look back at the photographs from this weekend and delight in how young and beautiful and happy you both look. Their only question will be, who is that woman who photo-bombed all the pictures?" BunnyLee raised her hand like a basketball player acknowledging a foul, "I'm just a girl who was having her fifteen minutes of fame. So I apologize for that. Mercifully, my larger than life status will soon run its course, whereas you, Heather and Joe, your love is forever. You followed your hearts and they led you both here."

BunnyLee raised her wine glass to toast the soon-to-be-married couple and people applauded…perhaps a little too vigorously, aiming their enthusiasm more at BunnyLee than at the Happy Couple. Was this response warranted? No way did she want to take any more focus away from them.

BunnyLee was having trouble gauging the authenticity of people's interactions with her. As she returned to her table, among the smiling faces, she looked to Ted for his reaction.

"How do you spell Bodhisattvas?" he asked.

"I think you need to find another muse."

"My muse. Right! That could get a laugh."

BunnyLee hung back as the evening wound to a close. She was preparing to slip out to her room to change when the cameraman stepped in front of her and thwarted her escape. He flipped his obie light on and took a wide stance.

"Yikes! Scared me!" BunnyLee said.

"Hey!" Rebekah was at his side. She wielded a handheld microphone. "Here's a face that many in our audience will recognize!" She mimicked, "'Operators are standing by!'"

"Right," BunnyLee said.

"I was wondering if you could tell us about that flight you were on this morning."

"Yeah, it was really something."

"Did you feel like you were going to die?"

"Like everybody, I guess. It was sure scary."

"Did you get banged around a lot? We see you've got quite a big bruise on your shoulder and what looks like claw marks above your other elbow! Did that happen as a result?"

BunnyLee hadn't noticed that her arm had turned black and blue from where the boy's head whacked her, followed by those falling drums. She reached for her other elbow where the Goth girl had held on for dear life.

"I suppose stuff like that happens all the time," she said.

"I'm guessing that you didn't know, because everybody got off the plane in time, but one of the engines caught fire right there at the jetway. It's been the lead story of the night!"

"The plane caught fire?"

She felt a wave of dizziness similar to the way she'd felt on the plane.

"How does it feel to have experienced a near death experience?"

"Well, um, actually I'm feeling kind of woozy. I'd been trying to put the whole thing behind me. But thanks for the interview."

Faint and perspiring, BunnyLee knocked over some chairs on her way to the emergency exit. She stepped into the courtyard. She hugged the trunk of an ornamental orange tree for support and leaned over. Nothing.

The wave of nausea ebbed.

Lovers tossed coins from the Japanese footbridge into the coy pond for good luck. BunnyLee saw splashes. She looked up.

The couple looked down.

"Love your smile!' the young man said.

"I'm not smiling," BunnyLee said.

The next morning her older sister, Lizette, called from Missoula to tell her that the close-up of her shoulder looked really gruesome on her new giant TV. Rebekah's human-interest report had gone national.

Her mom called right after and said that she and her dad hadn't known that BunnyLee was stateside.

"I just came for this wedding thing and I've got to go straight back. As it was, I barely got here in time. Anyway, I'm going to see you at Christmas. So, I don't want you to feel bad that I didn't have time to visit this time. You know you guys could always come visit me in Thailand!"

Her mom explained the ins and outs of it—so much political drama back home at their local church and what with BunnyLee's dad having recently become a deacon...

"I'm surprised you didn't have your hair done for the wedding, dear."

"That was the rehearsal dinner, Mom. I've got a hair appointment at noon for tonight."

"Have you been eating right? I know those cameras make a person look chubby, but..." BunnyLee could hear her father speaking in the background. "Oh! Your father wants me to tell you that there is a new young preacher at the church who wants to meet you! What did you say dear? Oh, right. He's single!"

On Monday BunnyLee called her agent, Angelo, at Theatrical Management Inc. to see what was up with all the billboards and, as always, had to remind him who she was.

"Yes, yes, Dial-a-Denture. They branched out into teeth whitening with Love Your Smile. And they exercised their option on a new contract. The amount of exposure this is bringing you is invaluable. You can't put a price tag on that. Couldn't ask for more."

"What about future work? Shouldn't I be using this as a springboard to something better? Shouldn't you be sending me out on auditions?"

"Best not to mess with a good thing. Be proud of what you've accomplished! Love Your Smile is a great gig. It'll run for years!"

"Years?!"

That gnawing feeling of desperation bubbled up. She expected this notoriety to be measured in weeks, not years. She heard the "Th-whack!" of a golf ball as somebody hit a scorcher to much applause. The head office of TMI was apparently now on the golf course.

"I'm way more experienced," BunnyLee said.

He couldn't have agreed with her more.

"Pretty much what everyone is looking for today is innocence. Someone like the actress Jadé, have you heard of her?"

"The Romanian actress? Yeah. She's young, but I'm not even

twenty-eight, yet…"

"Sounds young enough to me, too, but…Just remember, most of my clients would give their eye-teeth for an account like this… Well, not literally their teeth…" Th-whack! "Hey, sorry, gotta run…!" It must have been his turn to tee off.

Proud? BunnyLee didn't feel pride. Her face was now the corporate property of Dial-a-Denture. She would be the icon for dentures and teeth whitening gel for years to come. The idea of it was wearying. And to wait until she grew out of that 'look' was like waiting until she could no longer play the ingénue roles—an actress's most employable age.

The contract had its upside. Quarterly checks would be directly deposited to her bank account. There would be a modest amount to live on. How much was unclear, a few thousand for a regional campaign, lots more if it went national. But she wouldn't see any of it for months.

"I don't think you should listen to that guy," her sister said on the phone. "You've got to capitalize on this!" Heather had said the same thing.

So, 'just for the heck of it,' BunnyLee ventured out to an open-call audition.

There was a long wait to be seen and when it was finally her turn to read, the casting director immediately rolled his eyes and shook his head. In the jargon of the biz, BunnyLee was over-exposed.

She swallowed her pride and thanked him for his time. He suggested they meet later for a drink.

"Excuse me? To do what, commiserate?" She appraised the gawking faces in his company. Was he kidding?

He underlined his proposition with the provocative words, "Operators are standing by!"

"Ew! Gross!" Bunny said under her breath. She'd forgotten she was still on mic.

The term 'operators' took on a nuanced meaning—as in 'smooth operators.' This is what Ted was talking about. Her meme shifted in meaning depending upon who was doing the mimicking.

Apparently, show business still had its #MeToo side. From

studio execs to front office reps, the business was top to bottom oozing with skeevy types—gatekeepers who extracted a toll for their "professional help." So far, BunnyLee managed to steer clear of the casting couch. She'd side-stepped more than her share of close-calls.

As she left the studio, a scruffy lad waylaid her. He tried to hand her a copy of his screenplay. To him, BunnyLee was so obviously famous that she must surely be an insider who knew the ropes. She could see the photo caption now—Would-be Hollywood Screenwriter Makes It Big After Chance Encounter with Dial-a-Denture Girl!

Literally and figuratively, everybody wanted a piece of her.

BunnyLee ducked into the ladies room for refuge, then turned on her heels and exited as the cameras therein came out.

"That's it, I'm done!" she told Lizette on the phone.

"Done with Hollywood?"

"Acting, Hollywood... All this exposure makes me feel the exact opposite of what you'd expect to feel. The more everybody treats me as an insider, the more I feel like an outsider. I'm in a solitary place here. I'm in this alone. I'm numb. I feel emptied out."

"You just going to hole-up at Heather's 'til you leave?"

"Lizette, you have no idea how bad things are. I'm blindsided by fame. In Bangkok, I might stand out for being a Caucasian woman. Nobody there needs to memorialize the occasion as a forever-part of their online timelines. Further fame and fortune just aren't in the cards for me and I'm okay with that. I want to go back to feeling the way I felt back in Thailand."

"Which was?"

"That I was doing something important. That I was part of something."

Being an introspective person, rather than wallow in her feelings of isolation, BunnyLee doubled down on her journey of self-discovery and googled the word alienation.

Existentialists wrote long tomes about the emotion. Sartre,

whose musings about belonging won him the Nobel Prize, refused to accept the prize. He must have been feeling the same way that BunnyLee was feeling, or more accurately, not feeling, and it was to him that she turned for insight.

Compared to a supermarket self-help book, Sartre's prose was slow going. BunnyLee was two hours and ten pages into *Being and Nothingness* when Rebekah texted, asking her to sub in a tennis game on a famous person's private court. She'd be playing alongside notable guests. BunnyLee glanced at her book and decided that Being was a lot more fun than Nothingness. She texted Rebekah back, "What's the address?"

CHAPTER 2

BUNNYLEE PRESSED THE intercom at the ornate wrought iron gate and waited. The hedge and leafy grounds beyond were too thick to make out the house.

A man's voice asked, "Who are you?"

"Sorry I'm late. My friend must have given me the wrong street number."

"Who?"

"Rebekah. She couldn't make it. She was filling in for Gwendolyn." BunnyLee waved her tennis racket at the security camera. "I'm here to play tennis."

He buzzed her in. She climbed the steep curving driveway toward the Spanish style mansion.

"What's the address here?" she asked the African American man waiting in front of the carriage house. He was a big guy, handsome, maybe a few years older than she was.

"Number 10 Beverly Canyon."

She compared that to the number on her phone.

"O.K., well, whatever. Anyway, hi, I'm BunnyLee." She offered her hand to shake. His enveloped hers.

"I thought you said your name was Rebekah."

"Rebekah is the newswoman I'm replacing. What's your name?"

"Frankie. Mr. LeGrande's chauffeur." His easy Southern tone set her at ease.

"Buck LeGrande?"

"Yep."

"Really?"

"Yep."

"Will he be here?"

"Yep."

"Playing tennis?"

"Yep."

"Rebekah never said."

Frankie showed BunnyLee the way through the rose-garden trellis, down the path beside the pool that led even farther down to the court where three men were talking. And there he was, Buck LeGrande, in the flesh, shorter than she might have guessed, but otherwise, well, grand. BunnyLee was sensitive enough about her own newfound fame to know how annoying it was to be recognized. But talk about famous! This was the first time since she touched down in Los Angles where *she* wanted to record the event with a selfie. OMG! She couldn't wait to call Lizette and say, "You won't believe who I just met!"

The three looked like they were ready to pack it in for the day. She checked her phone. She wasn't that late.

She played it cool. She introduced herself all around with the confidence of an invited guest. "I'm the sub." She shook everyone's hands, "Pleased to meet you. Know so much about you." All very matter-of-fact, getting down to business, tucking in her blouse, pinning back her hair, adjusting her cap, pulling a white tennis glove tightly around her hand, then pulling the wrist of the glove up snug with her teeth. She was nervous. But who wouldn't be, meeting someone like him?

"So how do we decide who serves first?" she asked, taking command of the tempo of the game with the efficiency of a person who had somewhere to be later. "Should I spin?" she asked.

Everyone looked at her blankly.

"The racket...to see who goes first?"

"Oh, sure, go right ahead," Buck said. He and his guests exchanged puzzled looks.

Frankie stepped away.

+

Buck was used to being recognized by strangers, but not the other players. The 'Klingons,' as Buck referred to them behind their backs, were a gay couple that Buck met as a guest star on the set of *Star Trek*. Both played famous aliens. These days, they supplemented their income in special appearances, signing autographs, and by having their pictures taken with fans at Trekkie conventions. Buck knew that there was no way BunnyLee could have recognized them for one glaring reason: they made their Star Trek appearances in full Klingon garb.

Buck also wondered whether she'd seen the rather unflattering video of him in a dust-up with Kermit the Frog that surfaced on YouTube a couple of months ago. She didn't let on if she had.

It was never Buck's habit to let strangers insinuate themselves into his life. But the truth was, they needed a fourth and Frankie didn't play. Buck's regular mixed doubles partner had just called and canceled, leaving the rest of them high and dry.

"Who was it recommended you?" Buck asked BunnyLee.

"Gwendolyn, thru Rebekah."

"Not Ruth?"

"Who's Ruth?"

"She usually plays on Mondays..."

"Huh."

"...but she sprained her ankle."

"Gwendolyn had to go to Guam. She's a replacement in the USO show. She got the job last minute."

"Does Gwendolyn know Ruth?"

"Maybe, I don't know. Is Ruth a dancer?"

"Ruth is my accountant's wife."

"Huh," BunnyLee said again.

She unzipped her racket case with such a deliberate action that Buck found himself transfixed. BunnyLee was a well-proportioned, spry, graceful athlete whose only apparent imperfection, if you could call it that, was an asymmetric dimple that came and went in her left cheek whenever she smiled, which was frequently. She had a reliable serve, a serviceable forehand, and the most disarming single-handed backhand he had ever seen. Her cross-court shots came out of nowhere and left the Klingons flatfooted. Between important points, she discussed strategies with Buck in a deadpan Russian accent reminiscent of the femme fatale double agents of the James Bond era. "I vill hit to heez back hand, eet iz very veak, then vee rush net, da?"

"You rush zee net," Buck improvised in his own version of

pseudo-Russian, "I vatch your backside." BunnyLee gave him a quizzical look. He hadn't meant this to sound suggestive.

"Gud! Vee have plan!" BunnyLee said to cover the awkwardness.

Buck had to laugh. Her steady, unflinching gaze, coupled with her crooked smile, made him feel like a kid. Together, against capable opponents, BunnyLee and Buck won handily.

"Same time tomorrow?" BunnyLee asked when they were done, wiping her forehead with a towel.

"I only play mixed doubles on Mondays, Wednesdays and Fridays."

BunnyLee hardly gave the Klingons a second look at Buck's having described them as mixed doubles partners. This was Hollywood, after all, with modern interpretations of things mixed. And if you wanted to get technical, one of the men was wearing a tennis dress.

"Wednesday, then?"

He had to think quickly. "I do have a regular partner...Ruth. But I guess as long as she can't play…"

On Wednesday, against intimidating type-A producers, BunnyLee assumed a different strategy. With the aura of a ditz, she allowed her bust line and hips to define every movement as if her feminine features were a hindrance to her play. Her opponents, a husband and wife duo with an overabundance of team confidence, were lulled into hitting polite lobs. She returned them with little dinks just beyond their reach. BunnyLee would shrug, her body language portraying her good fortune as simple beginner's luck.

Comparing her to Ruth, Buck had to admit that BunnyLee was by far the better player and ever more entertaining. Then she unveiled her secret weapon. Facing double break point and BunnyLee serving, when their momentum might have slipped away, BunnyLee went to retrieve a ball at the net. She turned her back to her opponents. Bending over, the slipping waistline of her shorts exposed a modest area of her winsome cheeks.

"Oops!"

BunnyLee blushed.

Buck laughed. A thespian who can feign blushing was a rare

talent.

The husband, who had gotten enough of an eyeful, forgot that the purpose of the service return was to keep the ball in play, not drive it over the fence. Then when it was his turn to serve, he over-compensated by double faulting four times into the net.

It was an unconventional tactic, but when analyzed closely, not a move that would have worked against the Klingons. BunnyLee winked at Buck with a hint of that beguiling smile she had become so well known for.

"Same days next week, then?" Buck asked after winning their third match on Friday. She was clearly the best mixed doubles partner he had ever had. She looked quite at home on a chaise lounge poolside post-match, and she was good company. She was a keeper.

+

"I wish I could. I'm flying back to Thailand on Monday."

"What? Really? Why?"

"Well, first of all, that's where I live. And secondly, my housesitting gig is up. My friend Heather and her husband get back from their honeymoon on Sunday."

"But you can't. Who will I play tennis with?"

Buck offered her the use of the cabana to stay in. Then he added that he had three cars so she wouldn't have to rent one.

BunnyLee didn't have to think too much about her reply.

"Seriously?"

It wasn't unusual for BunnyLee to be a houseguest. It had been the norm. At her age, one thing just led to the next. There were many places on this planet where she would be welcome with open arms; friends were spread far and wide. But there was nowhere she absolutely had to be until the Fall term started. When her choice was staying in Beverly Hills at the house of a famous actor with a pool and a tennis court and a chauffeur-driven Bentley at her disposal, "Wow, okay, sure!" was the obvious answer.

Even still, it took her some thought to arrive at her decision and articulate it. Although it wasn't unusual for BunnyLee to be a houseguest, it was unusual for her to be the houseguest of a single man. She knew that he wasn't interested in her for her so-called fame. Buck was way more famous than she would ever be. He'd been in movies since he was a kid and he knew everybody in the business. But if Buck was anything, he was a single man. He was a famous single man. He was a man who was famous for being a single man.

"So, I'm going to be staying in the cabana, right?"

"Yes, I'm offering you the cabana," Buck reassured her. "You can come and go as you please."

"Are you sure?"

Buck assured her he was sure.

+

Buck's chauffeur, Frankie, observed BunnyLee with keen interest. In his six years working for Buck he had never known his boss to open his cabana to a guest.

Frankie had heard Buck ask his friend Sidney to look into the mystery of why she looked familiar. Sidney had a younger brother, Archie, a dentist, who recognized her straight away. BunnyLee was the alluring spokesperson for Dial-A-Denture in that late-night infomercial which had recently exploded all over the internet and beyond, with print ads everywhere promoting teeth whitener.

The only issue that neither Frankie nor Buck nor Sidney could reconcile was the question of who had recommended her for doubles.

CHAPTER 3

THE POOL HOUSE cabana was just a bedroom and a bath. Buck cleared a shelf for her in his refrigerator in the main house. BunnyLee pretty much had the run of the place. She read. She did her yoga. She worked on her tan. They were settling into a routine of having dinner together, ordering in. They worked on their short tennis game. But Buck made no demands on her time.

"I really like the guy," BunnyLee told Heather on the phone.

"Have you googled the Kermit the Frog outtake?"

"No! And I'm not going to. I've been here, what, a week? The man has been nothing but a gentleman. I don't know how long I can stay but it's fun while it lasts."

"He didn't say?"

"I guess I'll know it when the time comes. Meanwhile, my tennis game is getting lots better. And I like his friends. Anyway, he's a lot older."

"His homepage page says he's thirty-nine. But IMDB says he's forty-one. Does he have a girlfriend?"

"None that I've seen."

"Has he come on to you?"

"No! It's not like that."

"It's always like that."

"We're not dating! I'm just staying at his house."

"Sounds so innocent."

✦

On their second Friday together, Buck offered to take her out.

"There's this little place. The food is good. The waiters all know me. No one is going to bother you for your picture," he said.

Buck was parallel parking the Bentley off Wilshire Boulevard when BunnyLee pointed at the puppies in a pet storefront window.

"I once told my mother that the thing I wanted most in the world was a dog!" BunnyLee said.

Not the best of drivers, Buck was busy looking over his shoulder. He squashed the back tire into the curb.

"A dog would make you happy?"

"I didn't mean it like that. I'm very happy." BunnyLee touched his hand to reassure him. "Since I was a kid, I just always wanted a dog. But I was allergic. Now a lot of dogs are hypoallergenic."

Her innocent remark about happiness bothered Buck. He was happy hanging out with her. He'd been motoring along under the now questionable presumption that BunnyLee was just as happy hanging out with him.

Buck held the restaurant door for her. She paused at the window next door to watch the puppies playing.

"It's just that they're so cute!" she said. She touched his hand again to reassure him.

Buck knew that when she was a young teenager, BunnyLee's older sister thumbtacked a poster of him over her bed. A lot of teenage girls did that. Buck was pretty buff in a swimsuit in his teen-idol television days, known by his female fans more for wielding a six-pack than a six-shooter. With a little help from Photoshop, he still photographed pretty well. When BunnyLee described him as being really cute back then, Buck stopped himself from asking "What about now?"

Buck reminded himself that BunnyLee was his invited houseguest. He was her host. She needed a place to crash while she reestablished her footing in the biz. He was just helping her out. Romance was never mentioned as a possibility and, aside from a brotherly hug after a hard-fought doubles match or that sisterly pat on his hand while the two stood and watched the puppies in the window tumbling over each other with uninhibited joy, physicality had not been part of their equation.

Without that physical aspect Buck knew that BunnyLee could hardly be referred to as his girlfriend, which was annoying because he really liked her. For all of his sexual exploits, the idea of having a pal as a girlfriend was new to him. They had a good thing going and there was a singular risk in pushing it.

He didn't know what to make of BunnyLee. She had this overriding sense of sincerity that set her apart from the women who dotted the landscape in his rearview mirror. And now it came to the surface that she was a dog person. That revelation said something about the type of person BunnyLee was—nurturing, generous. But, like Groucho Marx, who would never join a club that would have him as a member, deep down Buck wasn't so sure that he was worthy of her. A woman as clever as BunnyLee would soon see through him, if she hadn't already. As far as disguises went, his toupee was just the tip of the iceberg.

On the other hand, the genuineness of BunnyLee's apparent sincerity troubled him.

Again the nagging question about BunnyLee kept rearing its ugly head: How had she appeared out of the blue that day at the very moment he'd needed a partner for tennis?

"Hey!" Somebody yelled from across the street. It was a photographer with a long lens aimed at them.

"Let's get out of here," Buck said to BunnyLee.

As the two were seated in a quiet corner of the restaurant next door, Buck tried to keep his demeanor jovial. He made a show of pulling out the chair for her to be seated. He joked with the maître d' about the wine list. But in his thoughts Buck was conflicted. He didn't need a mother to tell him that the world was full of grifters. Many women were out for fortune and fame. Even if BunnyLee turned out not to be a grifter *per se*, he knew there was a whole subset of women in the world who would say or do anything just to experience life on the inside. How could he be sure that BunnyLee wasn't one of them? There was an outlying possibility that she was using him.

✦

A woman at the next table gave Buck the tiniest wave with her pinkie finger and BunnyLee wondered whether there was any past history there. Buck didn't let on. He just smiled back. Buck LeGrande had a storied reputation in this town. BunnyLee wondered about the number of beautiful women he'd bedded.

An older man at a different table got up and ambled over.

"Excuse me, but my wife is too shy to ask. Would you mind if I took a picture?"

Buck was not at all perturbed by this intrusion. He turned his face to accommodate the man.

"You changed my life," the man said to BunnyLee. He turned to take a selfie only with her. "Brand new," the man said pointing to his teeth, "and they changed my life. I just married the girl of my dreams!" He pointed over to his table where his date, a woman in her seventies, silently toasted BunnyLee with her glass of wine.

"Well, that was awkward!" BunnyLee said to Buck when the man had left.

"Not at all. You're part of something bigger, now."

✦

Buck's usual dates were more like publicity events. No black-tie occasion was complete without a lovely lady in a sleek dress at his side. Eye candy. Just one more reason to have the cameras pointed at him. These were business engagements, clearly understood to avoid entanglements. Proximity to fame begot fame. Both parties profited by appearing in the company of the other. It was one thing to roam the world willy-nilly like BunnyLee, without a purpose or a plan. To be famous, one had to be calculating. Every camera flash was a unit of fame. The units added up for bonus points. Even the paparazzi who stalked him in packs during the height of the Kermit the Frog fiasco knew that photographers and actors had a symbiotic relationship. They dogged him for an explanation. He gave none.

Buck kept a cue card in his back pocket to remember each new date's name. If they were getting along at all, he might invite them back to Beverly Canyon. That wasn't the point. These were formal relationships, mutually beneficial to all concerned. These women were his invited guests; they arrived through the front door. BunnyLee arrived via the garden gate. BunnyLee was in the inner circle from the moment they met. BunnyLee and he were partners from the start.

After the wine was poured, Buck toasted BunnyLee's burgeoning career.

"You are not the first actress to stay in the cabana who went on to fame and fortune."

"I'm sure I'm not. I'm sure there have been many before me."

BunnyLee's tone was not lost on him, and he rather enjoyed the insinuation that he was thought of as a bit of a rake. "I was actually thinking before me. Before I owned the place."

"Who?"

"Audrey Hepburn, they say."

"Really?"

"Or Katherine Hepburn. One of the Hepburns. It's an absolute fact."

"Really?"

"With her dog."

"She had a dog?"

"Named Virgo."

"Virgo? That's my sign!"

That's how it came out that BunnyLee's birthday was only a few days away. When pressed, she admitted she was keeping it a secret because birthdays can be such a bother. She hadn't wanted to make a big deal of it.

Birthdays meant presents, and Buck wanted to get her something nice. He wasn't at all sure what that should be. The next day he asked Sidney. Sidney was knowledgeable in this arena. Sidney was an internet dater. Pictures of Sidney graced every single site: Sidney in a racecar, Sidney in a tux, Sidney holding a puppy. Sidney had so many girlfriends that he'd lost count. Sidney was a pro.

"I usually dump them before their birthday," Sidney answered.

"What about Christmas?"

"I make it a rule not to even date in December."

It was just so damned awkward that her birthday happened along so early in their relationship: just long enough that he couldn't let the occasion pass without presenting her with a significant token of his fondness for her, yet too soon to define his intentions, because he didn't know what his intentions were. The arc of their relationship had been so different from any other. They had never really dated, unless you classified mixed doubles as a date, which he didn't. Iced tea afterwards on the loggia was standard fare every afternoon, open to all players. He had offered to take her out before, show her off to the media, but she declined, preferring to stay in and order take-out. The fact was that the circumstances by which they had become friends were so unlike any other relationship he'd experienced that he didn't even know what to call it. He knew that he liked it. Loved it. It was comfortable. It was easy. It felt right. It was only missing that one physical component if he were to ever refer to her as his girlfriend.

Buck ended up going shopping alone. He assured himself that he could pick up some bauble from one of the notable purveyors of jewelry down on Rodeo Drive like Harry Winston or David Orgell or Tiffany's and be back before lunch.

It was the morning of BunnyLee's birthday; he pulled up behind the Beverly Wilshire Hotel and handed his car keys to the valet, who, with a couple of crisp twenty-dollar bills pressed into his palm, promised to keep the car positioned by the curb.

Instead of cutting through the lobby, Buck doubled back a couple of blocks to scope out the store with the puppies just in case he changed his mind. He had no intention of buying BunnyLee a dog, but having a Plan B was always a wise idea. Turning the corner on this quiet block, he stopped short. There was a picket line in front of the pet store. A handful of people from PETA and the ASPCA were stationed in front of the entrance, some with signs urging a boycott of pet stores everywhere. Buck was vaguely familiar with the numerous billboards around town decrying the assembly line breeding of puppies. Not being a puppy person, he hadn't given the subject of puppy production much thought.

A picket line presented a formidable obstacle. He was too well known in this town to window shop without being noticed, and he would look petty-minded if he ignored their noble purpose. So much for Plan B. Buck turned around and headed up to the famed shopping district of Rodeo Drive. He told himself that a jewelry store with its focused lighting and soothing music was much more conducive to contemplative gift-giving decision-making.

Like a candy store across from an elementary school, Two Rodeo Drive was directly across the boulevard from the pricey Beverly Wilshire and easily accessible via an exterior staircase to the right of Tiffany's. There was even a crossing guard in front of the famed hotel. Up those granite steps he knew of a small establishment specializing in the retail of gems.

It was early, but he was not the only customer. The Israeli owner turned and greeted him by name. "Mr. LeGrande, how nice to see you." The man was just finishing a weighty transaction with a Saudi woman. Her credit card wasn't a color that Buck had ever seen. It wasn't gold or platinum, more like the shimmering color of crude oil. The woman wore a full burqa; Buck couldn't tell whether she recognized him.

"How may I assist you today?" the salesman asked, and Buck's mood lightened at his tone. It was when the man started asking personal questions that his confidence waned. "How old is the lady in question?" he asked. "What is the relationship?" "What is it you would like to say with this gift?" Buck's hands began to shake. He knew earrings were probably the safest bet, but the salesman kept steering him toward the necklaces. The unblinking Saudi woman looked on.

"Women look better in diamonds," the woman said in a thick Middle Eastern accent. She made no move toward leaving the store.

BunnyLee had been living in the cabana going on three weeks. He suspected his buddies were beginning to wonder. He wasn't about to admit that the famed Hollywood sex symbol had so far struck out in regards to the classic Hollywood two-shot. Meanwhile, he had a partial view of the pool from his second-floor bedroom and had glimpsed what BunnyLee looked like going through her morning ritual of Tai Chi. He knew first hand that she looked just fine without any jewelry whatsoever.

The impeccably dressed salesman was guiding him to the necklaces across the aisle from the earrings, dangerously close to the wedding rings. The Saudi woman nodded approval.

Buck was starting to panic. He considered alternatives. He thought about lingerie, something sumptuous. But silky was so dangerously close to slinky. It was presumptuous. He needed a gift that BunnyLee could show off, and jewelry was a good example of an object that one could readily show off. Diamonds travel easily. Meanwhile, it was the whole showing off aspect of the gift that was so troubling. He obviously didn't want to appear a piker. The stone would need to be of a measurable size, something that could be admired without the aid of a microscope. But the subject was dodgy. There were resident experts in Los Angeles who could assay a diamond from across the room. Case in point, the attentive dark eyes of the Saudi woman in the store. Settings and cuttings had meaning. Carats were a language of expression that most men did not speak and most women were fluent in. For a pendulous diamond necklace that was featured in the store window, the salesman was pointing at a cool 1.45 million dollars.

"A good price," the Saudi woman said.

Compared to that, a pet-store dog would have been chump change. And Buck hadn't worked in a while.

He wondered if Arabic had a word equivalent to *kibitz* or if maybe this woman was working as a shill. He shifted his weight from one foot to the other. A crowd of tourists was accumulating at the open door, aiming their cameras at him. The blood was leaving his head to wherever blood hid when one was feeling faint. According to the salesman, who by the way he was beginning to loathe, a man cannot give earrings without consideration of a matching necklace. Throw a bracelet into the mix and he would have achieved a hat trick. A relationship that seemed like a pastoral drive in the country had now turned into a hairpin highway. Buck was no Le Mans driver, and jewelry was a slippery slope.

Buck LeGrande did not particularly like dogs or, for that matter, any animal with teeth. But he was a realist. He needed a present. Given the absence of other choices and in consideration of the time element--it was nearing high noon--the subject of dogs was a subject worth revisiting. He thanked the jewelry store owner for his help and doubled back to the pet store to see whether the situation on that front had changed.

It had.

Even before he turned the corner, he could hear the picketers chanting. He studied the mob scene from afar. The number of placards had increased ten-fold. Signs like, *Honk If You Love Dogs!* gave the passing traffic a reason to slow down and join in the fun. A camera crew from the local television station was poised at the far side of the action, taking it all in. The reporter was interviewing a policeman standing beside his cruiser. Buck was no stranger to a media event. Appearing in front of the press was his *forte*.

Using his phone as a makeshift mirror, Buck pointed the lens at himself to study his image. The sun's radiance can be harsh, but the smog indexes in Los Angeles on this late summer morning were mercifully high, lending a thick layer of bronze diffusion to the solar light source. His ruddy tan was nature's base makeup. It evened the undertones. He patted down his face with his handkerchief to wipe away any hint of sweat that could contribute to an unwanted sheen. He took a deep breath.

Buck made his entrance with a sense of purpose, making eye contact with everyone who looked his way. His rule of thumb was to hold each glance only so long as it took to ascertain the color of the other person's eyes. Any longer might seem inappropriate. A murmur went through the crowd as people recognized him. There was something exciting about seeing a movie star in the flesh. Even those with a casual interest in his work could become instant fans.

A woman handed him a leaflet entitled *Don't Shop, Adopt!* He gave it a fast read: through the efforts of the Humane Society and the Freedom of Information Act, the protesters were shining light on the dark underbelly of puppy mills and their brokers. Buck was a quick study. He was never one to memorize lines. A script to him was like a Google map that suggested various routes through the scene.

He waded deep into the throng and stopped at the epicenter near the glass entrance to the pet store. He chatted with a young volunteer who was taking a day off from her work at Greenpeace to canvass for the dogs.

The television reporter spotted him and elbowed her cameraman. The two moved in for the story.

He made a show of signing the anti-puppy-mill petition as the camera recorded the event. He wrote quickly so as not to allow his hand time to shake. Then he looked up and gave the newswoman his full attention. She was a nice-looking blondish lady about the same age as BunnyLee. Close at her side her heavy-set cameraman took a wide stance and prepared for a medium close-up. The camera was firmly planted on his shoulder, the lens eye-level.

"So you are here to support the boycott?" the newswoman asked. Was there a hint of giddiness in her tone? Buck thought so.

"I've always been sympathetic to worthy causes," Buck said. "What we should be doing and what all these earnest people here are proposing we do is instead of shopping at some profit-making establishment, we should all be supporting the shelters, making darned sure that there is an adequate number of adoption centers so that no pet goes without a home. Communities from all over the world look to Hollywood for direction. I applaud this action and am happy to lend my name to the effort."

Buck acknowledged a smattering of applause from the growing number of people who were within earshot. He returned his attention back to the news reporter, drinking her in. He flashed her his Emmy-nominee smile. She wasn't the first woman to be taken in by that smile.

The lens of the human eye can change focus at will, but the professional camera focuses manually. The cameraman determined what was in frame, and what was in focus dominated the storyline. With the lens centered on Buck's face, the demonstrators and their placards were relegated to the soft focus of the background, ensuring that Buck LeGrande would be the centerpiece of a human-interest story at the end of this evening's local news cycle about how much he cared about animals.

"A demonstration like this is about community, community coming together and saying enough is enough! Not in our town! Not on our watch!"

People responded to Buck with cheers.

"Of course, I also feel bad for these doggies in the window," Buck continued. "How can you not? So innocent, and so caught in the crossfire of this controversy. It's a matter of communication, having a dialogue. I feel compelled to walk inside this store right now and have a private word with the proprietor just to see if we can't work something out. Storeowners aren't bad people..." He reached out to pull the door handle.

"But Mr. LeGrande, we're boycotting this store," cautioned a middle-aged fellow with a clipboard pressed insistently against the glass door.

"That's right," added a pimply young man with a skateboard.

"Yeah," a third person added for good measure.

"Folks," Buck said to the assembly. He held his hand up in a plea for reason. "There is rarely an issue between levelheaded people that cannot be resolved with words." These were lines akin to many that he had spoken in the role of Nick Derringer in *Malibu Man*, his most recent television series. Never had they rolled so eloquently off his tongue.

"May I ask you to comment on your altercation with Kermit the Frog?" the newswoman finally had the presence of mind to ask.

"I will be happy to answer that question when I come out."

Once inside, Buck turned to reassure the booing assembly

through the glass. He held both palms up like an unarmed man. The mood on the sidewalk softened in his favor.

"How's that for a man of action?" Buck asked himself. Then he did something a lot less laudable. He turned to the owner with the loaded question. "Do you have a back door?"

"'Course I 'ave, mate."

The gaunt man wore a black leather cap with a matching leather vest and eye-patch. It took Buck a second to place him. Fading tattoos on his arms looked familiar, but it was the East London accent that gave him away. That and the missing left ear.

"Rex West?"

"Saw you out 'ere. Thought you'd signed on, joined in, struck up the band. Quite the natty crowd, 'at is." Rex proudly hailed from a long line of Gypsy horse thieves and scoundrels. He could hold his own in an angry mob. "Wha' a lot o' bother."

"What's with the eye patch, Rex?"

"Cat scratch. Bengalese tiger got the better o' me. Still got 'em the shot, I did."

"Good God, man! Still doing the animal wrangling, then?"

"Still in the game, mate."

Rex trained animals for the movies. Any time a script called for a live animal, especially if it was a dangerous kind of animal like a black widow spider or a grizzly bear or a rattlesnake, you name it, you could count on Rex to be the animal wrangler on the set. A snapping turtle? Child's play.

"Man, am I glad to see you!"

Buck crossed the store and offered his hand. Rex's version of a right hand was missing some secondary handshaking parts. His left was no better.

"So, you're working, then?"

"A little o' this and a lot o' that. A bit o' the worse for wear, make no mistake about 'at! Keep me eye on the store when The Biz is slow, ebb and flow, you know how it goes, weren't for hard luck I'd 'ave no luck t'all."

"Sorry to hear that…"

"Could be worse. Pirate pics is big again. Save 'em a pile on makeup, I do. What with 'aving the parrot on me shoulder, tis a win-win. Other day, I spied ol' Joey G. 'Member that horror pic we done back in the day, back in me pure thespian days? Bloke from the Kiwiland? Sees me in the state I'm in, asks, ain't it time you got out, mate? Had to laugh. What and quit The Biz, I sez? It's years I spent learning this trade. He's one foot out, says the numbers game's for 'im. Slipped 'im a bet right 'ere on the set, 'turned eleven to one, 'at 'ery night!"

Even on a good day Buck had trouble understanding Rex. With the throngs outside now making an unnerving racket, it was nearly impossible.

"Hey, listen, Rex, I'd love to catch up," Buck spoke above the din, "but I'm in a bit of a fix. I need a birthday gift. Today. Right away. I was thinking I'd get her a pet." A large contingent of the crowd outside began chanting along with a woman with a bullhorn. Buck's conversation with Rex was limited to short bursts between pauses in the chorus.

"PUPPIES AREN'T PRODUCTS!"

"I've a special on snakes, I 'ave."

"DON'T SHOP, ADOPT!"

"I was thinking a puppy…"

"BOYCOTT ANIMAL CRUELTY!"

"A monkey?"

"PUPPIES AREN'T PRODUCTS!"

"A dog."

"DON'T SHOP, ADOPT!"

"What! A frog?"

"BOYCOTT ANIMAL CRUELTY!"

"God no, Rex! I hate frogs!"

"DON'T SHOP, ADOPT!"

"Right. Forgot that. That whole YouTube thing."

"PUPPIES AREN'T PRODUCTS!"

Buck kept a wary eye on the window. The crowd was growing not only in size but also in self-confidence. Buck had to yell to be heard.

"A dog! A D.O.G! I need to buy a friggin' dog!"

As if on cue, there was a lull in the crowd noise. Buck's voice was loud enough to be heard outside. People looked in with startled expressions.

"You should 'ave said. It's one thing I 'ave, I've dogs. What kind you think?" Rex's one eye had Buck locked in full attention.

Buck turned his face away from the crowd and answered, "The thing is…I don't know the first thing about dogs."

"I've a good price on that mastiff," Rex said, pointing to an open cage and what looked like an overfed man in a dog outfit.

"I was thinking something smaller. A lot smaller."

"You already done this gal or you yet to do 'er?"

There it was again, the question of his relationship with BunnyLee.

"Something like that," was Buck's vague response.

"Wha' you need's a pup!"

"I was thinking one from the back room if you don't mind."

"In the back room I 'ave none. Animals in there for trainin' purposes only, not for sale, mate."

"Well, I can't exactly buy one of these out here! There's a faction on that sidewalk preparing to lynch me just for walking in here!"

"They do 'ave us outnumbered."

"Rex, how long have we known each other?"

"Long time, no question. Mere pups ourselves, sneakin' hooch behind the makeup lorry."

"You played my older brother. We broke into the business together!"

"Took the town by storm, you did. Buck LeGrande. A headline name is what you made. Hit and miss it's been for me."

"You know I got you work whenever..."

"Wranglin' the wild beasts."

"Sometimes you were on camera."

"Riskin' life and limb."

"Okay, so next time it'll be a role with lines."

"Time I played the leading man, it is. Arrrr!" Rex said, raising his mangled mitts.

He gave Buck such an astonishing one-eyed, unshaven, missing-tooth grin that Buck involuntarily stepped backwards. He banged up against an open-top glass cage; a startled a snake hissed at him.

"Jeezus!"

"Just pullin' yer leg, mate. But it's truly time I played a proper villain."

"Listen, you're right. Not that I have any work right now. But the next time somebody says they need a villain, I'm going to give them your name."

"Buck LeGrande, grand to see you, for you I cannot say no. I 'ave a dog back there, one in a million, smart as a whip. Been trainin' 'er. A veritable chick magnet is 'at one, get you laid straight away. Guaranteed."

"It comes with a guarantee?"

"Ironclad. But it'll cost you a lot of bucks, a lot of grands."

Buck was in no position to argue price. In exchange for safe passage through the back alley, he stood in the training room with his wallet in hand. What came out of his back pocket looking like a hefty lettuce sandwich was quickly reduced to two thin slices of pumpernickel as Buck handed over a pile of Benjamin Franklins for what was most likely the highest-priced pooch in the history of pet stores. As an added precaution, Buck signed a contract on the Puppy Passport: a joint account credit card in BunnyLee's name good for twenty percent off any pet need that might arise. He clearly had no idea then what that might entail. He was in such a hurry to escape with his prize that he would have signed anything. He did know the thing would need to be fed, but beyond that, he hadn't a clue. They sealed the deal with a "high five!" initiated by Rex that took Rex two hands to complete.

"Oh, no. Wait! What about allergies?"

"You're in luck there, too, mate."

They made their way through the narrow alleyway behind the store, sharing the weight of a cowering puppy in a carrier that was large enough to house a full-grown wolf. "Does it bite?" Buck asked over his shoulder as Rex limped to keep up.

"Everything bites."

Taken at face value, the whole episode of crossing a picket line was indecorous. Buck was a member of a labor union, the Screen Actors Guild, so he knew that. It was underhanded to the point of dastardly. It reeked of selfishness, bordered on narcissism. And on top of that, to be gloating about it later was improper. Yes, yes, a hundred times, yes. But he did get the dog, a hypoallergenic dog. And it came with that ironclad guarantee.

On his drive home, Buck rationalized his behavior. First off, he'd spoken up for and gone on record in support of the picketers. It aided their cause, so who could fault him for that? Secondly, he'd helped a failing businessman and old acquaintance by purchasing his most expensive product. He could have asked Rex for a discount, but had silently paid his price. That alone was an act of altruism, clear and simple. And thirdly, he was kind of afraid of dogs. So his motives were pure. It was all about making BunnyLee happy. This was his sole reward for further risking his recently tarnished celebrity after that Kermit The Frog debacle, and since when was acting out of friendship a selfish act? By the time he pulled into his drive at Number 10 Beverly Canyon and spirited the small sleepy canine into the den, he was beginning to think that the whole episode made him a candidate for a humanitarian award.

That night, BunnyLee came up to the house for a birthday dinner. The candles were lit, champagne was opened and, through the course of the meal, the bottle was adequately drained. The conversation turned toward the mechanics of acting, a subject they often discussed. BunnyLee filled him in on the merits of improvisation.

As far as Buck was concerned, improv was a fringe element of acting. He had never performed it. He was alarmed to hear that it came with hard-and-fast rules. The sketches were far more structured than he had imagined.

"Improv performers are trained to always say 'yes.' It's a Cardinal Rule. Because to say 'no' essentially ends the scene."

As an example of always saying yes, BunnyLee digressed to tell the story of her friend Heather and her boyfriend Joe, the ones whose wedding she had flown in for.

"He whacked her."

"You mean like mafia whacked?"

"Figuratively. Emotionally. He ambushed her. He hit her with the proposal of marriage when she wasn't looking and she had to say yes. Heather was performing at The Improv on Melrose. It was a big deal for her. She was in the middle of a scene where they take suggestions from the audience. She wasn't surprised to see a lot of friends were there. But she was surprised when her boyfriend jumped up on the stage."

"What did she do?"

"She said, 'Joe, funny seeing you here.' He knelt down on one knee and asked, 'Will you marry me?' I guess the stage manager was in on it because he brought up the house lights. Her parents had flown in from Cleveland."

"That's romantic," Buck said.

"I can't say. I wasn't there."

"Doesn't sound like you think so."

"He stacked the deck, that's all I'm saying. He never gave her the chance to say no. She was an actress; she was on stage; she played the part. Joe picked a situation where the answer was fixed. She had to say yes! That's whack."

"She did end up marrying the guy, didn't she?" Buck asked. "She had plenty of time before that to change her answer."

"Ah, but was her answer sincere? She felt pride about being asked in front of all those people and for him to profess his feelings in public. But public affirmation is what weddings are about. He jumped the gun."

"Hollywood sells a lot of tickets telling stories like this."

"They're called fairy tales. Moments like these aren't simple. A proposal is not a simple question. It's a big question: Is this the person I want to spend my life with? I like Joe, but did Heather really know in her heart that he was the one? Or was it her biological clock saying, 'Well, if you let this one get away, you're going to die old and lonely.' Meanwhile, there was always the possibility that someone better-suited for her was just around the bend."

"She'd have had those questions either way."

"True, that's true, that's absolutely true. It's about sincerity. I don't know about you, but my feelings often take me by surprise. Sometimes they blindside me. I can't ever be sure how I'm going to feel until I feel it. He never gave her the chance to experience it for real. And the moment passed. There was no way to go back and make it right. Anyway, I only mention this story because it says a lot about improv being rule-based. Which is counter-intuitive."

"Weren't they already living together? Wouldn't the idea of marriage have crossed her mind by then? Wouldn't Joe have already tested the waters?"

"Yeah, probably. I'm just saying it's not simple. Every situation is nuanced."

"Like what if the man was older than her, but famous?" Buck asked.

BunnyLee didn't say anything for a moment. She studied her famous, older host. "I'm not sure where you're going with this."

Maybe it was the champagne talking, he wasn't much of

a drinker, but Buck felt he knew where he was headed. He just didn't know how to get there from here. He launched into a short speech about wanting to do something special for her birthday. He was worried he had overstepped. "It's fully returnable, fully refundable," he explained, although how he might go about getting his money back seemed problematic. Knowing Rex West, the man had already bet and lost the money on the horses.

Buck could hardly breathe. He certainly wasn't prepared for BunnyLee's reaction when he led her to the den. Her tears. The last thing he wanted was to disappoint her and by first appearances he had failed in the happiness-making enterprise. He immediately filled her in on all the Puppy Passport perks, how all the expenses would be covered by him just in case the roadblocks to her happiness were monetary.

BunnyLee was holding the dog in her arms, wiping her cheeks, explaining that these were tears of joy, saying that this was the nicest, most thoughtful, most loving gift that anyone had ever given her. "I'm sorry to be crying. You just caught me off-guard is all." She smiled, "Hmm. I'm going to need to name her."

Buck looked at her carefully to see whether her feelings were genuine. The blood that had gone missing earlier in the day at the jewelry store was returning to his head. He felt rather good about himself. In a word, he was astonished. Like David against Goliath, he had slain the birthday present behemoth, and in so doing had made his delightful girlfriend happy.

She wasn't officially his girlfriend. Not yet. He had first to guide her upstairs into that realm she had yet to enter.

She went willingly. She led the way, part of the way, into his room, her bare toes digging into the thick nap of his Persian carpet. She stroked the wooden mane of the hand-carved horse from *Carousel Cowboy*, Buck's first movie as the leading man. She looked out his window. Her eyes widened at the partial view it afforded of the cabana and sun deck. She sat on his bed. The puppy nestled in the bosom of her silk dress. She lay back against his pillow, looking positively delightful. She gazed at him with that single-dimple smile.

From Buck's experience, the evening was a lock; the future was guaranteed. Had Buck been with any other woman, he would have now repaired to the bath to change into something appropriate. With BunnyLee on his bed, it was different. He didn't want to leave. He had yearned for just such a visit. What had felt long overdue now felt well worth the wait. There was no reason to hurry. He slid off his loafers and lay beside her. The soft puppy cuddled up between them. BunnyLee came in close and gave Buck a kiss. He was happy just to be holding her. Now it was his turn for tears to well up in his eyes. For one brief moment and for the first time in his life, he felt what it was like to be part of a family.

Then the puppy sneezed.

Having never had a dog, Buck had given scant consideration as to what went into having one. He'd given no consideration whatsoever as to what came out. That warm and fuzzy feeling presently turned cool and clammy. The dog had peed his bed.

BunnyLee was laughing uncontrollably, wiping the urine as quickly as she could with a Kleenex.

She tried to reassure him. "It's just a little puddle." She'd gotten most of it before it soaked through to the mattress.

Buck was distressed. He tried to laugh it off, too, but what can you say? Call it what you will, pee is pee. The thing had peed his bed!

BunnyLee sprang to action. She stripped the sheets. She washed the mattress with warm soap and water. She laid a towel out to cover what she called "The wet spot." Then she restored the bed to order.

"I'm going to name her Puddles!" BunnyLee announced.

Then she took her puppy back to the cabana to sleep. Buck stayed up for a while, thinking maybe she was coming back. The warm glow from the champagne had faded. The bed was empty. The moment was lost. He could see the cabana reflected in the pool from his window. The lights went out. He fell asleep on the duvet, avoiding as best he could the lump that covered 'the wet spot.' There was no getting around it; he was not a dog person. Which was a problem, because he really liked BunnyLee.

In the morning he ordered a new mattress.

CHAPTER 4

A COUPLE OF days later, Buck said to BunnyLee, "The Emmys are this Sunday. I was planning on skipping it this year but if you would like to go..."

They were in the kitchen. BunnyLee was eating an avocado out of the skin with a spoon. Buck was buttering some toast.

"I think I've had enough of show business for a while."

"Are you sure? These things are a lot of work, but they can be fun. You'll meet a lot of people."

"I know. It's just that you're used to it. You've been a star since you were, what, fourteen? For me, the cameras, the paparazzi, it's all so superficial and intrusive. I'd be too self-conscious. I just don't feel like I've earned any of this attention."

"It's a large part of the industry; you should get used to it."

"Doesn't it bother you that when you are out in public, you have no privacy?"

"When you are out in public, you are in public. There is no privacy; that's the point. There is no getting around it."

"Right. It's just that I feel like a charlatan. When I was fourteen, I was just another face on the outside looking in—like a commoner watching royalty cavort. Now, all of a sudden, I've attained this weird notoriety. People recognize me. They want to be near me. I can't even go to a department store without some woman chasing me into the dressing room to capture the moment on her cell phone. I wanted a new bathing suit, but there was no way I could try one on in there. She had her phone on a selfie stick and was framing the shot with me in the picture while I was starting to undress. 'Excuse me!' I said and she's like, 'Oh, no, stay right there! Just one more!' And what did I do to deserve this? Dial-a-Denture? It is all just so hopelessly ridiculous! To parade on that red carpet in some silly dress, I would feel like an imposter. I'm an outsider masquerading as an insider, caught in a... It's like I got tangled up in the velvet rope while I was trying to sneak under. I can't move forward and I can't back up. I'm stuck in some sort of fame-purgatory."

"Talent can only take you so far in this town. Show business is a business first and foremost."

"Sometimes it feels like high school multiplied by a thousand—everybody vying so desperately to stand out. But there is another reason. My parents think I went back to Thailand. Don't get me wrong, I love them dearly and I have tickets to see them at Christmas, but if I go to this event with you, it's going to be all over the press. Next thing you know my mom is going to be reading about me in the checkout line of the supermarket: 'Buck LeGrande and the Dial-A-Denture Girl, Details Inside!' They're my parents. They're conservative. They're beyond conservative. They're born again. This just isn't a conversation I feel like having with them right now. 'So you're boyfriend and girlfriend?' my father would ask. 'No, Dad.' 'Really? That's not how it looks in the magazine.' He's the kind of guy for whom science is fiction."

What she didn't say, but weighed heavily on her decision, was that the cost of a dress to wear to an affair like this, a dress that she in all likelihood would wear only once, might cost more than she made teaching in Thailand in a year. And then there was the subject of jewelry.

"We could skip the red carpet circus and go in through the side door," Buck said.

"Isn't that the whole point of going to these things, to be *seen*?" BunnyLee asked. "You need to go out and be seen. And not with some infomercial wannabe. You've got your own career to think about. You need to go with somebody famous!"

And that's what happened. His manager set him up with the Romanian actress, Jadé, through her agent. She was a sensation at Cannes that spring in a breakout love story shot in Prague. Her film hadn't even opened in America yet and her performance was already on the short list for an Oscar nomination. Buck was astounded that the girl accepted the invitation.

"See?" BunnyLee said.

Jadé arrived on Sunday just after noon while BunnyLee was in the kitchen and Buck was still upstairs. BunnyLee answered the door. She wondered whether the young actress knew English; her movie, after all, was subtitled.

Jadé spoke flawless English.

"Everyone who is anyone in Romania speaks English," Jadé said.

"I'm impressed. I teach English as a second language, so I know you must have started early."

"Everyone wants to come to America."

The woman was wearing an exquisite black dress with a sweetheart neckline and a simple cut above the knees. Bunny felt awkwardly underdressed in her tank top, cut-offs and flip-flops. "That's one of my favorite designers," she said.

"They lend it to me to wear."

"For free?"

"Just so long as I return it in one piece. I am so nervous to have it on!"

A pendulous tear-shaped diamond hung from a diamond-studded necklace nestled in her cleavage.

"And that necklace?"

"The Real McCoy! One point four five million. It was in the window!"

"Get out!"

"It is a big responsibility not to lose it. I can't wait to get everything off."

In BunnyLee's estimation, the young woman didn't look the least bit nervous. "Well, you look charming. Buck should be down any minute."

"Are you the daughter?" Jadé asked.

"No!" BunnyLee answered. She hoped Buck hadn't overheard. The woman was so innocent and stunning and all of nineteen. She wondered whether Buck might feel awkward about the age difference.

She needn't have worried. BunnyLee was explaining how she was his houseguest, staying in the guest cabana, when Jadé caught sight of the famous man. BunnyLee turned and the image of Buck in his perfectly tailored tux caught her up short.

"Wow!"

Here was a man who could wear a tux!

They say that the clothes make the man and that certainly helps. But this was on beyond clothes. Buck was right out of Central Casting, a leading man—a young George Clooney. Dashing was the word that her grandmother would have used. BunnyLee's pulse quickened as he stood before them.

"I watched every episode of your show, *Malibu Man*," Jadé said. "You are the symbol of masculinity in my country."

BunnyLee glanced at Buck and rolled her eyes in mock-disbelief. Buck smiled back. His look conveyed an intimacy between them that BunnyLee hadn't felt before. She felt a visceral tug at her core. And in that instant, she was his. No longer an innocent bystander, she was a light-headed, weak-kneed, full-blown fan.

"It is my pleasure to meet you," Buck said to Jadé.

This was a man BunnyLee had been pals with, had hung out with, traded barbs with. She had challenged him intellectually and he had humored her. She had even cuddled with him upstairs, in his private quarters on his bed. He had bought her a dog! But she had never really seen him before. Not like this. He had never used his weapon-grade smile on her. Not in the way he was deploying it on Jadé. BunnyLee couldn't help but stare as Buck turned his charms on the beautiful starlet.

Jadé was still gushing about how revered Buck was in Romania.

"In my country, people watch the Emmys," Jadé told BunnyLee. "Tomorrow I will be famous!"

"How nice for you, " BunnyLee said.

Jadé didn't have anything on her save for that little black dress, a million-dollar décolletage, and the irksome truth that her twenties, her ingénue-playing days, were ahead of her rather than mostly behind.

Buck took the beautiful starlet's arm and escorted her to the car. Frankie held the car door for Jadé and she sinuously took her seat in the back next to Buck.

BunnyLee bid them farewell.

The dress was free! Damn it! And that diamond? Precious! She felt like such a sap. She should have gone!

She watched the brake lights disappear down the drive and

sank to the stoop.

She had denied herself the rare chance to see life from the other side—from the inside looking out—in the vexing limelight. With Buck LeGrande, no less! This time the velvet rope of celebrity was being held open wide and she had declined the opportunity to step across the threshold—alongside a man she felt deeply about.

"Damn it!" she yelled.

BunnyLee felt snake-bit and she could barely stand it.

"Stupid, stupid, stupid!"

Later that evening, she was on the sofa fumbling with the remote to watch *Groundhog Day* when Buck got back. He popped in to grab a bottle of cold champagne from the bar fridge and startled her.

"Back so soon?" she asked. "I just made some popcorn. Care to join?"

Then she saw Jadé.

"Oh, of course…" BunnyLee said. "…I just hadn't expected… how silly of me…"

"No," Buck said.

"Are you two boyfriend and girlfriend?" Jadé asked.

BunnyLee and Buck looked at each other. Neither could answer that one simple question.

"Phew!" Jadé said, breaking their silence. "That would be so awkward. Buck was just telling me in the car about his carousel horse. How it actually works. I remember the movie it was from, *Carousel Cowboy*, so romantic. In Romania, everyone loves the romance. So are you going to let me ride it?"

Jadé was already halfway up the stairs. Buck turned to look at her, then back to BunnyLee.

"I should go. It's late," BunnyLee said.

"No," Buck said.

"I've got an audition lined up for the morning. The agent called out of the blue. So I should go."

BunnyLee turned and as she walked to the kitchen, she yelled up to Jadé, who had already disappeared from the top landing, "Have a nice ride!"

"BunnyLee…" Buck said. But she was gone.

✦

Buck felt like a heel.

As he climbed the stairs, he could hear the signature accordion music that played when his famous carousel horse was turned on: Kurt Weill's "Alabama Song," made famous in the Sixties by The Doors.

Buck paused in his bedroom doorway and studied this beautiful creature. Jadé sat astride the painted wooden horse, riding up and down, swaying along with the heavy beat, naked. He had to smile.

"I like to guess which plastic surgeon in our fair city did the enhancement. It took me a minute, but then it hit me. Your breasts are real."

"Boy, you're good."

Jadé was holding the pole with one hand and making believe that she twirled a lasso in the other. She mimed lassoing Buck. Then, hand-over-hand, she drew him toward her with the imaginary rope.

"Now I know what Lady Godiva felt like on her famous ride," she said.

"The first of the modern women."

"It must have been fun to cause such sensation. Although, if memory serves, she was riding sidesaddle."

Jadé swung her bare leg over the horse to face him. She spread her legs for him to see. "Like it?" Jadé asked. She was still rising up and down on the machine, so it was hard to focus on what she was pointing at.

"Just a second." Buck said. He set the champagne down beside her borrowed dress and necklace and switched the machine off. The music ground to a halt; so did the horse. Jadé's crotch came to rest at the high point of its cycle, eye-level to Buck.

"Now what am I looking at?"

"My bling!"

Jadé was pointing to a gold stud shaped like a miniature barbell that pierced the hood of her clitoris vertically with the lower part resting on that most mysterious of anatomical parts. "My mother makes them. I wear it all the time. I would feel naked without it."

Buck looked. Who wouldn't have looked?

"You shouldn't feel naked."

"My mother is a jewelry designer. If you look closely, the ends are set in jade, just like my name!"

Buck looked closely. Her jewelry was atop a well-tended area. Her pubic hair was waxed almost completely off, save for a tuft just above the subject of discussion. The hair was dyed, tastefully in Buck's estimation, with streaks of complimentary earth tones: a nice counterpoint to the green and gold jewelry. The whole design looked like a ceremonial arrow pointing down.

"They make great birthday gifts."

Buck had to admit that in his recent quest for a present he had not considered this choice. And so much simpler than a dog.

"She designs them with diamonds, too, but like I said, jade is my thing. Earlier tonight I was wishing I had worn the pearl. My mother makes this beautiful pearl pendant that dangles just so." Jadé pointed to where it would have dangled on that part peeking out from under the hood. "I was thinking it would have felt great when we were dancing tonight and everyone was watching. Go to clitbling.com and you can see it."

"Come again?" Buck wasn't at all sure he had heard her correctly.

She spelled it out, "Clit bling dot com. I did all the modeling for her website. You should check it out."

"I'll definitely do that," Buck said. If nothing else, this would be a story to rival any of Sidney's.

"I'm so glad you wore a bowtie. The other men who were there tonight who wore straight ties? They just don't get it. A bow tie is like the opening of an expensive gift." Jadé slowly undid Buck's bowtie. She leaned in and rested her arms on Buck's shoulders. Her big toe toyed with the pleats of his cummerbund.

Buck could see how Jadé was such a sensation on film. Close-up, she had a face that the camera would adore—her eyes were bright and doe-like; her eyebrows were exotic, their ever-so-subtle changes were exquisitely expressive and riveting to watch. Her looks harkened back to the actresses of the silent days in Hollywood when women seduced with their eyes.

She grinned. "When I heard it was you I was going with tonight, I was so excited. I wanted to do something extra special. You want to see?"

Buck wasn't sure.

Jadé whispered in his ear, "I had my anus bleached."

"Whoa!"

"Is there something wrong?"

"I think I need to close the blinds."

"Okay, I will just pop into the bathroom real quick."

This was uncharted territory for Buck. He felt as if the admonishing minds of the world were looking in through the window even though his house was on a hill and his room was on the second floor. As he lowered the blinds, he saw BunnyLee sitting by the cabana. The green light from the pool was casting an eerie rippling light on her face from below. Her hands were extended palms out in front of her. She appeared to be meditating. She looked like the divine goddess Bodhisattva Guanyin, hands-down one of BunnyLee's favorite Eastern deities, carved from jade. Puddles lay legs-out at her feet.

"Where do you keep the condoms?" Jadé called through the open door. "Never mind! Found them! Wow, interesting, I don't know this brand. They're from France? Size: *grande*. Awesome!"

Jadé came out of the bathroom and for the first time he marveled at the flawless beauty of the woman.

"Is that how you got your name?" she asked.

Buck wasn't following her question.

"Are you named LeGrande for your condom size?"

Hard to believe, Buck had never thought about his stage name in that way. He was a kid when his manager came up with it. At the time this stage name was just a stand-in for everything he felt he was not and everything he needed to be: larger than life. Looking out at BunnyLee, the sad irony of Jadé's question struck home. The name LeGrande appeared to mean only one thing right now: The Big Prick.

No. No. No way. No! He was not going to go there. Sex was part of who he was. Everything he did in life he did in a big way. He was not going to apologize for what he was!

"We should do this," Jadé advised. She looked at her watch. "I promised I would not be too late."

"I think you should take your watch off."

Buck left the window to join her on the new mattress. He unclipped Jadé's wristwatch and laid it on the side table. The sight of BunnyLee in quiet repose by the pool had clouded his thoughts. Even the touch of this sensuous woman was not enough to overcome the psychic reach of BunnyLee. Buck closed his eyes in an attempt to superimpose BunnyLee's face over Jadé's, determined to redirect his desire.

The psychology of transference was a treacherous and sometimes tortuous undertaking, one that was attained more through laziness of introspection than by force of will. Closing his eyes did not help Buck's cause because the jade-colored image of BunnyLee was seared upon his retina.

"Damn that woman!"

"Who?"

"Look outside, over by cabana, see for yourself!"

Jadé walked to the window and looked through the blinds. "All I see is your friend."

"What's she doing?"

"I think maybe she's chanting. Is that what you hear?"

Buck hadn't heard it, but now he did. He stood by Jadé's side. "Damn her!"

"Are you sure you're not boyfriend and girlfriend?"

"How could she be my girlfriend when I'm up here with you?"

"Exactly," Jadé said.

She reached for the short end of Buck's bowtie and pulled the garment off. She fingered the silk collar of his jacket.

"I love this material."

Using the ends of her painted nails she undid the top three pearl buttons on his shirt and stroked his chest hair with the back of her hand.

"You should turn around."

Buck obliged. Her hands reached around under his collar as she lifted his jacket off. She unclipped his cummerbund. One at a time, she lifted each foot to remove his shoes. He could feel her breasts through the back of his shirt as she unbuttoned his trousers. He stepped out of them. She slid his boxers down and he stepped out of them.

"Again, you should turn around."

Buck turned back around. His shirttails were all that separated him from his audience, and the Romanian woman was front row center.

"Act two, scene one, the curtain rises." Jadé lifted the tails of his dress shirt. "As they say in my country, the lights come up to thunderous applause."

"They say that here, too."

"I can see why."

Jadé stretched out on Buck's bed.

"What positions do you like?" she asked. "I like them all."

"The question is where do we begin?"

Buck was not well versed in psychology. He had not spent his days in the "Know Thyself" section of the bookstore. He hadn't given much credence to Socrates, who said that the unexamined life was not worth living. He had seen enough of life to know that the examined life wasn't exactly a picnic, either. You can leave the mental gymnastics to the experts was his credo. Instead, he asked himself, why not just enjoy the simple pleasures that life served up?

Sex was a perfect example: it was simple; it was pleasurable. It was like a game. It didn't matter whether you called it Hide the Sausage or Bury the Kielbasa; in the car coming home, Jadé had told him that back in Bucharest they called it Where's the Mititei? In every language, the rules were simple. Even with a girl as creative as Jadé, who offered so many intriguing avenues to explore, there were only so many places to put it. The act itself, however nuanced, was straightforward. And that was the direction Buck intended go. The road was clearly marked. Jadé's arrow pointed the way.

There was only one catch. As Buck had learned on his recent shopping trip to Rodeo Drive, even for a man with more than his share, blood could go missing when you needed it most. The straightforward approach to sex notwithstanding, there was only so much blood pumping in his veins.

Much had been said about men having two heads: the big head and the little head. Each functioned best when there was an ample blood supply. For some reason, God in His infinite wisdom had designed man with only enough blood to operate one head at a time.

This was not what you'd call an intelligent design. Maybe God hadn't heard of multi-tasking, yet, or maybe He was just messing with Adam the way BunnyLee was messing with Buck's mind now, but the simple truth was, Buck could not think with both his big head and his little head at the same time. It was one or the other. There weren't enough corpuscles for double duty. And even though the big head was so much bigger than the little head, his little head, being on the *grande!* side of the condom aisle, needed its share of the red stuff to perform.

On the other hand, Buck had not built his career around failure. Hollywood was a small town. It was a company town. People talk. The simple fact that Jadé had heard tales of Buck's carousel horse spoke volumes about the rumor mill. This was business. The stage was set. Go big or stay home. Failure was not an option.

"I want to show you my anus," Jadé said, returning to an earlier subject of note.

Buck had never heard of anal bleaching. The topic intrigued him. Plus, she'd gone to all the trouble.

He leaned in for a look-see.

"Ooohm…"

The chanting from outside seemed to be growing louder.

"Art is in the details, that's been my motto," Buck told Jadé as he took his first gander at the new art form.

"Mine, too," Jadé concurred. "They just opened a spa out near Palm Desert: The Final Frontier. I researched it; they're top of the field. What do you think?"

Buck lay on his side. Jadé lay on her side. He rested his elbow on the mattress and supported his head with his hand. Jadé rested her foot on his other shoulder. Anyone who ever said that intimacy was an abstract concept was mistaken.

It was intimacy with a woman that Buck most craved, whether sharing a bowl of popcorn on the sofa over a midnight showing of *Groundhog Day* or discussing the latest spa innovations over a yawning pair of velvety gams; it was the intimacy of closeness that pulled at his heart.

"It's definitely lighter, pinker than before. It's a little blotchy right here," Jadé pointed where.

"I like it," Buck said.

"Of course, you don't know what it looked like before," she said. "Do you ever feel like you are under the scrutiny of a microscope in this town?"

"Probably not to the extent that you do."

Buck's sight lines were way better than Jadé's. He was looking straight at what she was pointing to from memory.

"In bright light you can see." She sighed. "Don't mind me, this is an existential longing that we Romanians suffer."

The light wasn't bright and he didn't have his reading glasses. Buck couldn't see the imperfection. But he could see where she was coming from. Bright lights and scrutiny were the hallmark of their profession. Judging by the trajectory of her career so far, with an Academy nomination on the horizon, anyone could see that Jadé was going to the top. A lot of people were going to be paying close attention along the way. Her need for this spa treatment was a metaphor for her current life.

"It looks perfect."

"For the most part, I think they did an okay job. You like it?"

"What's not to like? I love it." He was surprised by her self-doubt. He had never met a woman more comfortable in her own body.

"*Dor* we call it—this emotion of longing."

"There isn't a square inch of you I don't find beautiful."

"Truly? I wasn't sure. That is so nice."

"Ooooohm." BunnyLee's resonant voice filled the night air.

Buck could have put some music on to drown her out, but no, he was stronger than that.

"I love your bling," Buck said, stroking the area that the bejeweled barbell pierced.

"That's nice," Jadé assured him. She adjusted a pillow under her ear.

The barbell had some heft to it. Jadé was on her side, her leg now draped across his shoulder. Buck lifted the barbell with two fingers.

"Really nice," Jadé reported in.

In the gym, lifting barbells was called bench pressing or pumping iron, ten reps and then a rest, ten more and then a rest and so on...Judging from Jadé's reaction, this technique carried over to the bedroom as well. Buck felt stirrings of his own. He assured himself it was only a matter of time before things were pumping in the right direction. In the interim, his tongue would do the heavy lifting.

"Ooooooohm..."

Now another voice joined BunnyLee's. He couldn't place it right away. He paused to listen. Buck breathed in and out in rhythm with BunnyLee's voice as he listened. He breathed deep.

The scent of a woman was heady. It was hormonal. It was carnal. There was something so basic and primordial about that aroma, something subconscious in the way it tugged at him. It was too much and yet...

Howling: that was the other voice. The dog was howling. BunnyLee's chanting had caused the dog to howl. With each long 'ohm' the dog raised its head to the starry heavens and joined her call.

"No fair!" Buck smiled to himself.

It was no longer a problem. The animal in him was aroused. The chanting made him feel even more powerful. He took in a deep breath and relaxed into the moment.

In rhythm with the tip of his tongue, it wasn't long before he now had all the females at Number 10 Beverly Canyon breathing as One.

CHAPTER 5

IN THE MORNING, after he kissed Jadé farewell and Frankie whisked the young beauty away, Buck headed to the kitchen to assuage a hearty appetite. "Alabama Song" was stuck in his head and he hummed The Door's version about asking the way to the next pretty girl. He hadn't expected to cross paths with his houseguest so early in the day.

BunnyLee lifted her gaze from her bowl of granola and watched him prepare his breakfast.

He felt bad—bad for BunnyLee. Bad for how things were working out between them. He was careful not to catch her eye. He went to the cupboard and poured himself a bowl of cereal. He also felt good, and feeling good also made him feel bad. He was having trouble reconciling these two conflicting feelings. In his mind's eye he replayed some of the highlights of the night before. He couldn't help but smile to himself, and it was hard not to show that smile on his face. And this, too, made him feel bad. He felt like a god, not the Big Guy upstairs, more like one of the specialty gods of the raffish, impetuous, Homeric type. Or if not exactly a god himself, he felt an affinity to the fraternity of gods who were elbowing each other and winking at his recent good fortune. He pulled up a stool next to BunnyLee and ate in silence.

BunnyLee was more circumspect about life.

"You really going to eat that?" she asked in an even tone.

"What's wrong with cereal?"

"Lucky Charms is not cereal."

"It says here the pieces are toasted oat-based."

"It's candy."

Buck chewed one of the marshmallow Marbits. He could totally relate to Lucky the Leprechaun who was dancing across the cereal box with glee. Some shaman in the Orient had told BunnyLee that she was five times lucky. Buck felt like he was the one who was five times lucky.

"Do you know what dyes they use to make all those brightly colored charms?"

"I really hadn't given it that much thought."

"You should."

"I will." Buck said.

He took another bite and chewed more loudly.

Bunny said, "I think I should leave."

"What do you mean?"

"I need to get back to my life. You've been so kind putting me up. I'm just spinning my wheels. I think it's time I left."

"I don't want you to leave."

"That's what you *don't* want, tell me what you *want*."

"I want you to *not* leave."

"You want me to stay."

"Yes."

"Well, I don't think it's healthy."

"What's not healthy? We have the pool, the sun, the green trees and fresh air, the calla lilies are in bloom again, such a lovely flower." Buck had suddenly become poetic. He took a deep breath. "We have tennis. Who would I play tennis with? I hope you're playing today. Remember the Klingons who you met your first day? They're coming this afternoon and they're expecting a heated rematch."

"You haven't looked outside. The Santa Anas are blowing. Nobody is going to be playing tennis for a while. And besides, I have an audition."

"You do? That's right, you said. When we talked last night."

"We didn't talk last night. We exchanged pleasantries and I shoved off to bed."

"You're mad."

"No shit, Sherlock."

"Tell me what you're mad about."

BunnyLee paused to collect her thoughts. She spoke carefully.

"You asked me to go to the 'Senior Prom' with you and I turned you down."

"First of all, it's not the Senior Prom."

"I'm glad for you that you went. In fact, I'm the one who insisted that you go. That woman is going to be a star. Everybody in this town is going to want a piece of her. And you were ahead of the wave. Your pictures together are going to be everywhere. How could I be mad at you for that?"

"You can't."

"I know. That's why I'm so mad."

"Don't be mad. I don't want you to be mad. I want you to be happy."

"I'm mad at myself. You had a great time. That's what I'm mad about. You had a great time and you didn't have it with me."

Buck chewed another charm. "I asked you first."

"You don't get it. I'd be crazy to fall in love with you."

For the first time in a long time they were looking directly at each other.

"Were you considering it?"

✦

Was he really expecting an answer?

She wished she'd bitten her tongue!

Saying she would be "crazy to fall in love" was shorthand for a whirl of feelings she was having which she could not possibly dissect on the spot—feelings that stirred up out of nowhere like a dust devil, invisible but for the debris it kicked up in her face—followed by the glaring fact that she was a guest in his house and had no right to be commenting on his behavior in the first place! And furthermore, who was she kidding, hanging out with this man? Was she really being truthful with herself that things could continue the way they had after last night! Hel-lo! Her feelings for him were naïve if not reckless and could only lead to jealousy and no way was she going there! She felt that all too familiar wave of dizziness that she had first experienced on the plane.

They'd missed their moment. That was it in a nutshell. Their chance for any kind of meaningful relationship, if there ever had been a chance, was now out of the question. She'd perilously opened a pathway to her heart. This was a mistake that any girl

could have made. She'd darned near opened her body! She knew
that she would forever regret it if she'd followed through with that!
Which was good, because she also knew that she would forever
regret it that she hadn't.

The man was looking at her and she dared not look away. He
was toying with her like a spider watching a fly. How could she
have risked getting herself entangled? She was flirting with danger
and it was just a matter of time before she got bit. The man couldn't
help himself. He was not emotionally available. He was put on this
planet to seduce and she was getting snagged in his web—a little
snack for later. How could she be so stupid?

The way he was looking at her, waiting for her answer, she
couldn't help but grin. He almost had her and he knew it.

✦

"None of your business," she said.

"I'm going to take that as a yes."

"Huh?"

"Please don't leave."

"It's not healthy for me! I mean, for instance, just as an example,
who eats like this?"

"I think we eat great."

"Well, if I were to stay, and I'm only speaking hypothetically,
because I need to be going, but if I stayed, then we would need to
start eating better."

"What's wrong with the way we eat?"

"Steaks and chops and burgers: meat, meat, and more meat."

"There are vegetables on burgers, what are those green leaves
sticking out?"

BunnyLee just looked at him with that even look of hers. He
was hoping for a guest appearance of the little dimple in her left
cheek that was so often followed by a smile. A thickening feeling
of guilt was beginning to ooze in and smother his earlier feeling of
elation.

"Were you going to cook?" he asked.

"No."

"Well, I'm not going to cook. When I'm working, they bring me
food. When I'm not, I order in." It's good to be king, he told himself.

"Couldn't we at least order in some Chinese for a change?"

"If you want Chinese, we'll order Chinese. What is that, Peking Duck?"

"No. Okay, we'll order one meat dish."

"Great. Let's do it!" King Buck decreed.

"Oh my God! Just like that, I won the debate!"

He knew she was being sarcastic, but he acted contrite. He was a benevolent king, the kind that people speak kindly of. In exchange for her not moving out, he agreed to eat healthier food.

When the Chinese deliveryman arrived on his bicycle that evening, Buck buzzed him in at the gate and met him at the door. He was expecting to pay for a couple of warm bags, tip the guy, and send him on his way.

"Jimmy Chan at your service!" The Chinese man saluted. "Show me kitchen!"

Buck ushered him in. "BunnyLee!" Buck yelled across the pool. "Dinner's here!"

He watched the man unpack an assortment of strange-looking vegetables and oddly colored oils. Buck still had a holdover hunger from the previous night's festivities and was eyeing the Lucky Charms. He watched as the man commenced to cook their dinner right there in the kitchen. BunnyLee breezed in to officiate, and she didn't seem at all put off by the ingredients. She was ooh-ing and ah-ing as she sniffed this and squeezed that. She nodded approval with every taste. She exchanged a few words with the man in French and they both laughed as if sharing a joke. Buck was busy watching for the arrival of the main ingredient. Even chicken would have been a welcome headliner on the marquee. He had missed the part about BunnyLee inquiring as to the man's availability. Maybe some of the negotiation was done in Chinese. Either way, before Buck had a chance to say, "You're kidding, right?" in English, she had apparently hired the cook fulltime in Cantonese. And, of course, Buck would be paying the freight. But what could he say? She'd won the debate.

They had Chinese food that night and again for lunch. And for dinner the next night? Chinese food. BunnyLee assured Buck that there really was meat in some of these bowls, but he would defy anyone to show him where. There was a leathery leaf called kale that appeared in every scene. Buck guessed it was the protagonist. And judging by the way BunnyLee savored it, a white gelatinous substance she called bean curd was the love interest. Mushrooms played the villain. These were slimier than the mushrooms he was used to but really looked the part. He suspected they weren't really mushrooms at all but some diabolical subspecies that slithered when you put them in your mouth and were very likely still alive in his stomach, turning his intestines into an amusement park ride. The cook couldn't make a soup without floating cloud ears in the broth. Buck was afraid to ask where cloud ears came from. He was pretty certain they were spawned in outer space.

He never let on that he knew, but the evidence was clear and simple: BunnyLee was exacting retribution.

Buck had to hand it to the cook; he was good. He was able to make some of this stuff taste edible. That was the miracle, but not the point. Buck had thought that by hiring a cook he had settled the argument, whereas in fact, it was becoming obtrusively clear with every grain of rice, with every bamboo shoot, that by having surrendered control of the menu he had lost control of the bigger argument. Or more precisely, he had never actually controlled the bigger argument. The evidence was glaring: BunnyLee's wonderfully crooked smile had gone on hiatus and a wickedly wry one was filling in while it was away. There was no doubt about it; King Buck was in the doghouse.

He sent a bouquet of flowers to her room on Tuesday via Frankie, but it did little to further *détente*.

The wind had been howling for two days with gusts up to sixty miles an hour, and there was no sign of it abating. Born in the Mojave, the Santa Anas joined forces with the Mono Winds of Western Nevada to create a maelstrom. Wildfires were spawned as far away as Mariposa up in the Sierras.

The hot dry air was the bane of Hollywood, and the movie industry was on edge. Nobody could shoot exteriors. Twenty-by-twenty silk frames used for sun diffusion became sails. Actors' wardrobe whipped around in the blustery weather and their dialogue vanished before the mic. Producers pulled their hair out, those who still had hair, as productions ground to a halt. In this town where show business was everybody's business, even the unemployed were distressed.

On the radio the rock group Steely Dan lamented that the Santa

Ana winds were here again, to which the punk group Bad Religion added that even the stars were edgy. That certainly described Buck. He hadn't been out for days. The Bobs likened the effects of the Santa Ana winds to the entire city of Los Angeles having PMS.

On television, people were blaming the Santa Anas for everything from Mother Nature to Global Warming. The conservative blogosphere referred to the Santa Ana Winds as Devil's Breath. They took a biblical perspective, arguing that since the winds emanated from the Gates of Hell, the hottest place on earth, this was indisputable evidence of our comeuppance for the loose moral fabric of today's society.

Talk of moral turpitude fueled the daytime airwaves searching for someone to blame. It was an ill wind that blows nobody any good, they said. A seasonal haunted house attraction in Las Vegas fortuitously named the Gates of Hell was enjoying a brisk business in which the Angel of Death appeared as a man in drag. Vegas being Vegas, reporters were hard-pressed to find a patron willing to share details about this adult Halloween attraction; only that at the end of the night the Gates of Hell's Lost and Found Department was swamped with queries about misplaced clothing. Had they found the culprit?

Buck had a parallel theory of his own creation: BunnyLee and her evil sidekick Puddles had conjured up the wrath of God with their poolside howling the night of Jadé. For evidence he looked no further than the weather map with its arrows pointing straight at Beverly Canyon. Number 10 was clearly taking a direct hit.

The air was bone dry. Tennis was out of the question. The red clay from the court was swirling in little dust devils, taking off for Catalina Island. The days were scorching hot, but you could freeze getting out of the pool on account of the stiff breeze. Not that swimming was an option—the pool was brown with debris.

Buck pretty much put Jadé out of his mind. He left her a voicemail thanking her for their date. After a couple of days went by, he was pretty certain he wouldn't hear back. She was a Romanian candle taking off. He was a dead man if he thought he could hitch a ride on that rocket into orbit. Someone from Warner Brothers sent over a script via Frankie along with a rewrite of the contract they'd been back and forth with. It was clear just how bored Buck was that he read the whole script. As a teleplay it wasn't bad: kind of a send-up of his old television series that they were calling *The Return of*

Malibu Man. The problem was, there wasn't a part in it for him: the lead in the pilot was a Black chauffeur, and his boss was an old, bent-over, washed-up Nick Derringer. Somebody in acquisitions was clearly delusional. The fact that they sent the script to him was just more confirmation of how skewed everyone's thinking had become. He sent the script back recommending massive changes.

Meanwhile, BunnyLee went about her business like the wind didn't bother her. She carried on undeterred. Buck looked for her by the pool, their common ground, but she was spending her days in the cabana with Puddles. That was, when she didn't have Frankie driving her around town.

+

Frankie ferried BunnyLee to an audition, the dentist, then a craft store; she was designing costumes for Puddles. On their way back they stopped at a Ralph's Supermarket for some groceries and a puppy treat. The Bentley was not one to be pushed around by the wind, but getting out was something else. The wind yanked the car door out of BunnyLee's hand.

Spawned behind dumpsters or between parked cars, dust devils were the real class-clowns of the weather world. These micro tornados appeared anywhere out of nowhere wreaking mini-havoc just for the heck of it. They might get fresh with the ladies—muss their hair and lift their skirts—or make off with a guy's baseball hat. They were especially churlish with the closeted bald.

Frankie waited with Puddles on a leash as BunnyLee trudged through the parking lot to the store. She covered her eyes from the dust with one hand and held down her sarong with the other. Inside, she glimpsed her reflection in the frozen food case. With her windblown hair and disheveled clothes she looked a bit unhinged. She pulled her largest pair of sunglasses from her bag to disguise her identity.

She was most careful not to be recognized in the checkout line. She kept her head down and scanned the tabloids while she waited to check out.

The cover of *American Celebrity* had a photo of Buck on the red carpet posing with Jadé at the Emmys. Their headline read 'Torn Between Two Lovers.' Next to the photo was a fake tear line and an insert photo of Buck with BunnyLee.

"Huh?" BunnyLee said.

In their photo the two were standing at the pet store window on the occasion of their only date out together. The picture was snapped at the very moment she'd touched Buck's hand to reassure him of her happiness. She remembered that the photographer had startled her. She did not look her kindest in the shot. 'Details inside,' promised more pix.

It didn't say where inside.

BunnyLee lowered her sunglasses to see over them. She leafed through the pages and stopped at a picture of herself on a billboard next to an article about Ted and his famous standup routine Ted Talks. It was now a multi-media extravaganza featuring a montage of BunnyLee's billboard pictures that Ted likened to Godzilla, the monster that devoured Los Angeles. BunnyLee remembered their conversation at Heather's wedding. Ted had stolen her joke! She leafed further and found what she had been looking for.

"Paper or plastic?" the cashier asked.

"What? Oh. Thanks, I brought my own bags."

The cashier noticed the article that BunnyLee was reading: a series of stock photos venerating Buck's career as a child actor and teenage heartthrob.

"I was at a protest a couple of weeks ago and Buck LeGrande smiled at me. I think that whole thing between him and Kermit the Frog was just more fake news. What I'd give to go to the Emmys."

"That Jadé is a real angel," a woman behind her in line said. "So innocent."

"Looks can be deceiving." BunnyLee said under her breath.

The man ahead of BunnyLee, groceries in hand, paused before leaving, "I'd pick the foreign one over that other woman. She's looks so...angry."

"Innocence," the woman behind BunnyLee said. "I think what everyone wants these days is innocence."

"Exactly!" the man ahead said, "Not someone hard-edged like that Love-Your-Smile woman."

BunnyLee pushed her glasses back up her nose to cover her face, but it was too late.

"Oh!" The woman behind her said. She discreetly pointed at BunnyLee for the man to recognize.

"Huh? What? Oh. I mean...I didn't mean...Sorry!" The man

said and took off.

"That was awkward," the cashier said. "Paper or plastic...oh, right, you brought. Don't pay him any mind. Everybody's just jealous when somebody with a little talent gets famous. I mean, not like your talent is little! But that Romanian actress is in a movie!"

"No offense taken," BunnyLee said.

"And so much younger," the woman behind her said.

"Yes, you said that." BunnyLee felt as unkind as her photograph on the cover suggested. "Everybody is entitled to his or her opinion."

Decisions, decisions:

Paper or plastic?

Jadé or the Love Your Smile girl?

In supermarket checkout lines, everyone was welcome to voice their opinion. Cashiers mediated the debate. Everyone in America who shopped, and that was just about everyone BunnyLee knew, read the headlines of *American Celebrity*. That would include her sister and her mother and all of her mother's friends. How BunnyLee measured up against Jadé was now the Question of the Week. She wondered whether they would hide the news from her dad; this shame of a Hollywood triangle embodied everything her parents warned her about when she was growing up. And then there was Ted, her standup comedian ex. BunnyLee's tabloid triangle would be fresh fodder for Ted's club act. Obviously having not gone to the Emmys with Buck had done nothing to insulate BunnyLee from her stifling celebrity.

She added the shoddy *Celebrity* to her bill and dropped the paper into her satchel for later.

It didn't stay there long. As she exited Ralph's, a dust devil ambushed her. It lifted the newsprint in its swirl and whipped it around her in a frenzy. Individual pages clung to her ankle, her elbow, her neck, her knee. Full color photos of all the Emmy gowns, the latest Cover Girl mascaras and blushes, polishes and creams—desperate stop-gaps for the has-beens and might-have-beens of the aging-out—and a merciless centerfold of debilitating cellulite. One page momentarily blinded her view, blown against her face, an ad for Dial-a-Denture. BunnyLee crumpled it in her hand. Pages did cartwheels across the parking lot. One stuck to an oil slick next to Frankie's foot. The angelic Jadé, posing in her designer dress and one point four five million-dollar diamond necklace, smiled up at them both.

Frankie was kind enough not to comment.

BunnyLee needed to call her sister to do damage control with her folks. She had half a mind to call Ted. She searched the backseat of the Bentley for her bag. Her phone was missing! Frankie drove them back to the store to see if she had dropped it there. Together they retraced her steps. They had no luck finding it and nobody had turned it in.

BunnyLee was technologically cut off from the world. She couldn't read the texts that would no doubt be piling up or answer her emails. She was in a Limboland, dizzyingly alienated in a swirling funnel cloud of disagreeable fame.

✢

Just when Buck thought things between them couldn't get worse, BunnyLee showed up at the dinner table that night with a yellowing copy of Søren Kierkegaard's *The Concept of Anxiety* which she cracked open as the main course alongside her dog-eared *Being and Nothingness*. Friedrich Nietzsche's *Beyond Good and Evil* was the surprise for dessert. BunnyLee was always reading something weird and he tried to humor her by listening, but truth be told, all these theoretical concepts made him nervous.

"'Man is condemned to be free,'" she read from Sartre, "'because once thrown into the world, he is responsible for everything he does.'"

She was introducing him to the philosophical ideas of existentialism and even though she didn't say as much, he suspected this all tied in with his extracurricular activities with Jadé.

"The point is," she continued, "is that man is forever at odds with nature. A person can say they don't have a choice, but isn't that itself a form of choice?" She then proceeded to enlighten him to the notion that 'anxiety is the dizziness of freedom.' He joked about how if it weren't for anxiety waking him up every night in the wee hours of quiet desperation he would never have gotten anywhere in his career—and then she informed him that, according to these philosophers, life begins on the other side of despair where a person chooses contentment.

"So despair is a good feeling?" Buck asked, trying to cover a note of panic in his laugh.

"I wouldn't say 'good.' Love is a good feeling, the most laudable of feelings. It radiates from within. It is illusive. It is everywhere when you feel it and nowhere when you despair."

Buck was having a bad case of longing for the old BunnyLee, the pre-Emmys BunnyLee. He wondered about that Romanian word *dor* that Jadé had used to describe this same feeling of despair. He wondered whether alienation was catching, like a sexually transmitted disease or the flu.

Then she started talking about Greek philosophy and the Greek gods that embodied human emotions.

CHAPTER 6

AUSTIN LOOKED AROUND for a spot of shade where he might get some shut-eye.

It was not yet midday in Vegas and too early to check-in. And it was hotter than blazes. Austin's Stetson was scant shelter from the unrelenting sun. His convertible no longer had a working top. The steel frame had buckled in the wind outside of Billings while closing for a downpour. Since then, rain or shine, this road-weary professional wrestler was exposed to the elements. His brother would have laughed and driven faster to avoid getting soaked through a series of thunderstorms, but even Laredo couldn't have outridden this unrelenting sun.

Austin slowed to a stop where Carson dead-ended into Casino Boulevard.

A row of palms along the boulevard offered scant cover. Las Vegas was not designed by its town fathers for the comfort of tourists lollygagging about outside in the sun. Not when there was all that fun to be found in the cool confines of the casinos like the Golden Nugget across the street. Its frilly canopy atop a white lattice façade looked like a chorus line of long-legged ladies lifting their petticoats to the marvels that glistened thereunder.

Austin was not immune to a promise hidden behind a sassy wink. His brother used to joke that they'd spent ninety-five percent of their money on wine, women and song and the rest of it they'd squandered. But the truth was buried deeper than that. In the Golden Nugget, years ago, they'd paid a heftier price.

The hotel breezeway was crowded with conventioneers checking out. Austin carefully negotiated the driveway crowded with luggage wagons and stopped the Cadillac before a dispirited group of men waiting for the airport shuttle. Austin knew the glassy-eyed look. Three nights of gambling and carousing relieved these men of their sense of wonder, a sizeable portion of their monthly income and a chunk of their self-esteem.

A man reached for his phone and framed a picture. Austin tipped his hat.

His white Eldorado convertible with red leather interior featured a pair of Texas longhorns lashed to the grill. DUSTDVLS spelled out the vanity plate. It was never the intention of the Sway brothers to blend in. Their mama used to lecture them, "Go big or go home!" Austin hadn't been home in years.

Austin needed more than a nap. He wasn't sure if this bootleg supplement he was taking was to blame, but he was jumpy and grumpy. Coffee made it worse. And he wasn't sleeping at night. Nightmares were troubling and he was increasingly vague as to what was real when he was awake. Time off was a luxury he could ill afford. Nor was it an option; he was under contract through the end of the year. But if ever a person deserved a break, it was Austin Sway.

Judging by the crowd it could be a long wait for the parking valet. He slid across the seat and leaned against the passenger door. He lowered his hat brim over his brow in a signal of "do not disturb" to the other men who were framing shots. He stretched his legs out on the seat. Austin had no intention of spending the night at the Golden Nugget. After this evening's big event, he was fixing to drive west, putting Death Valley and the Mojave behind him under the cool cover of darkness. He had some nagging business to attend. It seemed a waste, though; even one night in a better bed would have been nice.

Austin caught sight of a short, barrel-chested transvestite across the street waiting for the walk light. A sheer camisole top and fishnet stockings did little to cover her hairy chest and legs. Red hotpants, a wig of big green hair and a two-day-old beard completed the picture of gender dissolution. She took her time crossing the street. This was a performer who gave her all to audiences big or small, paying or not.

Austin fiddled with his new phone. Technology was not

his strong suit. Phones were all about interconnectedness and he wasn't in the mood to connect. To him, a phone was just a necessary fixture of a life lived on the road. His producer had shown uncommon kindness to set this new one up for him. All Austin had to do was remember his passwords. Texts and email were piling up.

Austin noticed the dispirited gaggle of men come to life as they surreptitiously elbowed each other and gawked as the cross-dresser sashayed close.

"I am the Angel of Death, and I have my eye on all you naughty boys." She made no effort to disguise her man-voice. "You and you and you and you!" she said.

Austin watched as these men averted their eyes and looked down at their feet. There was little doubt that each had enough scandalous dope on the others to ensure the covenant of *omerta*—whatever had happened in Vegas remained in Vegas. They stood guilty and confused. Thankfully for them, they were not the target of her interest. Austin was.

"I am come for you!" the transvestite said. She pointed her hairy red-nailed forefinger at Austin. This was when things turned momentarily surreal.

The transvestite walked straight toward his Eldorado. She used the longhorns as a step up, and stood looking down from the hood of his car. Just for a second Austin entertained the fear that he had conjured this woman whole cloth from his over-active imagination.

With expansive tattooed arms she addressed the chastened men.

"Gentlemen, gentlemen, if I may have your attention please! It is my great honor to introduce to you the spectacularly, incomparably, uncommonly gifted athlete, Austin Sway, America's favorite cowboy wrestler—a man whose exploits among the fairer sex, myself notwithstanding, are the stuff of legend! Please join me in welcoming The Dust Devil back to Vegas!"

Austin looked at her over his sunglasses as she knelt in deference to Austin's eminence. He woke to the realization that he knew her—not as a specter of his subconscious, but as a guy he used to work with and always went to great lengths to avoid.

"Whoa! You had me there for a second, Juan Carlos."

"I go by Juanita Carlita, now."

"Pardon me."

"Happy to see me?"

"I think you've got me confused with Laredo."

"And I am very sad to share my condolences."

"What's with the get-up?"

"I am the Angel of Death! I have come to save your soul."

"Charming."

"You underestimate me, Austin." As Juanita Carlita alighted to the curb, a bellhop asked her for a selfie and Juanita Carlita obliged him. The scrawny boy put his arm around her and framed the shot. She struck a comical pose. "I'm famous here, Austin. Am I not right, *amigo*?" Juanita Carlita asked the bellhop.

"She sure is, mister. Everybody loves JC."

"For being the ugliest tranny in Vegas?" Austin asked.

"I'm the marquis performer in this town's most infamous production, The Gates of Hell. They put me up here at the Nugget for the run of the show. Not bad, huh? Care to join me for lunch?"

"It's far too busy in there for the likes of me," Austin said.

"You dare refuse the company of The Angel of Death?" Juanita Carlita asked, one hand settling seductively onto her hip.

"I'm not looking for a savior, my friend. And besides, I'm already being stalked by the Angel of Death, so unless there of two of you…"

"Everybody needs a little divine intervention from time to time."

With that, Juanita Carlita nimbly hopped onto the trunk of the car, stepped over the mangled canvas top and slid into the driver's seat.

"I know a new place, Tex-Mex, you're gonna love." JC turned the ignition and dropped the sorry car into gear. "I usually don't go out all dolled up, but for you, I'll make an exception."

Austin's brother would have laughed at all this. Laredo once told JC that he was slipperier than deer guts on a doorknob and doubly hard to get off your hands, and JC took it as a compliment. Laredo believed in people and their right to be outlandish. He was everybody's greatest fan. Laredo didn't care about the authenticity of a man's story so much as the sincerity with which he (or she) told it. Austin had forever stood in the shadow of his brother's outsized personality and now he was squinting in the sunlight.

"Man, you are hardcore driving through Nevada with the top down!" JC said.

"Top doesn't close. Been like this for a while. Haven't been in one place long enough to get it fixed."

"What do you do when it rains?"

"A mechanic in Salt Lake was kind enough to drill some hole in the floor boards to let the rainwater out. Good thing, too, because I have driven through some real gully washers since."

Conversation came easy to JC as long as the subject was JC. Austin didn't feel like talking anyway and the stories were interesting enough. He sat across from him in a booth and listened.

"Nobody was as surprised as me when Vic cut me loose. Look at me, I'm five years younger than you, Austin, still in the prime of my career and then, dang, sorry buddy, nice knowin' ya! Thanks for the memories and all that. Never saw it coming."

"I expect I'm seeing my last days on the circuit, too," Austin said.

"This is what I'm saying. Vic, he can be friendly to your face, but turn around and you find a Bowie knife surgically installed in your ribcage. It looked like I lost everything, but I am here to tell you, because you have never had to deal with unemployment, there is a world of opportunity waiting for you when you finally set yourself free. Life professions are not so sacrosanct or hard fast as they were when we were kids. I know you come up doing the rodeos what with your pap being an announcer and all. Back then when you said the word rodeo, everybody pretty much knew what that meant. Not anymore. Nowadays you've got your Gay Rodeo Association, your Ladies with Lassos, your Cowgirls of Color, and on and on. Ain't nuthin' sacred no more and I am good with that. You just got to get a gimmick."

"I never knew you were gay."

"Austin, you miscalculate me. This ain't about straight or queer. I'm playing men's worst nightmare. I've hit the motherlode! Both sides of the border. Although the gimmick I came up with is way different south of the Rio Grande. I don't know if you knew this about me but my family on my mother's side are Mexican."

"With a name like Juan Carlos, I never would have guessed."

"Funny! You're funny! I forget that about you. But, yeah, I have roots down there. For years people were telling me about this cousin I had, José Luis. He wrestles in the *Lucha Libre* league. So I head south and look him up. Nice fella. Looks like an over-sized version of me."

"Is there no justice?"

"Ha! So together we concoct this new routine. Drag wrestling. It's a thing down there. Don't ask me why, but a man in a dress brings the house down. Luis and I take things one step further. We call it an 'I do' match. I play his harlot sister in a maternity dress with a *bambino* in the papoose and all my past boyfriends deny the kid is theirs. Family honor, it's big in Mexico. Jose Luis is trying to make an honest girl out of me. The referee is a priest dressed in parson's robes and it's a tag team event. The match doesn't end until I can slip a ring on one of our opponent's fingers and get him to say 'I do.' Of course, the would-be groom always wriggles free just before the priest declares us married. The Mexican crowds, they eat it up! When the heel tries to get away into the bleachers, the audience invariably gets into the act and tries to push him back. I'm not about to explain how a macho culture can cheer for a cross-dresser, but I can tell you that wrestling in drag is exhilarating. You got to try it."

"I'll take your word for it."

"Meanwhile, come to find out, off-season, witch-doctoring is the family business down there. Eerie, right? My *abuela* is a *bruja* remarried to a local shaman. It's like lawyers up here, a shaman moves into town and a couple of months later they need four more. Spells and elixirs and potions are flying this way and that. If you're sick down there, it's not because you caught a cold, it's because a neighbor thinks you poisoned his burro and hired one of these spiritual guys to even the score."

"My grandmother dabbled in herbs," Austin said. "It's part of our native culture."

"Right. There's truth to it, no doubt. The whole point of going to a shaman is to help you avoid calamity. They say that butterfly wings flapping in Michoacan can cause tornados in Texas. Which is to say that misfortune starts small and if you know the right shaman, they can help you side-step it initially before it bulls you over later. I think of it like pinball. The game is won or lost early when subtle nudges of the machine change the fate of the ball later on. Waiting until later, when a bigger nudge is your only hope, it's TILT! Game over! These shamans, they're like pinball wizards."

"That's an interesting way of looking at it," Austin said.

"It's like today, when I commandeered your car. If I hadn't come along or maybe had let you drive, who knows what could have happened, maybe a bad accident. Maybe that one little action on my part changed the whole course of your life."

"So on top of the cross-dressing, you've found time to become a shaman, too?"

"I've picked up a few tricks."

"Or maybe you're just full of it. Flags fly both ways, JC. Like maybe you didn't know what you were doing when you thought you did. How do I know you didn't nudge me into jeopardy when I was otherwise sittin' pretty?"

"Sittin' pretty? Earth to Austin! Look at you! You look like death warmed over! Where's the fun guy I used to know? No. Either you have the touch, or you don't. I think it's in my blood." JC stood and gave Austin a gentle shove on the shoulder and he shifted.

"Listen, I gotta take a leak."

"Tell me what you know about the Angel of Death."

"You mean the way I play her? Because the promoters, they've got this directing team, they have me wearing fishnet stockings held up by this lacy garter system. I have a hard time keeping it in place. It's a lot of fun wearing a skirt, very freeing, and this one is deliberately short because this is an R-rated form of entertainment. I get to tease a bit about what's underneath. And this red blouse? You'd be surprised how many guys are trying to look up my skirt or down my blouse. I mean, I have got to be the ugliest gal in the world and as long as I look sexy, they are sneaking a peak."

"Actually, what I was asking about was whether you thought the Angel of Death was real."

"How do me mean real?"

"I mean, do you think she takes different forms at different times depending on who she's stalking?"

"Austin, I know your brother just died and that has got to have been hell. But do you think she has come looking for you, too?"

"Laredo was the real star of our act. He would have fared just fine without me. He was my better half."

"Would you stop?!"

"I've had this feeling like I'm being stalked."

"By a woman?"

Austin nodded, yes.

"Is she pretty?"

"Her green eyes look right through me."

"In a good way?"

"No, not in a good way. It's a punishing stare. Like I am found guilty and she has come to collect the fine."

"Listen, I'll be right back. I got to go find the men's room," Juanita Carlita said.

"Aren't you forgetting something?"

"What? Oh hell, you're right. You think I need to use the ladies' room?"

"What do you normally do?"

"Normally, I'm not dressed like this out on the town. Normally I go straight home to the hotel, shower and go to bed after a long night. A person could get messed up going into the wrong restroom even in Las Vegas! What do you think I should do?"

"If it were me, I'd go around back and find a dumpster to go behind."

"You think? Oh! Funny! You want to come along as backup? No? Okay, well, wish me luck."

While he waited for JC, Austin asked for the check.

The waitress refilled his cup. "Careful, hon, coffee's hot," she said.

Something strange caught his eye. There was a woman outside in the parking lot. He could see her through the restaurant window. She was sizing up his car. And then she turned and stared right at him, those green eyes, like an aberration. This was a young woman, a teenager, uncommonly tall. The first time she appeared on his radar might have been as long ago as Calgary. He was appearing at the Stampede. Not that he much noticed the fans in the bleachers, but those green eyes, they gave him the willies.

This past year had been one big blur anyway. Then this summer from town to town there was this young gal in the stands: in Boise, in Missoula, in Billings, in Laramie. She was no ordinary devotee of the sport. When the audience stood and booed, the woman sat expressionless—pokerfaced and un-pardoning. The more he scrutinized that face for some sign of sentiment, the more he came to associate her with his mother. Or more precisely, regret he felt about his mother. When Austin was alone, which was now most of the time, he chewed over the notion that the Angel of Death had taken the form of a young version of his deceased mama to taunt him in his work. Magical thinking to be sure, but who could be cogent on the subject of death? And how else did you explain those green eyes?

There was a tap on his shoulder. He thought it was JC messing with him some more. He was mid-sip on his scalding coffee and he was afraid if he looked away from the girl, she wouldn't be there when he looked back.

"Austin Sway, as I live and breathe!" was an older woman's voice. "Fancy meetin' you here. Howdy!" She gave him a spirited slug on his arm to get his attention.

Austin was a wrestler hardwired to react. His body swung around, whereas his head remained behind. "What!" he said to the insistent fan. The coffee went everywhere and it was hot! Danged hot! He jumped to his feet. An awkward twist of his backbone and his neck locked up something bad. Not like it was one-hundred-percent perfect before, but in the parlance of his trade, this type of neck injury was a veritable career-ender. He'd wrestled some of the biggest men in the world, so there was no uncertain irony to being brought down by a mid-sized middle-aged female fan.

He held his neck in pain.

"Damnation!" The biggest event of the summer season was tonight and he was hurt. "And damn you, too for bringing me here!" Austin said to JC, who, returning from the washroom, stepped between Austin and the woman to tamp down further altercation.

CHAPTER 7

IT WAS LATE Friday afternoon on the evening of the fifth day of the eminent reign of the Chinese cook, Jimmy Chan. Buck awoke from his post-siesta siesta to the smell of beef cooking. His olfactory system was on high alert, and there was no mistaking that smell. He hopped off the bed and bounced down the stairs to investigate.

Chan was in the kitchen at the smokeless grill, and the flames were exuberant; a handsome specimen of filet mignon was sizzling away. Buck couldn't believe his good fortune. After five days of epic Dickensian deprivation, a steak. One steak.

He was wondering if BunnyLee was dining out because one steak divided two ways was not the way to serve filet mignon. In Buck's way of thinking, a filet mignon, when properly served, should sit proudly on a plate. Maybe a delicate garnish was tucked in on the side for looks, but for the most part a filet was a singular item that should be consumed singularly. There was never talk of sharing.

It wasn't even that large a steak, more of the practice variety found on the children's side of the steakhouse menu. But that was just splitting hairs. It was a steak and one of the best cuts around.

Buck watched as Chan poked the beef, determined that it was rare, and scooped it off the grill. The fellow then proceeded to cut it in half, and then into quarters, then into eighths and even farther until Buck couldn't keep track of the math. He wanted to yell, "For the love of God, man, stop! Cease!" but for the fact that the cook was armed with a sharp implement and BunnyLee had come into the room, he might have done serious injury.

"Oh, there you are!" she said and he smiled at the hearty welcome. "You're just in time. Frankie and Miguel are already at the pool." She kissed Buck on the cheek.

With his cleaver, Chan scooped up the meat from the cutting board and put it in a bowl for BunnyLee to carry outside.

"What's going on?" Buck wanted to ask, but he was careful not to, just in case he'd inadvertently dropped the ball on something important. Lack of meat in his diet had obviously addled his brain.

Frankie and Miguel, the elderly gardener, were standing by the teak chaise where BunnyLee so often lay. She set the steak down on the arm of the chair and went into the cabana. The tailwinds of the Santa Anas were still howling in the tops of the trees.

"The show is about to begin," she announced. She opened the glass door and held the curtain back. "Come on, honey, you're on!"

Puddles ran out onto the deck dressed in a tutu.

Jimmy Chan applauded. Miguel and Frankie joined in. Puddles ran around between everyone, greeting her audience one at a time and sometimes twice.

"Now, Puddles, sit!"

Puddles didn't sit right away but she did eventually. BunnyLee corrected the dog's posture.

"She's just warming up," BunnyLee assured everyone. "Now, lie down!"

Puddles lay down on cue and everyone applauded.

BunnyLee gave Puddles a morsel of meat from the bowl and Buck just about fell into the pool.

"Now for her latest trick," BunnyLee announced, "she's going to dance for you."

BunnyLee dangled a bite of filet above the dog's head and the dog went up on her hind legs. She moved her hand around in a small circle and Puddles did a pirouette. As the others applauded, both the dog and Buck's eyes were focused on the meat in BunnyLee's fingertips. She moved her hand forward, prompting her puppy to take a bow, and Buck very nearly took a bow himself. As the audience erupted, BunnyLee took even more food from the cache and fed the lion's share to the dog.

"Isn't she incredible?" BunnyLee asked, and Jimmy Chan was quick to agree. Buck was on the fence, although he was impressed by the amount that the little dog could eat.

"Dog got talent," Frankie said, and the others concurred.

BunnyLee was looking at Buck for his approval.

"I gotta admit, that was cute," he said.

"I know, isn't she amazing? I just love her!"

She had meant that as a compliment. After all, Buck had given her this terrific gift. He knew that. But suitors can be sticklers about semantics. Buck wanted her to say that she loved *him* for giving her the gift. Not that this was the time or place for romance—Frankie and Miguel and Chan were dispersing—but it would have been nice. Meanwhile, Buck was about ready to dance for his dinner. He would have jumped through a fiery hoop, anything for some attention and praise and a taste of reward.

BunnyLee had been doing a little reading on the internet, and she filled Buck in on what she'd learned: Puddles was two dogs for the price of one. A Labradoodle was a Poodle and a Lab. This was old news to Buck because Rex West had told him as much. But there was more. These different breeds had different traits. The Lab half was a hunting dog. They were bred to retrieve the quarry of their marksman master. Their sense of smell allowed them to zero in on a scent and follow it to its origin. They generally stayed on the scent until they found it. Their mouths were soft. They could hold a dead bird without fear of injury to the prize. This was why they were so safe around children. A child could stick its hand into the dog's mouth without incident. Labradors instinctively enjoyed holding a person's hand in their mouth.

"So how come she chewed my sandal?"

"She's just a puppy. She has to be trained."

Puddles was also a Poodle, and they were another kind of working dog. They had been bred as circus performers. The tutu was their native dress. As a breed they liked to be the center of attention and were easily trained to do astounding tricks involving both intelligence and agility. They did have a tendency to find mischief when they were ignored.

Buck sat on the end of the chaise next to BunnyLee. He watched as she fed Puddles from the bowl.

"She's so smart, she's like one in a million."

Rex West had said the same thing. He'd said a lot of things. Like that bit about a guarantee.

BunnyLee offered Buck a morsel of meat.

"What is this, beef?' he asked, sharing a taste in the feast. Puddles was looking for a little more attention of her own and she took Buck's left hand in her mouth. Then she sneezed. Buck instinctively pulled his hand back and he scraped his hand on a puppy tooth. That tooth was sharp! Or maybe it was her braces. Sometime during the last five days the dog had inexplicably acquired braces! BunnyLee looked at his hand. Little droplets of blood were forming along the line of retreat.

"It's only a scratch." BunnyLee said, kissing his hand and then going into the cabana.

Only a scratch? The dog had drawn blood! He was an actor. The camera was often pointed at this hand. He couldn't work with a mangled mitt! And what about tetanus? He was going to need a shot, if not stitches. He was about to yell for Frankie to take him to emergency when BunnyLee, who was coming out of the cabana with ointment and a Band-Aid, informed him that Frankie was taking her to an audition. She'd gotten a callback. Buck was trying to remember the three numbers you were supposed to dial in an emergency when BunnyLee suggested he drive himself to a clinic and get a precautionary shot.

It hadn't occurred to him that he might drive himself. If his arm swelled up on the way there, he wasn't sure whether he could drive and shift the standard transmission with one hand. If they amputated the arm, he was certain he wouldn't be able to drive himself back. He watched her swab and bandage the injury and longed for another kiss. He knew he was a big baby, as BunnyLee was pointing out, but big babies needed affection, too. She kissed him on the forehead and said, "Come on, let's go!"

Down by the garage, BunnyLee waved to Buck from the back seat of the Bentley as she and Frankie and Puddles sped off for her callback audition, leaving Buck standing in the empty drive. The cook was in the kitchen preparing Ramen noodles for dinner. At some point during the preceding week, King Buck had lost the reins of power.

The trip to Cedar Sinai Hospital wasn't that eventful. The wind in the convertible was making his hair stand up and he feared for his toupee. He didn't dare close the top, knowing that it was apt to get stuck halfway up. All this angst was making him sweat under his hairpiece, and sweat was the enemy of double-faced tape.

At the emergency room, Buck wore dark glasses. For the

most part, nobody gave him a second look. The first disquieting moment came when he raised his voice at the admitting nurse about the need to be seen by a plastic surgeon. He was holding a handkerchief over his mouth to avoid breathing in cancer or God only knows what else they had floating around in hospitals when the paramedics came into the waiting area to ask whose Mustang was blocking the ambulance bay on George Burns Road.

A tow truck was in full attack mode when Buck got back there and he started it in the nick of time. But when he swung around onto Gracie Allen Drive and pulled into the drop-off circle, there was no valet parking! By the time he found a spot on the street and got back to the nurse's window, they said they'd been calling him. He'd lost his place in line! He was in the process of pleading his case when the admissions nurse scolded him. "Sir, I cannot understand a word you are saying with that cloth over your mouth."

As the nurses were discussing his fate, a latecomer was escorted in ahead of him with two broken elbows and a gash on her forehead. It was all he could do to stop himself from crying foul. When he finally did see the doctor, he asked for morphine. The physician's assistant prescribed Tylenol. A nurse slapped gauze over his wound and secured it with white tape. He did get his tetanus shot and an antibiotic salve.

The ride home at night was significantly more eventful. To begin with, the Mustang was feisty. The danged clutch was a bother. He began questioning all of his latent driving skills. He had a brief lapse in memory as to which color light you were supposed to stop at. The wind was gustier than before. He had one hand on the wheel and was now holding the top of his head with the other when his cell phone rang. The phone was on the seat next to him, and he shouldn't have answered it while he was driving, but the call was from Jadé.

"Hey there."

"Buck. Everyone in Bucharest has seen our picture together. All are so very jealous. I have not been able to think of anything but you."

"I'm honored to be in the picture."

"I would have called you earlier, but I have been at sea."

"I'm so sorry to hear that. What's the problem?"

"No problem. I have been sailing."

"In this wind? Good God! Must have been a very big boat."

"It was."

Buck was imagining a storm-tossed Greek ship from the days of Odysseus, Jadé lashed to the mast, riding out the turbulent seas.

"When I was on Catalina Island, I was thinking how much I missed wearing the pearl. How I might have worn it dancing."

Buck knew exactly what pearl she meant and where it dangled.

"There is a celebrity benefit next week..." Buck said.

"No! No! And I am so sorry. Your manager, so difficult to communicate, has connected me with Alexei Long.

"Who?"

"Do you know him?"

Buck couldn't say that he did. "He has the same manager as me?" Buck asked.

"And so talented. So, how do you say...young? Everyone says that he is a young Buck LeGrande. I am withholding comment. He is a good sailor, but so lacking in one important feature from you."

Hearing this news about his one important feature was small consolation to the fact that Jadé was formally dumping him. Buck was having trouble steering. His phone was in his right hand and he was holding his toupee with his bandaged left. His knees were doing a heroic job of steadying the wheel but it was a lot to ask of them in this buffeting wind. A green light turned to yellow and then to red all in the span of time it took for Jadé to say she was moving on.

When Buck's foot went for the brake, his hands went for the wheel. His phone hit the floor, and his toupee caught the breeze. Apparently when double-faced tape gave up it surrendered unequivocally. His hairpiece took an unscheduled helicopter flight across the windshield of an oncoming convertible and onto the startled face of its driver.

"Pull over and keep your hands on the wheel!" was the amplified voice from an L.A. policewoman on a motorcycle who materialized alongside Buck's car.

Buck's phone was on the floor by his feet. He could see that Jadé was still connected. This would be such an awkward time to hang up on her. She would think it rude. Or worse, that he was inconsolable. The fact that she had called meant something. He tried to reach for the phone.

"Freeze!" came the order from the bike.

Buck's hands froze. As the car slowed, he tried to scoop the phone up with one foot, forgetting that both feet were integral to the stopping of a standard transmission car. The car lurched to a standstill and stalled with a sorrowful wheeze.

Any thoughts to being five times lucky were out the window. He was not lucky at all; he had simply lucked out. His show was running in one remote corner of the universe, and Jadé was the last woman on earth to get the news. He watched the screen on his phone go dark.

The five stages of an actor's career were the subject of a joke. Early in an actor's career people ask, "Who is Buck LeGrande?" After a little notoriety and box office draw, producers demand, "Get me Buck LeGrande!" Once the actor makes a name for himself and in order to save money, they demand, "Get me a Buck LeGrande type!" only to qualify it a few years later with, "Get me a *young* Buck LeGrande." And finally, when those same producers were out of the business sipping Mai Tai's in Maui, their young replacements would ask, "Who is Buck LeGrande?" That was the frightful question that kept Buck awake through the wee hours of the morning. For an actor who had recently been at the summit of his career, "Get me a young Buck LeGrande!" was the beginning of the end.

Jadé had just confirmed it. He was old news. Buck's career was now at step four of a five-step ladder. The next rung was oblivion.

The trooper studied his driver's license for the longest time.

"I don't know what it is," she was telling him. "From this picture I can see that you are who you say you are, and I watched you in your show, but something's different."

She pointed her flashlight at his picture ID and held the document next to his head for comparison. "Eyes: blue. Check. Hair: brown... Okay, I see the problem!"

She panned her flashlight to his naked scalp. It was lighter and pinker than the rest of his skin, and even without seeing it Buck could point from memory to the places where it was blotchy.

"You lost your hair."

By the time Buck got home, he'd composed an apology to BunnyLee. He knew he had wronged her. He'd had a one-night stand and essentially rubbed her nose in it. He'd been callous. He'd been vain. He'd allowed the little head to think for the big one. His conceit was so great that no one could possibly love him. He wasn't asking for an acquittal; that was beyond the realm of possibility. Absolution was the most he could hope for. He wanted to reconcile. He wanted to return to the days when they were friends, and tennis was a joy he would never experience again without the most joyful partner he had ever had. He wanted her to know that it was *she* that he had wanted to take to the Emmys, along with everything else that transpired that evening.

BunnyLee's light was still on. Buck ran up to his room to find his backup toupee. For one brief moment he entertained the idea of appearing without it. There was enough of his real brown hair to comb forward, but that left the left side of his scalp bare. He even entertained the idea of just combing the hair straight back and flaunting a new look, but the script from Warner Brothers was languishing on his bedside table. One glance in that direction was all it took for him to abandon these unhairy thoughts and hurriedly tape on his backup toupee. He blended the mane with his own. It was clear that if he intended to spend his future time free of the faux fur, he did not intend to start that night.

BunnyLee came to the door when he knocked. She pulled the curtain back slightly to speak with him through the screen.

In the movie version, BunnyLee would come out, no, she would 'emerge from her lonely boudoir' wearing nothing but her wispy sarong. She would ask about his hand. There would be tears in her eyes, her worry having gotten the better of her. He would assure her that it was only a scratch. There would be an awkward moment while each wrestled with the right words. He would apologize. He would spill the grief in his heart and she would reveal hers. Any doubt about the trueness of his heart would be swept from her eyes.

But that's not quite how it happened.

BunnyLee did answer that knock wearing nothing but her backlit sarong and, as always, she looked angelic.

"I wasn't sure if you'd still be up," he said.

"I was about to turn in."

"My hand is all right. It was only a scratch."

"You were right to have it looked at, just to make sure."

"They gave me a tetanus shot. And an antibiotic."

"It was wise that you went."

He had ached for her to invite him in. Then something unexpected caught his eye. She did not appear to be alone. There was a shadow of what seemed like a larger than life figure moving in the background. On the wall behind BunnyLee, Buck saw the unmistakable shadow of a man in a ten-gallon hat. She asked Buck whether they could talk in the morning. She bid him goodnight. Eyes can play tricks on us, but the shadow was clearly that of a man in a cowboy hat.

Now, with all due respect, BunnyLee was Buck's guest. "You can come and go as you please" were Buck's exact words when he first invited her to stay there. They had an understanding: "I have three cars, so you won't have to rent one" was part of the understanding. Things were cordial; that was the spoken part of the agreement: Buck's largess.

In other respects, their understanding now seemed woefully insufficient even though no amendments to their agreement had ever been made. The prospect of romance had barely been breached; it lurked as a snake in the underbrush. This was where things got dodgy. They had also never discussed other guests, for instance, nor how BunnyLee might entertain one in private.

By the time Buck finally got to sleep, in his dreams the shadow of the man in the cowboy hat stood ten feet tall. He awoke in the dark at 3 a.m. in a cold sweat. He could ask BunnyLee to leave, of course, but then he'd likely never see her again. And besides, this was a debacle of his own doing, this undoing, this business in pursuit of the spotlight, this hollow endeavor alongside Jadé called Fame.

Fame. It was a force of human nature, a sinuous seducer, invisible and invincible as the Santa Anas. It was the dust-devil of Buck's childhood imagination, the monster under the bed, the sleepless ogre that teased his imagination to set sail for distant lands, puffed the sheets with wanderlust for odysseys afar, then forsook his willful soul in irons, this tortured heart of his like a castaway on a distant shore far from home.

Damn BunnyLee and her existentialist teachings! Buck had a bad case of Despair.

CHAPTER 8

THE NEXT MORNING, BunnyLee peeked out from behind the curtains of the pool-house cabana. The trees were no longer bent over in the wind. Things were nice and still. And there was no sign of her host. They say that houseguests, like fish, begin to stink after three days, and she'd stretched her stay at Buck's to almost a month. He'd been nothing but the perfect host, but in the last week their friendship had soured.

Should she stay or should she go? BunnyLee was at one of those proverbial forks in the road.

For five days, the Santa Ana winds blew furiously across Southern California, and she was now pale and antsy from her time trapped inside.

Seizing this sunny day, BunnyLee scooped up Puddles and held her in one arm. In the other she cradled a mostly-read television pilot script that she'd promised Frankie she would read. She made her entrance poolside wearing a wispy sarong around her bikini and exchanged pleasantries with Miguel, who was cleaning the pool filter, about the positive turn in the weather.

"*¡Que buen tiempo!*"

Then she set about her routine. Sunbathing was a work of yogic diligence what with all the twisting, the adjusting, and the rolling over—nourishing her inner goddess while discreetly attaining a seamless tan.

Birds returned from wherever birds hid during gale-force winds, and they chirped about on the ground. BunnyLee watched

Puddles bound after them; there was no danger of her catching them. She settled onto the chaise lounge and assumed the lotus position. She took stock of her present life.

What had become of BunnyLee's philosophical journey of self-discovery? What did she have to show for her four years in Southeast Asia exploring the incredible lightness of inner peace? She'd moved lithely from one experience to the next. Unencumbered. Enlightened. On a higher plane. She was the helium in a balloon un-tethered.

She breathed deeply.

No. She wasn't flighty. She was happiest when she skated above the fray, but that wasn't always possible. She still had her feet on the ground. Her feet had lost their footing; that was her problem. She'd followed her heart and lost sight of her path. She was mired in an uncharacteristic indecisiveness. What did you do when you followed your heart and it led you down a blind alley?

She tried quieting her thoughts with another long, deep breath. They wouldn't settle. She should have moved out on Monday! If it weren't for the bad weather, she would surely have moved on by now.

And now? Now that the weather was improving?

"I'm damned if I do and damned if I don't."

"*¿Perdón?*" Miguel asked.

"Oh. *Nada*," BunnyLee answered. But it wasn't nothing. She was damned if she left and never knew what she had missed or damned if she didn't and stayed to be a snack for the insatiable spider who had spun this sticky web.

Life in the Olympian hills of Number 10 Beverly Canyon gave her a privileged view of Hollywood, not all savory, and for this experience she was forever in the debt of her host. Alas, she was mired in that quagmire of contradictory Western values.

Puddles tugged at her towel in a playful way. BunnyLee pet her puppy.

The inconvenient truth about values was that there were so many to choose from.

BunnyLee opened Frankie's teleplay at her bookmark and stretched out on the chaise. She concentrated on the storyline to allay her thoughts. A shootout was in progress at the end of the second act. She read to the end of the story. In television, simple crimes led to simple justice not found in real life. In this pilot, an insidious Hip Hop crime syndicate had whacked the patriarch of an Italian crime family, and now the hero of the series—a sanguine African American who drives a limo for an aging-out private eye—was taking them all down. BunnyLee made a mental note to google 'sanguine' just to be sure.

In real life, she doubted there was ever justice for misdemeanors of the heart. She appealed to her higher self, and the verdict was in. Her feelings were hurt. Or would it be more accurate to say her feelings hurt?

She looked up from the last page. Puddles had disappeared.

"Puddles?"

She couldn't say how much time had elapsed since her puppy slipped away. It was a while. Being a neophyte pet parent; she wasn't at all used to the unsettling sense of responsibility that it entailed.

"Puddles?"

She leaned on her elbows to get a better view of the surroundings. Her top straps were untied. It took some doing to bundle everything back up.

"Miguel, *vistes* Puddles?"

"*No, Señorita* BunnyLee."

"Here, honey! Here, girl!"

Once standing, she scanned the fenced-in area. Debris from the storm was everywhere. Ominous black shapes lined the bottom of the pool. Fortunately, Miguel had already skimmed the top surface, save for a rogue leaf or two, and after a moment of dread BunnyLee determined that her chocolate-colored dog was not down there. She wasn't that worried about her falling in. Miniature Australian Labradoodles were born to swim. Her dog just wasn't big enough to crawl back out.

"Puddles!"

BunnyLee checked inside the cabana, under the bed, in the closet, in the shower. She pulled back the long set of full-length drapes. There wasn't anywhere else to hide in a glass-walled guest cabana. And besides, Puddles was good about coming when she was called.

"Puddles?"

BunnyLee studied the white picket fence that bordered the pool area; there was probably enough space between the wooden slats and the grass for a determined animal to wriggle under. She unlatched the gate and looked around.

The morning sun rippled across the stately Spanish terracotta tile roofs; its rays illuminated the hillside estate in a warm glow. Leaves from tall oaks dappled the lawns like a well-lit movie set.

Of the two paths that Puddles could have taken, the one to the right wound down to the tennis court. A large oak branch, broken by the storm, lay across the net. To the left, the other path climbed past the garage, through the thorn-rose trellising to where the main house loomed. Puddles was a social animal; there was little doubt which path she'd chosen.

Up at the house, Jimmy Chan carved vegetables on the veranda. BunnyLee shaded her eyes and looked for signs of her host. He was normally out and about by this hour when it was nice, puttering around the flowerbeds to the *bossa nova* beats of Brazilian music. But today Buck was nowhere to be seen.

She pondered what to do. She was loath to go up to the house. BunnyLee was no dummy when it came to affairs of the heart. She had every right to her feelings. Two weeks ago she might have moved into that house.

But that moment had passed.

Buck knocked at her door after midnight last night and she'd bid him an awkward goodnight. It was pretty obvious that her tenure in the cabana was over. Who was she kidding?

If there was one simple truth about where her feelings lay, it had taken her all week to come 'round to admitting it: she suffered the unshakeable heaviness of the lowest of the lowest of emotions. She was jealous.

"Puddles!"

It was time to get her dog, collect her things, and find the words to say goodbye.

✦

The sound of BunnyLee's voice entered the open window of the upstairs master suite. It seeped into the subconscious of her slumbering host and added substance to his tangled dreams.

Buck often lay awake into the wee hours, mulling the downward slope of his career. He hadn't worked in two years, and, judging by the quality of scripts being handed his way, he wasn't about to any time soon. Actors were inherently apprehensive, and anxiety was often the cause of insomnia. He knew that; it came with the territory. It took years of hard work, along with a share of good luck, to establish his career. Then one misstep, an unfortunate dust-up with Kermit the Frog, and his success was derailed.

But last night, existential angst was only the subtext to Buck LeGrande's present despair. He knew perfectly well what caused this night's misery, and the effrontery of it had robbed him of his sleep, until dawn, when he finally found a slumber.

✦

Puddles nudged Buck's bedroom door open with her nose and stole across the Persian rug to his bedside. She studied the sleeping thespian. His youthful good looks, looks that he'd been trading upon since childhood, were surrendering to a hint of middle-aged pudginess, a thickening neck, the beginnings of a second chin tucked in comfortably beneath its sculpted first. Puddles wagged her tail. She sat on her haunches. She waved her front paws for attention and sneezed. It was an impressive sneeze given her size, and the force of it sent her tumbling backwards.

Buck flinched. He didn't wake. But the sudden movement of his head shook his hairpiece free from his scalp in what was clearly another failure of his off-brand roll of double-faced tape. The wig dangled precariously on the edge of the mattress for a moment, then fell to the floor. Puddles sniffed at the toupee and then at Buck. She sneezed again.

One eye blinked open. It scanned the room.

✦

Buck realized immediately that the waking world was not how he'd left it. For starters, the bedroom door was open. He focused on the wad of webbing lying hair-side down on the carpet and slowly recognized it as his back-up toupee. A touch of his scalp confirmed it. Worse yet, the pink tongue of his archenemy, Puddles, was licking the thing.

As a maturing actor, especially one who'd made a good living playing the willful kid, the young rebel, and later the bad boy, appearance was an ever-increasing full-time obsession. Daily tennis, working out in his home gym, even the time he devoted to sunning his ruddy complexion was no accident. Twenty-four-seven, even in his sleep, Buck was intimately aware of the importance of a full head of hair. The fact that BunnyLee had never seen him without it was evidence of his commitment to it. Now it lay on the floor in harm's way.

Puddles shook her head and wagged her behind. He lay motionless. Puddles sneezed again. That dog had done nothing but sneeze since she got here.

Buck could have petted the puppy and acted as if he were happy to see her, but he knew firsthand about the sharpness of that puppy's teeth. Literally. Or her new braces! Either way, showing affection to this mutt was how his hand had come to be cut, the event that precipitated last night's descent into despair.

If Buck had learned anything from playing a modern-day cowboy private eye on his long-running TV series, it was that a gumshoe must never take too lightly the cunning of an adversary. He knew that once he showed the least bit of interest in the hairpiece the thing would become fair game. His sandals, his socks, his tennis racket grip, all had met their demise in one of Puddles' games. And Puddles would make a game of anything.

He estimated the distance between him and his hair. He could lunge for it, snatching victory from the jaws of defeat, but it would take his full reach. At best he would have only one slim chance.

On the open market, the resale value of a used, custom-woven hairpiece, if anything, paled in comparison to the value of the signed photographs and movie posters, the curios and iconic props that decorated his master suite. Try putting a price on the fully operational carved wooden horse from *Carousel Cowboy!* But at this moment, Buck would have traded it all for the safe return of his toupee. Memorabilia merely proved his past; the toupee prolonged his youth.

Its worth was incalculable. Good hairpieces were difficult to procure discreetly, and this hairpiece, this perfectly coifed, backup, emergency hairpiece, was his sole remaining toupee, owing to the flight of his favorite toupee while driving his convertible last night. He had a do-or-die meeting on Monday with the Acquisitions Department at Warner Brothers about signing the contract on a new show, and he certainly couldn't attend a production meeting without hair. What was he going to do, surrender to aging and go bald? So much rested upon the safe recovery of that toupee that Buck started to shake.

✦

Puddle's eyes tracked Buck's bandaged hand as it emerged from under the duvet. She growled friskily at it.

✦

Shaking was one of those things that actors who play cool guys really shouldn't do. Not that any cameramen ever mentioned it in a wide shot, but many a director complained about it in a close-up; the evidence was right there on every playback monitor. Puddles was close enough to notice the shaking. It was hard to miss. The loosely fastened gauze bandage that covered the cut on Buck's left hand was quivering like a play toy.

The thought crossed his mind to hit the dog with his pillow, but then again, Puddles was not one to play fair. She would surely yelp, raising the alarm. BunnyLee was so taken with her new pet that she was liable to call the ASPCA on him. He'd had his fill of bad press. And he was already in the proverbial doghouse. Truth be told, he knew he had only himself to blame for whatever dalliances BunnyLee undertook the night before.

Puddles crouched.

Buck knew little about Puddles' genetic makeup other than that bit about her being a cross between a poodle and Labrador retriever. In both Rex and BunnyLee's estimation Puddles was an extraordinary animal, but she was only half retriever. Her poodle half was more your mischievous bury-the-bone-where-no-one-can-find-it type of dog.

He should have pulled his hand back to the safety of his covers. Instead, he took a swipe at the toupee and deftly grabbed it.

"Ha!"

Those who faced him in doubles across the tennis net knew something about Buck's quickness.

Puddles' poodle legs were like springs. She snagged the finely crafted hairpiece with her teeth and wouldn't let go. The delicate weaving stretched to its limit.

"Help!"

✦

Outside on the patio, the new cook sculpted radishes into roses and set them to blossom in a large tub of ice water. A portable television was tuned to the closing credits of *Rawhide*. "Rollin', rollin', rollin', keep those dogies rollin'," Jimmy Chan sang along with the music. It was through television that this Chinese expat gained his unique command of English.

Puddles dashed through the French doors onto the patio. She was sneaky fast. Chan only caught a glimpse of her as she passed. She held what looked like a small animal in her mouth. The famous actor came charging after her wearing only his boxer shorts. He picked up a tennis racket.

"Where is she?" Buck asked. "Where did she go?"

Chan pointed to the rattan sofa with his cleaver.

The phone rang. Jimmy Chan expected Mr. LeGrande to answer it. His superior didn't even appear to hear it, occupied as he was with poking around under the furniture with the racket. Chan looked at the phone, then at Buck, and then at the phone. Being new to the job, Jimmy Chan was unsure of his telephone answering responsibilities.

BunnyLee arrived from the garden. She was fifteen years younger than Buck and a good thirty years younger than Jimmy Chan, who was as much a connoisseur of the female form as the next guy. Because this was only his sixth day on the job and only the first day fit for sunbathing, he averted his eyes so as not to be caught staring.

"Buck," BunnyLee said, "she's only playing."

The phone rang again. BunnyLee ignored it, too.

✦

BunnyLee was having trouble making light of the situation. Buck, now on his hands and knees, turned. His face was crimson. BunnyLee gasped. It was true what people said; Buck LeGrande was bald! She'd suspected he was bald, but not that bald!

Buck dropped the tennis racket and covered his scalp with his bandaged hand. He held his other hand out in front of him in a feeble attempt to block her view.

BunnyLee laughed.

She'd meant it to be the kind of laugh that lightens the mood, the kind of laugh that glistens, the kind of laugh that says it's okay, doesn't matter, I like you just the same. But there was panic in its tone as she focused on Buck's expression. On a scale of one to ten of the worst reactions she might have had at that moment, her awkward laugh was an eleven. BunnyLee winced. She should have listened to her intuition and moved out last week while they were still friends.

The phone rang again.

Puddles seized upon this break in the action to emerge from under the sofa and head out to the garden with the toupee in her mouth. She sprinted down the stone steps and proved small enough to squeeze back under the gate to the pool, giving her an added measure of distance. Buck chased the puppy. BunnyLee followed.

✦

Jimmy Chan pointed at the phone. It was as if he was the only one who could hear it ring. Growing up in China, when the phone rang, people stopped what they were doing to answer it. Nobody had time to just call and chitchat. The telephone meant business.

"Oh, Puddles, not in the pool!" BunnyLee called out.

✦

"¡*Cuidado!*" Miguel yelled. He had the filter spread out in pieces on the lawn.

✦

There was the sound of a splash as Chan saw Buck enter the water, too late to catch the toupee. A loud screeching sound came from the pump as the hairpiece entered the machine.

The phone ringing had stopped.

Chan watched a news report on the escalating drought and wild fire threatening Mariposa up north. Switching the station, the cook watched a recap of the previous night's Pay-Per-View professional wrestling event in Las Vegas. Chief Tenaya, wearing an Indian feather headdress and multi-colored spandex tights, held the Dust Devil, Austin Sway, Jimmy Chan's favorite wrestler, around the neck in a death grip. The cowboy wrestler, also in spandex, wore a red-white-and-blue-striped Stetson cowboy hat. A very short referee dramatically counted down from ten by slapping the mat with each number.

The cowboy wiggled free from the Indian's hold and climbed to the second rope of the wrestling ring at the corner stanchion. He balanced precariously on the cord with his back to his opponent. He seemed poised to step up to the third rope and do his famous back flip over his advancing opponent, Chief Tenaya, but he hesitated. The audience jeered at Austin's reticence to jump.

"Jump! Jump! Jump!" Jimmy Chan joined in the chant.

In a close-up shot it was clear that Austin was in a great deal of pain. He held his neck and cringed.

A string of party lights that hung on the patio above Chan's head, flickered. The picture on the television pixilated and went blank as the power at Number 10 Beverly Canyon went out.

The telephone began to ring again. Jimmy Chan watched it. He drummed his fingers on the cutting board. The landline rang again and again. On the sixth ring the cook couldn't stand it anymore. He picked up the phone.

"Howdy!"

Chan strained to understand the voice on the other end of the line.

"What? No. He not come to phone right now. He swimming. I write down message, yes?"

Jimmy Chan opened a drawer and found a pen and Post-it pad.

"Okay, pardner, shoot!"

CHAPTER 9

THERE WAS A quick knock at Austin Sway's motel room door, then the sound of the passkey card in the slot. The door opened. Austin cowered at the sight of a silhouetted figure. For the past year he'd had dreams about dying. In his pre-awake stupor he imagined the Angel of Death was upon him.

"Housekeeping!"

The maid gasped, probably at the sight of a powerful athlete sprawled out on his back, looking not unlike a model in one of those underwear advertisements in *Gentleman's Quarterly*, except minus the underwear. Austin made a feeble attempt to cover himself; the sprain in his neck caused his hand to reflexively detour to the pain. His private parts remained public while the maid stood there. She giggled.

"My bad!" she said.

When she finally did close the door, he heard her cackle even louder outside. It was clear to Austin that the woman had recognized him. To his mind, she had taken advantage of a man when he was down. This was his lot in life.

For what it was worth, he was still a celebrity. No longer the baby-faced audience favorite of his youth, he was now the one cast as the bad guy or "heel," the wrestler who raised the ire of the crowd. People would boo. They would shake their fists. They would spit as he made his entrance. It was all in good fun, but he didn't like being cast as the man that people loved to hate. And, as the adage went, when the bad guy suffers, he suffers alone.

It took some doing to get out of bed. He tried first to wriggle his torso toward the edge of the mattress and slide off frontward. That put too much stress on his neck. He inched back to the center and with a bit more pain managed to roll over onto his stomach, then exit feet first.

When he was finally standing with his head precariously balanced above his shoulders, Austin assessed the damage. He could turn his neck slightly to the left, but to the right, no way. He shuffled into the bathroom, thinking a hot shower would do the trick. He slid back the shower curtain; the plumbing controls were too low to reach without bending or squatting. Overnight, muscle stiffness had progressed downward to his lower back. Bending and squatting were presently out of the question.

With effort, he swung one leg over the tub wall, then the other. The valves were still too low to reach with his hand. The simple act of bathing was now an ordeal.

He curled his toes over the knurled plastic knob and turned the cold-water valve with his foot. It was slow going. The hot water wasn't forthcoming. In the interim, the showerhead spewed a generous flow of icy water squarely down onto his face, his shoulders, and his aching neck.

It was at times like these when even the most focused athlete should be forgiven for having second thoughts about his chosen profession. Not that Austin Sway had any other marketable job skills. The last thing he and his brother did before joining the wrestling circuit was work the rodeos entertaining the crowds as rodeo clowns.

Originally that work had been limited to pleasing crowds with their antics between bull-riding events, and they were good at it, maybe the best ever. But, more and more, their duties involved sharing the arena with an angry bull to serve as alternate targets for the bull to attack when its rider was thrown from its back. It went without saying that daily exposure to large, spirited messengers of death, however exhilarating, had its downside. Being mauled, gored, gouged, or trampled was commonplace. In fact, rodeo clowns were now more aptly called barrel men because a barrel was the only place in the ring to hide from the twelve-hundred-pound bull.

At this moment the idea of dodging the horns of an angry animal whose balls were cinched in a leather harness as it was released from the bucking chute, with the primary assignment of serving as a decoy, however amusing to the crowd, seemed preposterous. Professional wrestling was a whole lot safer, but that too had taken its fateful toll. Austin and his brother used to tell people that when the time came to hang up their spurs and spandex they would return to the ranch. Now his brother was gone, and there never had been a ranch.

The hot water valve loosened. The water began to warm. Austin let it beat against his neck. The spasm finally relaxed enough to step out, dry off, get a t-shirt over his head and pull on his sweatpants. Fortunately, he had a rare night off before his next scheduled bout up in Fresno.

Digging into the bottom of his duffle, Austin rounded up a syringe and an ampoule of Dianabol. He punctured the seal of the bottle with the needle. Holding it upside down, he drew out the amber liquid. That was the easy part. Finding a muscle to stab was tricky. His rule of thumb was to place these injections in out-of-the-way areas because needle marks created scar tissue. His gluteus maximus was the biggest candidate, but today he lacked the mobility to reach around back. He knew there were people who drank the "juice," but he preferred to keep the steroid out of his bloodstream and away from his liver.

Looking in the mirror, he rolled his eyes at where life had led him. Desperate times called for desperate measures. He jabbed the needle into his neck and watched the contraband chemical enter his stiff muscle tissue.

It was approaching midday when Austin opened the drape of his second-floor motel room window and surveyed the scenery. He could see beyond the outside walkway handrail that the parking lot was empty. The only vehicle within sight was an old Ford pickup with a camper shell parked behind the recycling bin of the Crystal Palace next door. The sight of it gave Austin a start. It was the same pickup that he'd seen yesterday afternoon, parked near his car as he was being led out of the Tex Mex restaurant in Las Vegas by Juanita Carlita. The license plate was hard to make out at that distance. It looked like a Nevada plate. And even though you saw a lot of campers on the road, being modern-day covered wagons, you didn't see many pink Ford Rangers with lace curtains in their windows. Now it was becoming clear that yesterday afternoon's encounter was no coincidence. He didn't like the looks of it, not one bit.

He rooted around his duffle for his phone to take a picture. He wanted to zoom in on the vehicle for closer study, but his phone was downstairs in the trunk of his car.

As for his injury, it was more a question of timing as anything else. Otherwise, that casual run-in with a fan before last night's debacle of a performance could be explained away as just more bad luck. The innocuous voice of a middle-aged woman in the crowded restaurant should have been just that—harmless.

"Austin Sway! Fancy meetin' you here!"

Her face was as familiar as her voice, where had he heard that voice before?

Austin zipped up his duffle bag. He opened the motel room door and stepped out onto the walkway. Below was his convertible backed into the parking space. To his right, the nosy maid pushed a housekeeping cart. Behind her, a woman tried to squeeze by. Sure as sugar, it was the same woman who'd tapped him on the shoulder in Vegas. Austin yelled to the maid, "Stop her!" It seemed like the least she could do considering their recent intimate moment together, and the maid obliged. To his left, at the far end of the motel balcony, an elevator door noisily opened.

"Oh, golly!" he said aloud, not being one to cuss in the presence of ladies, no matter what their intention. But here she was again, the one with those emerald eyes.

The wraith remained in the shadow. She raised her open hands and outstretched her arms toward him and beckoned him to join her where she stood—under the flickering EXIT sign.

"Jiminy Cricket!"

Performers had their fans; it came with the territory. And, like rock stars, professional wrestlers had groupies. Some men saw it as a perk—any comfort received along the way being much appreciated when they had no permanent address and no family to call their own. But this felt like being stalked.

There was only one way out, and it involved scaling the handrail and jumping.

The second-story railing of the Bakersfield Best Western differed from the specifications of a wrestling ring. The handrail was not pliable, and it was some thirteen feet above the parking lot, rendering it far less conducive to impromptu exits. And, whereas exiting the wrestling ring via the third rope was an action more or less expected of a professional wrestler, checking out of a motel via the second story balcony was a move rarely attempted, even by an athlete in tip-top shape. When the athlete was five years past his prime and suffering from a wrenched neck, such action was ill advised.

The adrenalin was flowing; the older woman squeezed by the maid and was closing in fast. Austin tossed his bag over the railing. It landed squarely in the back seat of his convertible. He scaled the ironwork and looked down. It looked a long way down. With a little trajectory, he judged he could hit the trunk of his car, shortening the fall by a few feet, but that would mean jumping away from the building. He lowered himself to the concrete ledge and lined up with his target. He would have to bite the bullet in regard to his neck. As he balanced on the precipice, he weighed his options. He could face providence or jump. His brother died from a stunt seemingly less dangerous. Being a Western boy, full of spit and moxie and from a land of big skies and wide-open spaces where the motto is "Don't fence me in," Austin chose the course of least resistance.

"Oh, I left the shower running," Austin called out to the maid. He was a conservationist at heart and, what with global warming and the recurring California droughts…

He jumped. The sound of a body hitting sheet metal was louder than one might expect. It diminished the athletic beauty of the action.

✦

The motel desk clerk sitting at reception looked up and closed his laptop when he heard it. On his security monitor he saw a man writhing on the trunk of a car. His first thought was suicide. Then he saw two women on the balcony enter frame and wondered if the man had been pushed. He lifted the phone to call 911. The fallen man was up now, crawling forward into the driver's seat; he was starting the car. The desk clerk hesitated. He saw the car exit the frame. He watched it appear in person around the front of the building and pull out of the parking lot onto the state highway, heading north. The clerk returned the receiver to the cradle. Death at a motel was never a good thing. Homicide would bring out the sheriff, along with ambulances and squad cars with their sirens and flashing lights, none of which was ever good for business. The clerk opened his laptop and set speculation aside. He had a screenplay that he could never seem to finish.

✦

Austin skipped the Interstate entrance. The surface roads afforded him the best likelihood of throwing his stalkers off his trail. He had a general sense of the terrain. He hadn't strung together six days in a row in California since he could remember, but of any state, this one was closest to his heart. Austin had spent his childhood traveling up and down the central valley with his parents on the county fair circuit.

He felt his legs for serious damage and came up negative. His neck was surprisingly loose. He knew from past experience that any freedom of movement in the neck department would be short-lived. In the manner of all great professionals, he evaluated his recent exit: how he might have perfected his jump with a little practice. In his rearview mirror he could see that his landing had imparted an impressive cavity in the sheet metal trunk. He shrugged. All things being equal, it wasn't too bad for a guy his age: a close call in a life littered with close calls. It was all too crazy, though. His imagination had gotten the better of him. He needed to cut back on the steroids.

Oil wells gave way to walnut groves. Their limbs hung heavy over the road. His tires kicked up the tough-skinned fallen fruit and it bounced around in his wheel wells like dice in a cup at the craps table. Then came miles of Mandarin oranges cooked on the sunbaked pavement. This was the valley of plenty, bordered by rugged mountain ranges, one of which he caught glimpses of to the east. He checked for the pink Ford Ranger. So far so good.

Those two women were in cahoots; that was now clear. The younger one most likely wasn't a she-devil, but she surely gave him the creeps. And the older one was pushy. Whoever they were, they seemed to know his itinerary better than he did. He wasn't taking any chances. He turned onto a gravel road that led northeast, out into the grasslands of the sub-Sierra. He had a nagging promise to keep. Austin punched the radio and listened to the Grateful Dead sing "A Friend of the Devil." He sang along.

CHAPTER 10

THERE WAS NO ICE! The cook had raided the fridge.

Every last cube had been called into service to curl scallions and sharpen carrot spears. They were floating in a tub on the kitchen counter separate from the one the cook had set to soak radish rose garnishes out on the veranda. Who even ate radish garnishes?

Buck read a Post-It note stuck to the refrigerator: *Urgent! A-Number-One Pick! Top Dog! Call Mr. Morris!* It wasn't clear who had written it, although all evidence pointed to the cook who Buck had just sent to the grocery store armed with a fistful of cash and instructions to buy American food.

Who was Mr. Morris? He scrolled though his Contacts. There was no Morris, first name or last.

Buck trotted into the den to check the old Rolodex for a clue. No luck there either. And the ice machine under the bar had been pillaged!

There was no hope of ice. The power was out throughout the house. Buck caught a dismal glimpse of himself reflected in a silver platter over the bar. It was an honorary award he received years ago from the LAPD and the intricate engraving played tricks with his reflection. Even still, with what he could make out, his hair looked a mess. He was feeling around under the bar counter for the light switch that of course didn't work, when yesterday's unopened mail caught his eye.

He eased the tongue of the manila envelope open and slipped out the contents.

It was a contract from Warner Brothers via his lawyer along with a revised script for *The Return of Malibu Man*.

The contract was the usual fare. Sidney had poured over it again and ultimately given his o.k. But the cover letter had a note attached. It was uncommon for Sidney to comment on anything other than the nuts and bolts of the legal stuff, so Buck was intrigued that his old friend had added his two cents to the artistic merits of the script and more specifically to the part Buck was to play. 'Wow, quite a departure from your previous role!' he wrote.

"I'll say!" Buck said. The chances of his taking on this part were zilch. Sidney should never have even been in the loop on this one. What was the point of having his manager okay the contract for the part of an old man. Hadn't Buck sent it back for a massive re-write? When was when? Tuesday? Just four days ago?

He was thirsty as hell and not only was there no ice, the soda dispenser was dead to rights! All there was to drink was an open carton of orange juice. Buck sniffed its contents, shook the container and sipped a little. Not bad, but not good either. At least it was still cold. He poured a glass, sipped some more. The carton was a month past its last sale date. Buck added a healthy splash of vodka to kill whatever might be growing in it.

Sidney was right. The TV pilot was dead on arrival. What could they have done in four days to revive it? The character of Derringer was still so vastly different than the debonair, smart-alecky, joke-cracking part he had embodied for four seasons. He could tell as much from the first page—the character's sanguine African American chauffeur still got all the meaty lines, whatever the hell sanguine meant.

Buck drank a little more. The concoction was a tad tart and not particularly quenching. He added a bit more vodka just to be safe.

When he stepped out the front door of the house, Frankie was outside the garage polishing the Bentley.

To the typical sightseer, or for anyone who has ever dreamed about being rich, by all appearances Buck LeGrande lived a fairytale lifestyle in a hillside bungalow with three bedrooms, not including a maid's quarters or Frankie's digs above the garage. And then, of course, there was the cabana where BunnyLee was a guest. Buck had a pool long enough to do laps, and a clay tennis court shaded to the south by giant oaks. Add to these amenities the fact that this estate came with a Beverly Hills address and the average ticket holder on the Tour Bus to the Stars could justifiably conclude that Buck LeGrande was cradled in luxury, that he lived like King Midas, dined on Kobe beef and beluga caviar, and showered in Dom Perignon champagne.

Appearances were deceiving. On this Saturday morning, Buck felt like King Lear: slowed by age, surrounded by traitors, his grasp of power weakening.

Looking out from the open-air deck of the tourist buses at the curving streets on any one of the numerous Hollywood Hills guided tours, most camera-wielding tourists only came away with pictures of Mission-style roofs. Few caught glimpses of life beyond the giant hedges and gated drives. Buck's estate was as private and secure as any other. His mail slot was welded into the motorized gate. But in years past, on a regular basis, a lucky number of passersby saw the celebrated actor enjoying one of his favorite activities, a stroll down his manicured driveway to collect his mail.

In those days of over-abundance, if a tour group happened upon Buck in the act of sorting his mail, he thought nothing of giving them a jaunty wave with his fistful of white envelopes. Clicks from their cameras were too many to count. And why not smile? Those envelopes contained royalty checks from movies he could barely remember being in, checks from long-ago television guest appearances, and of course—the dollop of whipped cream on the lemon meringue pie—checks from his long-running series, *Malibu Man*, which came with such regularity back then that he could tell which day of the week it was just by looking at the return address.

What Buck was slow to notice, but grew glaringly obvious over time, was that even though the same number of royalty checks continued to arrive, the size of those checks diminished with each passing year. Not so the property tax bill, which just grew bigger and bigger. And even that bill, if it were the only bill, might not have been so bad. There were so many others. Keeping a house in Beverly Hills, keeping the driveway manicured, keeping the pool clean, the tennis court rolled, the marble floors sparkling, all took money. And that was just for necessities. Recently added to that ledger was a Chinese cook and Puddles, whose lifestyle yielded its own potential mailbox full of surprises. He was waiting to see the one from the canine orthodontist for Puddles' alarming mouthful of braces—a Puppy Passport medical expense that Buck had unwittingly signed on to pay. Mail like this would take the fun out of anyone's day.

Then there was the shadow of a man in a ten-gallon hat that Buck encountered last night in BunnyLee's boudoir.

He took a long sip from his vodka and orange juice.

Buck had feelings for BunnyLee, jumbled feelings, feelings he might have trouble finding the right words to describe, even if he could sort them out. Adding insult to injury, the power was off and they were out of ice!

He would have happily yelled at somebody if anybody were around. Jimmy Chan had yet to return from the supermarket and Miguel had been dispatched to the pool supply. BunnyLee was in the cabana trying to cure Puddles from sneezing. The only candidate was Frankie, but it was hard to pick a fight with somebody who was voluntarily polishing your car.

It wasn't in Buck's nature to wear his emotions on his sleeve. The types of characters he portrayed showed few outward signs of distress. They faced down danger in a devil-may-care manner. Hiding their emotions was their charm. These were tough guys and wise guys, cool guys and cons—guys who succeeded in spite of their inner fears and with a sparkle in their eyes. Early on, Buck's agent promoted him as the next James Garner until too many in the coveted younger demographic asked, "Who's James Garner?'

When a part did call for a character's feelings to show, an actor like Buck needed to look no farther than the script; because in every script, a character's emotion was written in parentheses right there above the dialogue, right there in black and white.

As for Buck's own feelings, these remained buried in the subtext of his life.

And when his feelings happened to come uncovered, like this morning, they arrived unscripted. The fact of the matter was it was not easy to understand one's own feelings, especially while one was feeling them. It could take a lifetime to sort that stuff out and Buck didn't have all day.

Take despair. People called it an emotion. But dig a little deeper and you'd find that Buck's desperation was a hodgepodge of ingredients, a simmering *bouillabaisse*, an alphabet soup of emotions. It contained a lot of anger focused around that dog mangling his hairpiece this morning, but if you were to dig even deeper, stepping gingerly through this unpleasant psychological sortie, you would find that combining the pressures of his daily life, the maintaining of a lifestyle which lately seemed untenable, along with all the detritus of his childhood--a mother who died when he was one, a father who dropped him on the doorstep of a great aunt at two--alongside those slights and disappointments and periods of loneliness that often welled up again when he experienced similar setbacks in his present-day life, this was no clear broth. Indeed, you had the makings of a fricassee. Certainly the shadowy appearance of last night's visitor was a large part of Buck's froth. But the ladle that stirred the stew was the laugh that BunnyLee laughed when she saw Buck this morning *sans toupee.*

Buck touched the top of his head and tried to flatten his damaged hairpiece. It didn't fit so well after this morning's overland journey in Puddle's jaws and its subsequent whitewater voyage through the pool's unfiltered recirculation system. Buck held the Post-it in his hand and strolled down the driveway toward Frankie.

Frankie was sitting on an upside-down bucket, attending to the finer points of detailing the Flying B, the iconic hood ornament that rode atop the classic Bentley Silver Shadow grille. As Buck approached, Frankie stood and addressed his quasi-employer.

Frankie was a good-looking Black man, bigger than Buck and ten years younger. He still had his Virginia accent and spoke at half the pace of the Southern California norm. His deep and resonant voice put people at ease.

"Hey, boss, Miguel took the impeller into town like you said. I told him I'd finish detailin' the car. I don't mind doin' it unless you need somethin'. Got to have the car lookin' nice for Monday."

Buck held out the note. "You know anything about this?"

Of the two mysteries Buck was anxious to solve this morning, determining the author of the pink Post-it was first on the list. Unmasking the owner of the ten-gallon hat in the company of BunnyLee last night would take more sleuthing.

"Looks like a phone message."

"You didn't take this call?"

"No sir. I know better than to answer the phone."

"Nobody should be answering the phone. That's what I keep that old answering machine for." Buck squinted to read the note, then gave up on vanity and pulled his reading glasses out of his pocket. He read aloud. "Urgent! A-Number-One Pick! Top Dog! Call Mr. Morris!" He gazed at Frankie. "It sounds important. But what does it mean?"

"Thing to do might be call this Mr. Morris and ask him."

"Brilliant! If I knew who Mr. Morris was. Who even calls a landline anymore? I'm racking my brain. There's nothing in the old Rolodex. So who took the message?"

Buck showed it to Frankie.

✦

Frankie stroked his chin while he studied it. Not being one to willingly get others into trouble, he was slow to answer.

"If I had to guess, I'd say Jimmy Chan."

"He shouldn't be answering the phone."

Frankie soft-pedaled the importance of the matter. "Thing is, if it was Chan, maybe it isn't so important."

"It says urgent. How could it not be important?"

"Because Chan, he doesn't know too many words. Or..." Frankie paused. He tried to explain it away. "Or it could have been a wrong number."

"An urgent wrong number?"

There was really nothing to say, but he felt the need to say something. "You think this message is for you, Boss?"

"Frankie, who the hell else could it be for? There's just BunnyLee and me and she's got a cell phone."

"Not since she lost hers she don't."

"She lost her cell phone? Why doesn't she just get a new one?"

"I guess she's hopin' it turn up. It only went missing yesterday." The subject had now drifted to BunnyLee.

"She been out here?"

"Who?"

"Who? Who else? BunnyLee. Has she been out here?"

Frankie didn't like talking about BunnyLee any more than Jimmy Chan. He hadn't survived six years around this famous man by stirring things up.

"No, sir, I have not seen BunnyLee. Miguel said she wanted to take her puppy over to that vet if she doesn't stop sneezin'."

"Frankie, under no circumstances are you to take that dog to the vet."

"No?"

"There is nothing wrong with that dog."

"No?"

"No."

"BunnyLee's been thinkin' maybe Puddles has a breathin' disorder. That's why she wants to bring her dog to the vet."

"From inhaling too much filet mignon? That dog is costing me a fortune. What kind of dog you ever met wore braces?"

"A winning smile goes a long way in this town..."

"On a dog?"

"BunnyLee loves her Puddles."

Buck nodded. He sighed. He looked at his feet. There was a curious new look of desperation on Buck. Frankie had first noticed it around the time the Kermit the Frog outtake debuted on YouTube. But this morning it lingered around the edges of Buck's famous face.

"You two talk a lot," Buck said.

"No, sir, not us," Frankie answered.

Buck was leaning in. "But sometimes you stand and chat."

Frankie stepped back against the Bentley. "Hardly never... I mean now and then, I'm more of a listener. Sometimes when I'm out drivin' her to auditions and whatnot we talk about stuff. Not important stuff. Things like the weather, or the other day about how Cheyanna was in the waitin' room..."

"Cheyanna, the singer?"

"Yeah, BunnyLee had a good time hearin' stories about this Native American dog whisperer they have up in Mariposa."

"She ever talk about me?"

"Nope."

"Never?"

"No, sir. Maybe about what you and she had for dinner or where you'll be going later... nuthin' like..."

"She talk about our relationship?"

"Boss, that's none of my business."

"You've met these veterinarians. They're a lot younger than me..."

"Boss, I bring her there and I take her straight home..."

"I'm just saying it would explain a lot, if one or more of them... or maybe the dog's dentist..."

"Kinda hot out here. What say I go mix up some ice tea?"

"Yeah? With what ice? That cook used it all." Buck took a healthy swig of his drink. "I might be paranoid, but that doesn't mean they're not sneaking up on me. A guy like me can never relax."

"Nuthin' that a new television series won't cure."

"Enough with the free advice."

"I'm just sayin'..."

"What are you saying?" The two men stared at each other. They would have been eye-to-eye had Buck been standing on an apple box, or the way they often photographed him from a low angle looking up. In real life, Frankie was more than a head taller, and broader across the shoulders.

Buck took a step back. "Don't mind me. I've just been playing the private eye too long. Can't help but put two and two together, though, and it just doesn't add up." He gazed at the Bentley and then back at Frankie. "If not them, who? Miguel's too old, and what's-his-name, Charlie Chan, the cook, hardly speaks English. So that just leaves you, Frankie."

"Me? What's that suppose t'mean?"

"I'm just saying, who spends more time with her than you?"

"Now that there is the liquor talkin'!" Frankie said, pointing at Buck's drink.

"It's my imagination that BunnyLee suddenly has no time for me?"

"Right now, BunnyLee's only got eyes for Puddles," Frankie answered.

"Puddles? I have had it up to here... Like it's my fault the dog has a sneezing fit every time I come near? You should see her bedroom!"

"It isn't that bad."

"How would you know? When were you down there?"

"Tuesday when I delivered her the flowers you bought." Frankie was desperate to change the subject.

"Oh, yeah. Well, somebody was in the cabana with her last night."

"Huh? No, Boss, there was no one with her."

"You know that for a fact? Last night, when I got back from the hospital, I dropped in to say goodnight. I saw the shadow of a man in a ten-gallon hat!"

"There ain't no way in hell..."

"I know I've got no justification..."

"Nobody could have gotten in through that gate without me knowin' about it."

"So I should believe you or my lying eyes?"

"Boss, now that you've got this new series, there is no time to be stewin' about none of this."

"Yeah, well, it's only a pilot. Sidney looked over the contract. It's straightforward stuff, but I haven't agreed to anything yet. They would have to agree to some changes."

"It's never too late to stage a comeback. Look at Perry Mason way back when... Guy as talented as you, you'll be back on the talk shows in no time, just you wait and see."

"Raymond Burr? I knew him when I was a kid."

"Yeah. That man made a comeback."

"Working out of a wheelchair. Not a lot of sex appeal in that."

"Show ran for years..."

"He got old."

"No sin in gettin' old."

"In this town there is. Good thing I read that script."

"You read the script? All of it?" Frankie asked.

Buck nodded. "It's about a sanguine African American private eye who works as a chauffeur for an old cripple." He said. "An old cripple named Nick Derringer. Which is kind of a coincidence what with Nick Derringer being the name of the *young* character I recently played."

Frankie had never known Buck to read a script, at least not until he had to. And even then, he only read his own lines. Frankie was pretty sure that his reading this new script was not good news.

"I almost agreed to the stupid thing before I read it!" Buck said. "What do you think they'd be saying about me in the trades if I came out walking with a cane?"

"No, the bad guys think you're old, but all the time the audience knows otherwise. They know it's just your thing."

"My thing."

"Your cover. Everybody knows you aren't really bald and don't need the cane..."

"Everybody but the bad guys...Why is that, Frankie? The bad guys don't watch TV?"

"All I'm sayin' is it's never too late to start anew. This producer, he's a smart man. You sign a contract Monday, you're back on top with busloads of pretty young fans throwin' themselves at your feet again."

"Right. Busloads of pretty young things fresh from Nowheresville just itching to be with some bald guy with a cane. What do you think someone like BunnyLee would say if I came out all bent over and walking with a cane?"

"You really care that much about what BunnyLee thinks?"

"I'm just using her as an example."

"Well, it's none of my business, but I would have thought that you'd've taken her to the Emmys."

"She didn't want to go." Buck said. "But you're right. I should have." Buck looked Frankie straight in the eyes. "I am not going to sign some contract just because the phone hasn't rung in a while. Which reminds me, when Chan gets here, you tell him I want to see him about this message!" Buck turned to leave, then turned back, holding up his empty glass. "When is the electricity coming back on?"

Frankie filled him in on what Miguel had told him. "Power company said that when that pool pump jammed, a big spark took out that transformer across the street. Which started what they called rollin' blackouts. Power's out to the top of Laurel Canyon and down the other side into the Valley. Miguel left the gate open, so I need to watch the drive."

"Does my hair look alright?"

"Yep."

"You sure?"

"Yep."

"Good. I've got tennis with Sidney and the boys. So, don't go taking BunnyLee anywhere behind my back. I want to talk to her first." Buck turned back to the house.

Frankie sat in the driver's seat of the Bentley. He could have written a dissertation on the temperament of Buck LeGrande, but today's mood was way off the mark. Frankie felt desperate; he had to do something. His next career depended on Buck taking that part. The meeting at Warner Brothers was two days away, and he wasn't at all sure that Buck intended to go. Rather than convincing him to reprise the role of Nick Derringer, it seemed like he'd made things worse by bringing the subject up.

He needed a backup plan: to enlist the help of BunnyLee. Her opinion carried a lot of weight; Buck listened to her. But getting to BunnyLee was easier said than done. Frankie couldn't risk being seen in her company. She spent most of her time in the guest cabana these days. Frankie was not about to chance getting caught hanging around down there. Especially now that Buck suspected him of spending quality time with BunnyLee.

CHAPTER 11

AUSTIN HADN'T SEEN a service station since leaving the Central Valley. Settlements were spotty here. Where there was water, he saw the occasional ranch, fenced for grazing. Further up into the grassy foothills, he didn't encounter much of anything but open, untamed chaparral.

Twenty years ago, he and his brother explored this feral backcountry. On horseback, there was no need to follow the road. A cowboy or Indian—and they were partly both—traveled with impunity. Few would have the skill to trail men intent on losing them. He checked his rearview mirror periodically for signs of the pink Ford Ranger. He was fully aware that a car plying these dusty roads would be easy to tail. His white convertible Cadillac Eldorado with red leather upholstery would stand out no matter where, even without that set of Texas longhorns lashed above the front grille.

The road was tough on his neck. To maintain any speed at all meant to endure a constant jostling. He slowed to let the air clear behind the car. He was pretty sure he'd shaken his pursuers. He stopped the car.

Getting his door open and easing his stiff body out of his seat was a minor ordeal. Walking around back of the car, he diagnosed another. The trunk latch was jammed. This was most likely due to the rather large imprint he'd made landing on the trunk lid earlier this morning. It would take a pry bar to pop the latch. He could hear his cell phone beeping, but it was his neck brace that he wanted. Both were trapped in the trunk. There was nothing he could do but drive on and look for help or turn back.

He drove on.

A handful of folks in these parts were here to get back to the land, and some had never left it. To say that they were communing with nature would be pushing it. More likely than not, this was where their ancestors staked a claim for gold or had simply broken down. These were his kind of people, Austin assured himself. If they owned a working TV, they would recognize him straight away and even go so far as to offer him their last beer.

But then again, TVs don't work so well without power. And some of the men in these parts weren't the type to lend out their crowbar to any passing stranger, either. Especially not while they were holding it menacingly above that stranger's head.

Scattered alongside a meandering seasonal brook were rudimentary encampments, target practice ranges, the occasional vintage trailer. He knew he was in man's country after counting half a dozen army surplus M.A.S.H. units. One room and portable, they were perfect for a guy to move into after the wife had shown him the door. Austin sized up a number of these places without stopping.

The road veered close to an adobe homestead with a ragged blue tarpaulin for a roof. Austin caught sight of the barrel of a rifle poked through a torn window screen. It glistened sunlight as it casually followed his progress.

He checked his gas gauge. This was not the kind of place you wanted to run out of fuel. It seemed like the end of the line for any number of folks, and he didn't want to be counted among the missing. He half-expected the hooded Angel of Death to step out from behind a boulder to tell him his time was up.

On a hilltop, Austin spotted a landmark—a small Spanish chapel. Two decades back, a Jesuit priest had battled against the elements to keep it standing. On closer inspection, it looked like time had won the war. The iron bell clung to the broken timber in the arch above the doorway; the door was missing. The roof of the church had succumbed to gravity and daylight shone through to the altar. Gnats swarmed in the light looking like smoke from an extinguished votive.

More likely than not, the kindly pastor was now six feet under among the tilting headstones in the churchyard beyond. In

Austin's mind's eye, this would have been a proper place to lay a man to rest, but in the clear light of present day, the place looked godforsaken.

A few miles further, along the edge of a mesa, the road passed under the wooden arch of an abandoned RV retirement community—The Trail's End. Empty hook-up sites were arranged along both sides of the road and on their far sides they hugged the rim of a cliff—not the safest place for children or sleepwalkers. At the far end, he came to a lone Mexican ranch-style building. He read a sign above its sagging porch: *Nursing Home, Crematorium, Good Used Clothes.* To the looks of things, this was a service establishment built on a bad business model—no repeat business. An *Open* sign hung in the window.

Austin's neck hurt like heck. He turned the car off and got out. A murder of crows cawed and shifted vantage in the needle-bare ghost pine overhead. He looked through the barred window. Used boots, belt buckles, a modest collection of previously owned prostheses were featured items. There was no substitute for a neck.

Austin tried the door. It was locked. A hand-written note taped above the handle read, 'AROUND BACK!' An arrow pointed to the right and down.

Austin walked to the edge of the ravine. This did look very much like the end of the trail, not just figuratively. The road descended precipitously into a steep gulley to ford a trickle of a stream, and it was pretty much just a washed-out slope from here to there. A Road Closed sign lay by the wayside. Down below, a freestanding chimney poked through struggling oaks.

Austin considered his options. Being of a class of men who never turned back when they were stymied, on principle he didn't like turning around.

Additionally, he was a guy who lived in the present. He viewed the future with caution and cringed at the thought of looking back. His recent past in particular was full of heartache too fresh to revisit.

Below, a woman stepped out of the shadows and waved up at him.

Austin waved back.

"Down here!" she said. She struck a solemn figure in a black hat, black jeans and a black silken shirt. Her long sleeves, loose shirttails and black hair hung like feathers at her side; her bangs were cut straight across her brow.

"My trunk is jammed!" Austin said.

"What?"

Given the distance between them and the unpredictable wind, long sentences were imperiled. "I...need...a...pry...bar!"

"I've an andiron," the woman said. She waved him down.

What was left of the road was deeply rutted. Austin took a step down in her direction and his foot slipped on the gravel. He wasn't anywhere near the steepest part of the slope and his neck was telling him not to do it. He knew that climbing back up with the andiron would be equally problematic.

"No! Bring the car!"

"Drive down?" That didn't look like the wisest thing, either. He wondered whether the woman was crazy.

"You gotta bring the car!"

"Not sure she'll make it."

"Back 'er down!"

Austin had a high threshold to pain, but it was hard to think straight with his neck hurting so much.

"Is the road okay beyond?" he asked.

"Better than this."

"Does it continue north?"

"As the crow flies."

It was said that when you reached a fork in the road, you should take it. Meaning that sometimes life's decisions boil down to a flip of a coin or a roll of the dice. Austin didn't have any ready adages for facing a chasm other than to admit that sometimes there were no good choices. He backed the Eldorado to the edge where he'd been standing. His neck already hurt too much to ignore this glimmer of salvation. Twisting his body to see in reverse was like doubling down on the dicey bet; once the decision was made, there was no turning back. He inched the car over the crest and eased it down the embankment.

The woman shouted encouragement, "Turn! No, left! The other left! Too much!"

The back wheel found a rut and the car bottomed out with a jolt under the driver-side door. It jarred him from his coccyx to his collarbone. He tried easing the car out of the channel; the tire spun on the loose roadbed and the car moved sideways. Crows mocked him. Some decamped to the sparsely leafed oak branches and now sat ringside. He gave the engine more gas and burned some rubber. The tire caught and the car lurched free. The brakes and steering weren't much good after that as the Eldorado bucked and gyrated out of control. It was all he could do to hold onto the wheel with one hand and his neck with the other. The car spun around onto the leveling ground below and stopped, facing forward. He'd lost rodeos on the bucking backs of less spirited creatures.

"Been years since somebody tried that," the woman said. "Most folks come from there." She pointed across the stream.

Austin's door wouldn't open. He put his shoulder into it, but no luck. He slid across the seat to the passenger side and got out. He tipped his hat.

"Ma'am."

The woman came across older close up. Her richly tanned, sun-dried face was deeply rutted like the land around them, with a beak for a nose.

A crow landed on her shoulder and she fed it a morsel from her breast pocket.

Austin's veins flowed with enough indigenous blood to be wary. Dozing among the elders around the campfire late at night, safe in his grandmother's lap, he'd absorbed enough of the native lore to be mindful of crows. Crows messengered between the here and the hereafter.

"Sorry to see you come alone," the woman said.

"Were you expecting somebody else?"

"I'm no help when it comes to lifting bodies is all. But yer strong."

"I just need a tool to get my trunk open, so if you have that andiron?"

"It's leaning beside the oven," the woman said. She pointed along a path that followed the stream. "Just started the fire. Take a few minutes 'fore she's up to temp."

If Austin was paranoid, he had the steroids to thank for that. His harried dreams got the better of him at night, and again he wondered whether they were seeping into his waking world. He looked back at his car. A crow landed on the hood. Another alit on the crooked longhorns lashed to the grill. The Eldorado looked like carrion lying there. He glanced up and saw vultures circling.

"You have paperwork?" the woman asked.

"For what?"

"Government's got their fingers into everything. File a form for this, get a permit for that. Now you gotta tell 'em what yer gonna do with the ashes. Like it's anybody's business. Nobody can afford to die anymore."

One of the crows hopped from the windshield to the seat and looked cock-eyed at the dash. It jumped to the steering column and began to work the shiny keys out of the ignition with its beak. Austin waved his hat and hustled back to the car to rescue them. The woman followed.

"Body's in the trunk?" she asked.

"Whoa! Slow down! You've got me mixed up with somebody else."

"You don't have a wife in there?"

"No, ma'am. Is that what you do here?"

"Burning the body helps free the spirit."

"Well, I never had a wife and my brother's already cremated. His ashes are in the trunk, as a matter of fact, along with my neck brace and my phone."

The woman looked at him sideways. She leaned closer. Her one visible pupil stared fixedly at him.

"How long...?"

"How long what?"

"...you been traveling with the ashes."

"I'd have to think back..."

"Three months?"

"More."

"In my way of reckonin' a year's the limit! You gotta get rid of 'em! After a year yer just lookin' for trouble."

Her words sent chills.

It was said that crows would sometimes pass information to humans; there were tales where crows took human form. She certainly fit that bill. Austin stepped back. His imagination was getting the better of him. Physically, he could look out for himself. Metaphysically, he wasn't so savvy. He could imagine her flying up into the oak branches to be with her black-feathered friends.

"I had in mind that old chapel a mile or so back, but it's bleak. And besides, Laredo wasn't fully Catholic..."

"You gotta let 'im go!"

A truck stopped in a cloud of dust at the crest of the ravine up by the store. The crow-lady waved.

"That must be them now."

The air cleared to reveal what Austin already suspected—the pink Ford pickup with lace curtains. It was the women who'd been hounding him.

"Well, don't that beat all," Austin said. "Uncanny how they know where I am."

"Down here!" the woman said to them.

"I best be going. Just one thing. What do folks do with the ashes?"

"Spread 'em."

"Where?"

"Wherever it suits ya. Just don't tell nobody. Especially when it's private property. Nowadays, everybody wants a say in what you do. State says ya got three months to do it."

"What happens after that?"

"It'll cost ya. They got a fine for everything."

Standing by the pink pickup was the younger woman—the one with the emerald eyes.

Like a wounded deer, Austin hightailed it. He slid over the car door into the driver's seat and gunned the engine. He was clearly being hunted.

Beyond the dry riverbed, he followed the one-lane dirt road. According to the sun, he was heading generally north, which was a good thing. Other than that, he really wasn't making reasoned choices today.

Jumping from a second-story railing onto his trunk, driving backwards down a washed-out embankment; these were not the actions of a man who was thinking clearly. He wondered what was in those anabolic steroid shots. Big Eddie, his producer, knew a guy who knew a guy who was bringing this stuff up over the border. It was anybody's guess what was in it. Austin was cautious with the dosage, but maybe this bootleg version was cut with something, or maybe it was too pure. He was new to juicing. Aside from building muscle mass, Austin didn't know what indications to expect. This didn't feel like Roid Rage even though paranoia was said to be part and parcel. He was sad, but who wouldn't be? The trail ahead was long and lonely without his only sibling at the wheel.

If he could find the trail!

Tall grasses overtook the road. It was hard to say which way to go. He slowed to a stop. The Crow-Lady's firm warning about the ashes had him thinking. It felt portentous. Omens were warnings one did not ignore. Like the ripples that came before the bow of the canoe, subtle disturbances foretold outsized events. That was one thing he and Juanita Carlita could agree on.

From the glove box Austin pulled a folded newspaper. Under a medium-sized headline, Laredo's official wrestling photo was like looking in the mirror. Austin checked the date on the page. He crosschecked the wrestling schedule for today's date—September 23rd—and did the math.

Damned if his brother hadn't died a year ago today.

Laredo and he went everywhere together; it was hard for Austin to move on from that. For his own sake, if not for Laredo's, it was long past time to let him go. He needed to find a fitting place and put Laredo to rest.

CHAPTER 12

FRANKIE SLOUCHED LOW in the driver's seat of his boss's Bentley. Monday's meeting with Warner Brothers was only two days away, and he needed to do everything in his power to get Buck to the table if he was to achieve his ambition.

Not that long ago, Frankie and Buck had been closer to being friends, back when Buck's contract negotiations fell apart and his series came to an abrupt end. Buck had been holding out for a large pay increase against all advice.

His agent had suggested that a contract extension with the same terms and same pay level would help propel the show into its fifth season—the point at which a popular show has enough episodes on the shelf to make it a desirable production for syndication. Buck disagreed. He argued that the potential for syndication gave him a bargaining chip to seek a raise.

The producers saw things a third way. They looked at the ratings as a curve over time and noted that the curve had taken a downward dip. In their minds, a fifth season would be a roll of the dice even if Buck would agree to certain southerly adjustments in his pay. After all, it wasn't the last season of *Gunsmoke* or *Bonanza* or *Dallas*, they pointed out.

The first four seasons of *Malibu Man* did make syndication after a while, but not on a channel anybody had ever heard of. It played to a mostly camp audience that found entertainment value in what his critics called its melodramatic plots, cardboard characterizations, and sentimental outcomes. And, of course, it appealed to those women, and subset of men, who thought Buck still looked hot in a Speedo.

Things got very quiet around Number 10 Beverly Canyon after the show was canceled. Buck was blindsided by the turn of events. He became melancholic, introverted, and thoughtful. He continued to have Frankie drive him places even though their destination was unclear. They would talk on these rides, Frankie at the wheel and Buck in the back seat. Or more precisely, Buck would talk and Frankie would drive. Sometimes Frankie would park up on Mulholland Drive so that they could watch the lights come on in Studio City until he realized that Buck was too afraid of heights to look down. Heights were the upshot of fame. The higher Buck climbed, the further he could fall.

Other times they headed out to Malibu. Frankie would take Sunset Boulevard; the irony was not lost on him. At the beach, they revisited the numerous locations where Buck's character had ferreted out all manner of crime and corruption and spousal indiscretions. Buck still wouldn't get out of the car. Frankie began to think his reticence to appear in public stemmed not from his fear of people recognizing him but, worse yet, a fear of them not. After years in the limelight, Buck was slipping into obscurity. Despite all the hard work of burnishing his public image, more and more people were now scratching their heads and asking, "Remind me, who is Buck LeGrande?"

It was around this time that Buck marked his fortieth birthday without fanfare. For anyone who had approached this signpost in a culture that celebrates youth, it was a peek over that hill into the precipice below. Buck wondered aloud whether it was his time to ride off into the sunset, while Frankie wondered silently whether he would be expected to drive him there. For the first time in Buck's life, he was showing an abundance of humility. He was accepting and warm. And, for the first time, Frankie was actually starting to feel a kinship.

Then, a couple of months ago, an unfortunate outtake surfaced from a years-old appearance on Sesame Street. It showed Buck LeGrande in an altercation with Kermit the Frog, the world's most endearing puppet. In the video, Buck gripped him around the neck as Kermit struggled for air in slow motion.

Miraculously, now everybody remembered who Buck LeGrande was. A lot of people wanted to know what he had to say for himself. Buck wasn't talking. His childhood buddy and present-day manager, Sidney, advised him to lay low for a while and wait for things to blow over.

BunnyLee's voice woke Frankie from his reverie.

✦

"Psst! Hey, Frankie, is he gone?" BunnyLee called out from behind the cedar tree at the far side of the carriage house. Frankie sat up in the car and looked for her in the rearview mirror, then he cast a wary eye up toward the house.

"Don't see him. But that don't mean anything."

Frankie got out of the Bentley, only to be interrupted by the sound of a car ascending the drive. Sidney and the boys arrived in a newly painted red vintage Dodge Charger convertible.

Even on a good day, Frankie would have preferred to avoid seeing these men. Archie called to him before he could get away.

"I'll be right back," BunnyLee whispered. She ducked out of sight.

"Frankie, my man! How's it shakin'?"

Frankie gave a half-hearted wave back. He was used to Archie's pseudo-ghetto slang, delivered in a *mano a mano* familiarity that was just so lame.

Sidney was slow to get out of the driver's seat, so Archie hopped out of the backseat over the side. From the front passenger seat, Ziggy scolded him about scuffing the new paint. Archie hurried to get to Frankie.

"Why's the gate open?" he asked.

"Power's out."

"Is she still here?"

"Who?"

"Who?" asked Archie. "The big question mark. The enigmatic woman. The inimitable BunnyLee."

Archie circled around behind Frankie and positioned himself in a spot in the driveway near a break in the hedge where he could see down to the pool.

Since her arrival and meteoric rise to residency, Buck's friends had an abiding fascination for BunnyLee. She was blonde and personable and disarmingly attractive. But she also presented a palpable danger. Before her arrival at Number 10 Beverly Canyon, there were no women around. Aside from Miguel's wife providing housekeeping service, things were estrogen-free. Their Saturdays often devolved into boisterous clubhouse humor. These days they still enjoyed their refreshments by the pool, but the topics now turned to headier matters. They'd never known as worldly a woman as BunnyLee, who could speak of Daniel Day Lewis and René Descartes and Realism versus Naturalism in the same sentence. She was well versed in Darwin's influence on Method acting. When Buck proclaimed that his method of acting was to shoot from the hip, BunnyLee had a name for that too. To her mind, when you boiled it down to its essential element, art was not a complicated idea. Art was simply the active expression of an emotion. Buck was a Naturalist, she explained, which had everything to do with feelings and, it turned out, nothing to do with nudism. BunnyLee could recite Baudelaire from memory. In an electrifying performance, she told them:

"Be Drunk.

"You have to be always drunk. That's all there is to it--it's the only way. So as not to feel the horrible burden of time that breaks your back and bends you to the earth, you have to be continually drunk. But on what?

"Wine, poetry, or virtue, as you wish. But be drunk. And if sometimes, on the steps of a palace or the green grass of a ditch, in the mournful solitude of your room, you wake again, drunkenness already diminishing or gone, ask the wind, the wave, the star, the bird, the clock, everything that is flying, everything that is groaning, everything that is rolling, everything that is singing, everything that is speaking . . . ask what time it is and wind, wave, star, bird, clock will answer you: it is time to be drunk! So as not to be the martyred slaves of time, be drunk, be continually drunk! On wine, on poetry, or on virtue as you wish."

All cheered the devil-may-care attitude, but later they wondered among themselves whether she diminished them by her virtue.

BunnyLee explained how Baudelaire was channeling Dionysus. This wasn't the first time that she had mentioned Dionysus. He was the Greek god of the grape harvest and everything that an abundance of wine entailed. Buck didn't have a clue where she was heading with all of this.

"Dionysus is the god of epiphany," BunnyLee said, as if that explained everything.

Sid and Zig held back as Archie spoke with Frankie. They showed more constraint around the topic of BunnyLee. Both had careers in show business and they exhibited an insider's diffidence toward fame and its trappings. As an entertainment lawyer, Sid knew the value in keeping his nose out of his client's personal business.

Zig wrote screenplays about vampires. His Eastern European accent lent an authenticity to his command of the genre, and he'd even had a script optioned a few years back. It was like finding a nugget of gold; Zig kept thinking there was more where that came from. Frankie wasn't too sure. Even with vampire stories, there was a saturation point.

Archie never let them forget that he made a better living as a dentist, but of all of them, he was the most star-struck. Whether in a restaurant or out on the freeway, Archie was forever pointing out famous people. His knowledge was encyclopedic, even extending to the minor players of bit parts whose few lines of dialogue entitled them a mention in the credits. It was an education. Actors whom Archie's pals had never heard of turned out to be having decent careers. When Archie bragged that one of his new patients was an adult film star of some renown and versatile skill-set, Sid and Zig felt compelled to google her so as to fully acquaint themselves with the depth and breadth of her *curriculum vitae*.

"Is she out?" Archie asked, clearly hoping for a glance at BunnyLee through the hedge.

"She's in her stable," Frankie answered, dryly, as if BunnyLee were a prizewinning filly grazing in some rich rancher's corral.

"So she's still here? I have a bet with Zig she won't last two months, and this is week four," Archie said, looking through the hedge just in case Frankie was mistaken. "You wouldn't happen to know if she's got a tan line?"

"Why you ask me?" Frankie answered. No way did he want to be resident expert on all things BunnyLee.

"Why don't you ask Buck?" Ziggy interjected. "I'd say he ought to know."

"That's a good one. I'll have to do that."

"Come on, you guys, we're here to play tennis," Sidney yelled from the gate. Of the three of them, Sid was on the surest footing. His friendship with Buck went well beyond the others, all the way back to when they were child actors together with Rex West on the set of a coming-of-age movie.

Sid held the gate for Ziggy and then waited for Archie. "You playing tennis?"

"Yeah, I'll be right there," Archie called back. And then to Frankie, who was heading for the driver's door of the Bentley to back it into the garage, Archie asked, "What about her hair? Is she a real blonde? I bet that she is."

"I find out, you be the first to know," Frankie said.

"Thanks, Bro, I knew I could count on you." Archie fist-bumped him then walked off past his brother, who closed the gate behind them.

"Psst! Psst!"

Frankie turned but could not see BunnyLee.

"Any sign of him?" she whispered.

"He's supposed to be playing tennis."

BunnyLee stepped out from behind the cedar. She carried Puddles in a large satchel with a strap slung over her shoulder. She was still wearing her bikini. "Where's Miguel?"

"BunnyLee, you've got to put something on!" Frankie would risk being caught alone in the company of BunnyLee, but only if she was fully dressed.

"I've got some clothes in my bag." BunnyLee lifted Puddles out of the satchel. "Hold her for a sec, okay?"

She handed the dog to Frankie. Frankie was no expert in the art of holding a puppy. While he struggled to control the wiggling animal, Puddles licked his ear. BunnyLee moved behind the cedar hedge where Frankie could only see her feet.

"Frankie, I've just been so worried about Puddles. You have no idea."

"You're worried? Jeezus, BunnyLee, Buck can't see me near you undressing! Go to the cabana!"

"I'm sorry, but I don't have time," BunnyLee said from behind the bushes. "And besides, I can't go back there without him noticing."

Frankie backed away from where she was standing and leaned

against the Bentley. He looked up toward the house. He felt uneasy just holding her dog.

✦

BunnyLee unhooked her bikini top as she spoke. "The material in this suit is unbearable, you have no idea. But how can anybody order a bathing suit online and expect it to fit?" She dropped it into her bag and fished around the gigantic purse for her blouse. "It's not like I can go to the department store anymore."

She pulled a light cotton print blouse from the bag. "Tada! Here it is!" She turned it right side out, shook the wrinkles out of it, picked off an errant dog hair, and slid her arms in one at a time. "Where's Miguel?" she asked again as she buttoned the blouse.

"Went to the pool supply," Frankie answered.

"Hold on just one more sec, okay?"

"BunnyLee!"

"Well, the bottoms itch worse than the top! And you can't see me."

"That's not the point."

✦

Frankie could see BunnyLee's bare feet at the trunk of the tree as she slipped out of her sandals, then her bikini bottom, one foot at a time. With any luck he could have put to rest either of Archie's pressing questions about her tan line or whether her carpet matched her drapes. Frankie was a better man than that. He turned away and let the woman's secrets remain secret.

"I went online just now and omigod!" BunnyLee said. "They say these sneezing fits may belie something deeper. I read about one dog that sneezed a lot and ended up needing a heart transplant! I know you're not supposed to believe half of what you read on the internet but I am so worried!"

"Yer scared? I'm dyin' here!"

He relaxed a bit when BunnyLee emerged in a pair of shorts and a blouse. As she came back around the car he handed her the dog.

"Listen here, BunnyLee--"

"I mean, what if Puddles is really sick and I don't do anything?"

"Heart transplant? For a dog? Now there yer talkin' big money. BunnyLee, you overhear what Buck was sayin'? I think we've got us a situation here. Now he's saying he's not gonna sign that contract!"

"What contract, remind me again?"

"For that script that I've been writing! *The Return of Malibu Man*. The one that Warner Brothers picked up."

"They did? Wow! Congratulations! I just finished reading it. I loved the part with the shootout in Frontiertown at the end. I know you've been talking about this script, but I just assumed, you know, everybody in Hollywood's writing a script. Does Buck know you wrote this?"

"I took my name off his copy."

Archie pushed through the garden gate.

"I forgot my racket," he said, smiling at BunnyLee. "Hello, BunnyLee. How are you today?"

"Fine, thank you, Doctor. And you?"

"Just fine, thanks."

Frankie watched as Archie went to retrieve his racket from the backseat of his brother's car. He looked for any hint that he had seen BunnyLee changing or had overheard what they were saying. "Steer clear of that one," Frankie said under his breath.

"He's harmless," she replied over her shoulder as Archie fished his racket out.

"He talks too much."

"He's impressed by my 'fame'. Every dentist in America is supposedly jealous that he knows the Dial-a Denture phone bank operator personally!"

"And how is Puddles?" Archie asked as he returned. He stopped to rub the dog under her chin. He pulled back the dog's lips to inspect her braces. "How's my favorite patient? Looks okay, but if there is any redness or bleeding, you come see me right away."

"Thanks, Arch, that is so nice of you. I'm more worried about her sneezing."

"She seems fine to me."

"But sometimes she has these sneezing fits."

"Nice day for tennis," Frankie said.

"It is a lovely day," Archie replied. He seemed to Frankie to be settling in for a long conversation.

"You don't wanna keep 'em waitin'," Frankie said.

"No, you're right. I should get back. Well, okay, nice to see you, BunnyLee."

"Nice to see you too, Doctor."

They watched as Archie disappeared through the gate.

"Now he's gonna say you and I have been talkin'."

"I don't think he's going to mention you at all. Tell me again about your script. It's got Nick Derringer in it."

"Right. That's why I call it *The Return of Malibu Man!* Where I bring Nick Derringer back from retirement."

"Right. And Buck would do the part again?"

"That's exactly right."

BunnyLee couldn't help but scoff at the idea. "Frankie, he's not gonna do this."

"The details are all worked out, BunnyLee."

"He's not going to play an old man. And another thing, he's not going to play second fiddle to a younger character. Remind me what 'sanguine' means?"

"One of the four temperaments, like pleasure-seeking and sociable. Like, on top of the world."

"Right. So wasn't Buck the sanguine character in the original *Malibu Man?*"

"Yeah, but this time, not so much."

"That's what I'm saying! The younger character gets all the best lines. I just don't think he's gonna go for it. But then again, what do I know?"

"I don't see it like that, BunnyLee. First off, he hasn't worked in a while. And secondly, he needs the money."

"He does? I didn't know that. Don't get me wrong. I really liked it. It's fun and it's funny. But it's a long shot. The main character is his chauffeur, right? Frankie, he's going to know that the main character is you."

"They always say, 'Write what you know!' And besides, I got the part."

"Really! No fooling? You're going to play the chauffeur yourself?"

"Darn straight. Guess all those college drama classes paid off. This time, the Black man gets to be the sanguine guy."

"Frankie, that is awesome!"

"Just so long as I get him to sign the deal. BunnyLee, you have got to take my side in this. In Hollywood, they're always lookin' for new voices. Quite frankly, I need the job, too. I don't know if you know this, but I don't technically work for Buck."

"How's that?"

"I used to get paid by the film company. Since his series was canceled, he kept me on in exchange for free rent and per diem. It's a nice gig, I don't have to drive him too much."

"So all this time you've been driving me around you've been doing it for free?"

"Something like that. But don't get me wrong. Buck, he needs this work, too...after all that business with the YouTube video."

"You mean with Kermit? I was out of the country when that came out."

"Things have settled down, but that Kermit video? That was a big deal. Everybody was talking about it."

"Why did Buck strangle Kermit the Frog? It is just so not like Buck!"

"He never did say. And I was there that day. But for Buck to act like that... Buck, he never loses his cool. All the pressure, it can get to a person. Even to someone like Buck. Whatever. He needs to get past this. He needs to work."

"I don't know...I guess...I mean, yeah, I know. I mean, who am I to throw a wet blanket on it? But Nick Derringer was a hip young stud! My older sister was in his fan club!"

"In this script he'd be...more grown up."

"Well, yeah! As in—an old man? Going bald and carrying a cane? It's a big change for Buck."

"I never saw him read a script in depth before. Now I've got to convince him there is fame in older types. AARP is full of feature articles about actors who made a comeback later in life. All Buck has got to do is go Monday and sign."

"AARP? Okay, whatever, I'm all for it. But it's a big change. He'd be going from leading man to comic relief. He's a good enough actor if he puts his mind to it. With character actors, it's okay to be flawed. Their flaws are their strengths."

"Would you tell him that?"

"Right." She laughed. "First he'd have to admit that he has flaws. Meanwhile, I just need to get to the vet."

"You know I can't do that, BunnyLee."

"Frankie, I have to!"

"Buck, he came out specific. Something's got him ticked off. All I know is I have got to get him to that meeting Monday!"

"He's upset about this morning. Puddles snuck into his room while he was asleep and made off with his toupee..."

"Buck wears a rug?" Frankie asked.

"Like you didn't know."

"How was I supposed to know?"

"Everybody knows. It's the best-kept secret in Hollywood. Even Puddles knew, didn't you sweetheart? You're lucky you missed it. She was tearing down the path with Buck after her. She had his hairpiece in her mouth, shaking the living daylights out of it. Frankie, the look on Buck's face, I had to laugh. I was trying to make light of the situation. First I thought she was gonna bury it in the bushes, but there wasn't time, so instead, she went for the pool. Miguel found it jammed up in the impeller. You didn't notice Buck's hair?"

"How could I not? It looked somethin' awful." He shook his head. "You shouldn't have laughed."

"Oh, God, I know, the look he gave me. I just wish I could take it back. Then he put that mangled thing back on his head! I just wish I could take it back."

"Just stay out of sight!"

"How am I going to do that with Miguel in town and you refusing to drive me? Unless you want to give me the keys to the convertible..."

"Buck's Baby? He'd have my neck. What if Buck wants to use it?"

"When I moved in, he said I could use any of his cars."

"Yeah, but that was then."

"What if I told him that I read your script and I thought it was good and that if he put his mind to it, it could be a new beginning for him."

"You'd do that?

"I don't see any harm in it. It's true."

"Just don't let on that I wrote it."

"Right. I mean, after all, since he needs the work. He stopped at my door last night. I'm afraid I've been a little harsh with him since...well, you know...the night of the Emmys with Jadé sleeping over."

"BunnyLee, you've got to understand that Buck, he has a reputation..."

"I've heard all about his reputation."

"What I mean is, he has an image to uphold. He's always been a Hollywood sex symbol. That's his shtick."

"His shtick."

"He's always played the playboy. And besides, he said you had some friend over last night."

"What? No, I didn't! Is that what he said? I just had the place pulled apart to take some pictures of Puddles."

"He thinks you had a man over."

"Frankie, I would never…I mean, it's his house. It's his life. He should be able to do whatever he wants without me admonishing him. Or rubbing his face in it! There is no way. I would never do something like that, no matter how I felt about the Emmy's."

"So you minded? About Jadé?"

"You think?"

"It's a dangerous business, jealousy."

"I hate how I feel! This is not me. This is not the person I want to be. It's poison. I have to move out."

"Not before Monday! BunnyLee, you got to promise me! Don't move out before that contract gets signed! You drive a stick-shift?"

"I drove my friend Heather's Pinto. That had a clutch."

"You gotta understand, that thing in there's a whole 'nother animal, four-barrel, you name it, suped up."

Frankie was referring to the stall that held a yellow nineteen sixty-four-and-a-half Mustang. He worked the keys off his key chain and handed them to BunnyLee. "Can't start her in the garage. Makes too much noise. I'll push her out. Just let her roll past the bend in the drive before you pop the clutch. Gate's propped open."

Frankie pushed the car out of the garage with BunnyLee at the wheel.

"Go to the vet's! Then go somewhere safe! Drive out to the beach!"

Frankie gave the car a shove.

"The beach? I don't think so. Come on, Puddles, we're going to get you cured!"

"Just go easy on 'er! Those valves are sloppy." There were a hundred things to know about that Mustang being spirited and temperamental. "And you can't put the top up!" Frankie yelled after her.

CHAPTER 13

AFTER AN HOUR of slow-going miles, Austin came upon an inhabited trailer park where they'd circled their wagons around a watering hole—a saloon named The Last Roundup. A group of motorcycles leaned on their kickstands at the hitching post. As a rule, Austin didn't go into biker bars.

Taking in the surroundings, he noted that it was a community made up of vintage Airstreams and park models tucked into the thick vegetation: an oasis in an arid landscape. In these parts, this would be counted as a town. They must have found a reliable water source here long ago and stayed. Austin was hoping to find a backyard mechanic. He drove around the encampment of neatly kept trailers but the only business establishment appeared to be the bar. He approached the building again, this time from the side parking lot. He wasn't taking any chances. He parked behind the dumpster so it wouldn't be spotted from the road.

Walking around the building to the front, he heard the distant sound of a truck approaching with a missing muffler. He stepped behind a propane tank just as the vehicle cruised by—the pink Ford Ranger with lace curtains. It must have dropped its exhaust system at the ravine because it was making a hell of a racket. He waited for the sound to fade into the distance. He then proceeded around front to take a closer look at the bikes. He studied the bikes for telltale signs of trouble.

Harleys and Indians. All hogs. There wasn't a foreign bike in the lot. For starters, this was not a good sign. He sized them up for any indication of gang affiliation. A tricked-out turquoise and beige Dark Horse had a bumper sticker on its tasseled saddlebag, "I'm dumb and I vote." Austin didn't know what to make of that, although it sounded like a political statement. He didn't personally go in for politics even though his profession was steeped in it: the more controversial, the better.

Controversy sells. No two words better expressed the formula for the success of wrestling on television. The more outrageous, the more offensive, the more politically incorrect, the more attention it garnered. With much fanfare, he and his brother had recently wrestled against a duo who wore turbans and called themselves the Rug Riders.

Austin channeled the persona of the lonesome cowboy as he pushed through the swinging louvered doors into the saloon. Two men sat in the corner playing checkers while four others looked on. Another man drank alone.

A couple of things immediately struck Austin as odd. The first was how quiet it was. There was no conversation. No jukebox spilled some mournful country ballad about love lost. A television above the bar was tuned to Fox News with the sound off and the man who was sitting alone seemed to be reading the closed caption. The second thing that struck him as odd was how no one looked up when he walked in even though the louvered doors continued to swing loudly back and forth behind him.

"Excuse me, Gentlemen," Austin addressed the room. "I would be much obliged if one of you would lend me a crowbar. The latch on my trunk is stuck and I need to pry it open."

The barkeep emerged from a back room carrying a case of beer. She was a Mexican American beauty with dark hair pulled back in a ponytail. Her black eyes focused on Austin.

"Won't do you no good. They can't hear."

"They can't hear anything?"

"Not a stitch."

"Even if I talk loud?"

"Makes no difference. Besides, you don't want to mess with them. They're trouble." She set the case down on the bar and began to unload it into the ice chest.

"What kind of trouble?"

"Gunslingers."

Austin pushed his hat back on his head and scratched his

scalp. "Deaf gunslingers?"

"The Deaf Bikers. You never heard of 'em?"

Austin shrugged. He was beginning to like her. "I'm not from around here. Used to be, but that was a long time ago."

"I know who you are."

"You do?"

"Yep."

Austin was not sure whether this was welcome news. She looked at him in such an odd, head-cocked–to-the-side way, he wondered whether there was any history there. He'd been a tad impetuous in his youth, and he knew as well as the next fellow how those days could come back to bite you.

"I never heard of 'em either," she continued, "'til I took this job. It's a whole settlement of deaf persons that's kinda regimented. They only drink Coors beers from the bottle for one. Something about them Coors beer ads just speaks volumes to 'em. The Rockies bein' the backbone of America and all that stuff about pure as a mountain stream." She took the empty case and began filling it with empty Coors bottles. "Frankly, I don't get it. All beer's just made in factories, ain't it?"

Austin was wondering whether he'd slept with her. He calculated the math. Seventeen years ago, when he and his brother were riding a local wave of rodeo fame, she couldn't have been older than sixteen, tops. Not that that would have been entirely out of the question, but even in his youth he had respected the swift hand of the law. Maybe she had an older sister? And then there was the chance that she had known his brother, a case of mistaken identities that often happens with identical twins.

"But it does make my job easier servin' but one type of beer." Sliding a deposit bottle underneath the bar, she added, "Seeing as how I can't get this other cooler open."

It had been a long time since a woman had stirred his blood like this: certainly not since Laredo bashed his head in the ring.

"So what is it y'need?" she asked.

Austin could have answered that question in a number of ways. There was a whole laundry list of needs that pertained to him. But getting that neck brace strapped under his chin was currently at the top of the heap.

"You wouldn't happen to have a pry bar, would you?"

"I sure don't." She smiled. Her smile was intoxicating.

"Wouldn't the other end of yer lug wrench do the trick?"

"If I could get into the trunk to get it, then I wouldn't need it."

"Copy that." She shrugged. "Well, maybe one of these boys can help." She didn't sound too hopeful.

The saloon patrons were now milling about, moving closer and, in a manner of speaking, had him surrounded where he leaned at the bar. To turn his head even slightly he had to turn his whole body. He had no idea what they were saying with their hands, but the whole room was engaged in a heated discussion. He understood enough to know that he was the topic of discussion. He turned back to the bartender. She was in a safer spot behind the bar.

"I can't help reflecting upon the fact that there is still a lot of wide-open space in this county without their having to stand so close. Do you know what they're saying?" he asked her.

"Yep."

"Do you care to enlighten me?"

"They want to know what happened in Vegas."

"You watched the Pay-Per-View last night?"

"The whole tavern did," she said. "Johnny in the middle there is askin' why you didn't just finish things off."

"You can read their hands?" he asked her.

"That's how I got this job."

"Then could you tell them that I'm injured?"

"You can tell them so yerself. They read lips."

"They can understand me but I can't understand them? Seems hardly fair."

"Ain't nuthin' fair about a lot of things," the bartender answered aggressively, then added, "I didn't say that, Oscar over there did." She pointed to the man who had been sitting alone. He looked like the meanest of the bunch.

Austin turned back to her so that they couldn't see his lips. She seemed to be enjoying all this tit-for-tat a lot more than he was.

"I'm afraid I missed your name."

"Kat."

"Whose side are you on, Kat?"

"They pay me to serve 'em beer. And from time to time, translate."

"Could you tell me if I'm in some kind of danger?"

"There ain't a man in here you can't take."

"That might be true, on a good day."

"Rumored to have wrestled a twelve-hundred-pound steer to the ground with your bare hands, that's what they say about you on TV."

"On a good day, perhaps."

"Quite the crowd in here last night."

"That's good for business."

"And they all thought you threw yer match with Chief Tenaya," Kat said.

Austin could see where this was going. "Professional wrestling on television is presented as a family entertainment," he said, stating what to him was an obvious fact overlooked by many. The implicit statement being that if you cared to wager money on a wholesome television event, you did so at your own risk.

Four of the men were standing, moving closer, forming a circle around him.

"My family is not entertained by the fact that I lost a week's wages on a sure bet. And when a guy deliberately throws a match…"

"You had money on the match?" Austin asked Kat.

"Not me, Johnny. I'm just tellin' you what they say."

Austin addressed Kat in confidence. "In my experience, when folks have money riding on the outcome of a sporting event, they tend to take it personally when the outcome is contrary to their wager."

"Especially when they throw the fight," Kat answered, then added quickly, "I'm just tellin' you what Johnny says."

"But I have my back to him."

"He can see yer face in the mirror," Kat said, pointing over her shoulder with her thumb at the mirror over the bar.

"Backwards?" It took Austin a second to sort that one out, noting how it is harder than heck to read a book backwards in a mirror or stab oneself in the neck with a hypodermic needle full of steroids. He turned to address his detractors. "Now that there is an untruth!"

"If you are as injured as you say you are, mate, then why the hell aren't you wearing a neck brace?" Kat said with an Australian accent.

Austin turned back to her with a quizzical look. He felt like he was in a bees' nest of trouble.

Kat was glowing. "Adam's an Aussie born and raised there in the Outback. He signs with an accent."

Austin studied Kat. He liked her a lot. But he wasn't at all sure whether he should trust her. As attractive as she was, the others were equally menacing.

Austin had long ago learned that the best way to diffuse a heated situation was with language, the more long-winded the better. He turned his body again to address the bar patrons. "The neck brace in question, a state-of-the-art neck brace as it so happens, presently resides in the trunk of my car, the very car that is stationed outside. But for a twist in fate, the latch is stuck. Otherwise, the sooner I lay eyes on that brace, the better I will feel." The men were all signing at once. He forged onward, not sure whether anyone was listening. "I can assure you that I made every effort to continue that match last night, but in wrestling, as in other sports, the functioning of one's neck is integral to one's success..." He was mindful that there are truths specific to pro wrestling that are difficult for a fan to swallow, especially when the truth was the size of a horse pill.

"And another thing, of all sports that are broadcast with any regularity on television, pro wrestling is the only one that odds makers in Las Vegas decline to take wagers on." That should tell them something, Austin thought to himself, but decided not to delve into any more specifics. Divulging too much was like giving a youngster the low-down on Santa Claus or the Easter Bunny. These were the post-*kayfabe* days, when only the wrestlers were in on the ruse. Yet there were people all over the country, those easy marks, who still believed in the authenticity of wrestling as a conventional sporting event. He knew how they would be dismayed to discover that wrestling did not conform to the everyday principles of competition.

"I am aware how disconcerting it may feel, especially in cases of live events such as last night's Pay-Per-View, when things do not go as they are planned. Take for example the grudge match between Chief Tenaya and myself, which I am told was widely advertised on local stations. One could make a case that I did not perform up to my fullest potential." Austin had made so many extemporaneous post-match speeches to the unblinking and silent camera that he was even beginning to feel at home in front of such an unusual live audience as this one. "I am no stranger to adversity. So believe you me, I feel your pain. The fact that there are those among you who wagered your hard-earned money on my reputation does me a great honor, and I am sorry that I let you down. I let myself down. All I can say is that your faith in me gives me the strength I need to make a comeback..." He wasn't expecting cheers, but the silence was still deafening.

"Sounds like the second coming," Kat said, in an ironical tone that caught Austin off-guard.

"...if my body holds out," Austin continued. "Wait a minute, who said that?"

"I did," Kat responded, "but you don't need to worry. There is such a shoutin' match going on, nobody's paying any attention to what you say."

"That's a shame, because I do feel compelled to let them in on a trade secret so as they don't make the same mistake twice. If these men were to find out that all my victory speeches were pre-recorded weeks in advance of the victory itself, then that should tell them something. If anyone were listening and if I was truly forthcoming, I could give them an earful, no disrespect intended."

Admitting that all his matches were choreographed might have struck the ardent fans as a bit of a scam. And as difficult as it was to impart this type of information, the reality was that it was only half the story. The fate of most wrestlers was actually in the hands of those passionate enough to subscribe to fan magazines and fill out the questionnaires, because in a convoluted way it was the fans who determined the outcome of these matches.

A person's feeling about pre-determinism said a lot about their makeup. After they had given it some thought, many were very comfortable with the notion that the future was already decided. Whether they subscribed to the ebb and flow of Taoism, the causal laws of Karma, Einstein's quantum physics and the Big Bang, or to the many Christian theologians who posited that the future was already written as scripture, they would notice a trend: cosmologies derived from determinism.

Conversely, the concept of free will gave a lot of people the willies. It was just so much more consoling for some to believe that the universe could only unfold in one given way and that an omniscient narrator of that future had a determining say in that outcome. Like the reader of fiction, one needed to have faith in his or her author, faith in the belief that the narrator knew how best to tell the story, faith that what may have seemed like irrelevant philosophical digressions were in fact well-crafted artifices both necessary and sufficient to the telling of a compelling story.

Long story short—as much as a wrestling fan might have initially felt offended by the deterministic course of a wrestler's career (even though that course was set by the fan base), many later took solace in the realization that 1: professional wrestling was in fact the most democratic of sports and that 2: the fan who filled out the survey, however unwittingly, had assumed a certain godlike power over the fate of the current pantheon of wrestlers by voting for his favorites. The inconvenient truth of wrestling was that, whereas in traditional sports such as baseball or football or even bull riding, for that matter, a player's success and consequent fame was determined by his or her athletic prowess on the field, in pro wrestling prowess and success were determined by the wrestler's fame. The more popular he was and the more votes he got, the more he was scripted to win.

This was an early form of social media, preceding Facebook, in which ones 'likes' dictated the kind of content that one would see later on, often at the exclusion of controverting opinion. Innocent in its formulation, sinister in its results, a heel might end up winning a championship match or become the President, thanks to an electorate that subsisted on fake news.

Austin surveyed the room again. If he had learned anything in his seventeen-year career, it was to approach wrestling fans as a politician. His maxim was that he never met a fan he didn't like for, as any politician can attest, fans were his constituents. It was they who voted him into power. But, since no one appeared to be currently interested in hearing any more of his discourse, he took the opportunity to change the subject.

"Is there a mechanic in the house?" Austin asked the room.

The men stopped their signing. The room grew still. Men in front stepped aside to allow the shortest among them to saunter forward.

"That's Jason," Kat informed him. "His nickname is The Mechanic."

"Have you ever worked on an Eldorado?"

"There ain't a car I ain't fixed," Kat translated. "Just needs to be whacked."

"Whacked?"

"Whacked."

Austin wasn't sure he was familiar with the term outside of how a mobster might mess with someone on a television show.

And its literal translation appeared to be the quick draw and firing of a six-shooter. Austin was startled, thinking for a moment that the man was armed.

The Mechanic led the way out through the saloon doors. Austin followed the parade of men. He stopped at the door to see if Kat was coming. She hesitated, then accepted his non-verbal plea for help.

Outside, The Mechanic was tapping at the damaged trunk, feeling the vibrations with every knock. Kat stood in the parking lot and translated. "You want I should open her up?"

"I would be much obliged."

The Mechanic went to the saddlebag of the turquoise bike and pulled out an Army Special, sliding the barrel of the weapon into the waist of his jeans. He then returned to the Eldorado and stood with his back to the trunk.

"Whoa, there," Austin said, having strong doubts about The Mechanic's methods. Not that anyone could hear him.

The biker strode ten paces away, turned, and emptied six rounds into the trunk. The first two broke through the Cadillac insignia trunk lock cover. The remaining four blew out the barrel latch and continued on to parts unknown. The Mechanic returned to the car to inspect a one-inch hole in the sheet metal. He inserted the barrel of the gun into the hole, twisted it upward and the trunk popped open, exposing to the world the detritus of Austin's life.

Anyone who has ever traveled for extended periods knows that the longer you are at it, the less you tend to carry. That being said, if one were to look over Austin's shoulder at this moment in his life, one might be saddened by the observation that for a man who lived out of his trunk, there wasn't much in it. Some t-shirts, sweatpants, zippered hoodies, and free weights vied for space behind the spare tire and the silver canister with Laredo's ashes. There was a bag of ointments and lotions and painkillers. The biggest bag contained an assortment of braces that, starting at the ankle, continued upward and outward to the knee, the shoulder, the elbow and the wrist. In short, for everything that bent, they made a brace, and in his time Austin had occasion to need at least one of every type.

A silent cheer went up from the crowd when Austin held up a white cloth contraption. His neck brace now sported a bullet hole through both sides. He also retrieved his cell phone, which indicated a number of missed calls and texts. He palmed a couple of small plastic figurines that were lying beside it.

He threaded a piece of rope through the empty latch hole and secured the trunk lid to the bumper.

As he pulled tight the Velcro straps of the brace, the Mechanic stood next to him and snapped a selfie with his phone. Austin winced: not the kind of publicity photo he would want floating around the internet. Austin was a freelancer with no compensation clause in his contract, meaning he was always only one debilitating injury away from joblessness. It was a simple act of self-preservation that he kept the news of this injury to himself.

"I am much obliged for your help, ma'am," Austin said to Kat, tipping his hat. "If there is anything I can do for you…"

"You could grab yer lug wrench and help me pry open that cooler in there. Then I'd be happy to make you some lunch if yer hungry and offer you something other than a Coors to drink."

Austin touched his stomach at the proposal. The offer to pause for a moment in the company of one of God's loveliest creatures seemed too good to pass up. The fact that the offer included lunch sealed the deal. He brought the lug wrench inside and watched Kat pop the cooler lid open.

Austin stood at the bar. He studied her through the pass-through into the kitchen as she readied his meal and wondered to himself how it might be to have someone this nice to come home to. Truth was, he was unskilled in the nuances of dating. He had never really dated on his own.

One of their jobs as rodeo clowns way back when was to entertain the ladies in attendance, especially those sitting with their cowboy dates. You could easily pick them out in the stands, all dolled up, cringing at the harrowing events transpiring below. The twins, dressed in exaggerated western attire and clown faces, blew kisses their way. They held their oversized hats over their chests, miming wildly pumping hearts. They held up rigged flowers whose proffered stems were designed to wilt before their eyes. And if the women were single, there was another set of protocols altogether.

The brothers had learned the hard way that if only one of the twins was in a relationship, the other was high and dry. So they concentrated their charms on those women who were out on the town in pairs; western gals who enjoyed the spectacle of risk-taking cowboys performing perilous stunts, recognizing that ladies, too, had a lust in their loins to ride. This was what Austin and Laredo called their extracurricular rodeo events. The boys were mirror twins; one parted his hair on the left and the other on the right. Otherwise, no one could tell them apart. In the ladies' room, between innings so to speak, young women didn't need to compare notes. They only had to agree on two simple notions, 'They're so cute' and 'I can't believe there are two of them.' No competition, nothing more to discuss.

Standing at the bar with Kat in the kitchen, Austin wasn't at all sure of the ground rules. He hadn't a clue how best to proceed; he was a comic without his straight man or the other way around. Laredo used to say, if you climb on a horse, be ready to ride. That was sound advice. But on that aforementioned laundry list of his existential needs, it was dawning on him that not growing old alone was squarely at the top.

He heard the fateful sound of the pink Ford Ranger with its missing muffler returning from the other direction.

"Damnation," he said under his breath, even though no one in the room could hear him. No way did he want to be confronted in some distant outpost of civilization by whatever these women cared to dish out. He was not about to allow a repeat of what happened in the Golden Nugget yesterday in Vegas or this morning at the Best Western.

He left the saloon doors swinging noisily back and forth behind him, his half-empty beer on the bar. Next to the bottle he placed a small figurine of himself in full wrestling regalia as a token for Kat to remember him by.

Outside, he crouched behind the propane tank while the pink Ford pickup passed the other way. They were zeroing in on him. When they were out of sight, he loped to his car.

Back on the trail, Austin didn't feel at all good about his premature departure. His tracks were littered with memories of disappointed ladies. He now added Kat to the list.

The land grew hillier, the grasses greener. The road flirted with the foothills of the Sierras, heading generally north. He came to a stop at a two-lane highway and waited for a caravan of lumber trucks to pass. They were big rigs bearing the fruit of Nature's bounty: massive felled redwoods lashed to their trailer beds from what must have seemed to his father's fathers to be a limitless supply of alpine forest, there for the taking. Waiting to fall in line behind the last of these trucks as they descended into the valley, Austin took stock of life. The old West was vanishing faster than the polar icecap. On the seat beside him, his cell phone flashed notices of numerous unanswered calls and texts. "Can't Find My Way Home" by Blind Faith played on the radio. He was back in the modern world.

Further to his right, an old-style general store at the intersection was open for business. Austin had a vague memory of stopping at this intersection as a tyke with his parents on the rodeo circuit. His old man had been a rodeo announcer in a lineage of rodeo performers harking back to the early days of Slim Pickens, who was so named because the work of the rodeo clown yielded so little money. Their family migrated like carnies from one county fairground to the next, northward in the spring, back south again in the fall. One of the last, best rodeos of the year happened to be held up ahead in the high chaparral near a town named Mariposa.

On the front porch of the store, a young boy dressed in cowboy boots and hat sat in the saddle of a mechanical horse. Lack of money didn't hinder his imagination. The boy rocked back and forth in simulation of a canter. And when he caught the eye of the cowboy in the white Eldorado convertible with the Texas longhorns lashed above the grill, the boy dropped the rein from one hand and tipped his hat.

Austin nodded back, touching the brim of his own hat in salutation: two cowboys out for a ride, enjoying life on the wide-open range.

Austin remembered another thing about this place—butterflies. Everywhere there had been swarms of migrating butterflies meeting and mating. His mother, whose heart pumped a few pints of Native American Ahwanee blood, spoke plainly about her beliefs. "Those are the souls of dead folk headin' home," she said.

His dad's Spanish forebears followed the route opened up by Franciscan monks who plotted an inland chain of missions through the San Joaquin Valley some two hundred years before. These men could not have anticipated the stream of prospectors who would follow their tracks in pursuit of gold. Much to the annoyance of the native population, they stayed. Some comingled. But for the most part, they didn't make good trading partners with a people whose staples consisted of insect larvae, acorn flour and, when in season, grasshoppers. The Forty-Niners devoured the resources, hunting local game with their rifles and cooking the carcasses over countless campfires, decimating countless black oak trees for their firewood. Austin wasn't generally one to take sides, but he saw this thorny history as a darned shame.

Austin was due at a technical run-through in Fresno, but in an act of free will he turned right, onto the highway heading up into the Sierras. It was high time he did something with those ashes. His recent run-in with the crow-lady doubled down on that truth. It could be years before he was back in these parts. His brother's remains had clanged around in the trunk for a year. If he was going to do this, now would be the time. He knew the way and it would set his mind to rest to get this over with.

The Sways had been, in effect, a family business. When the twins joined the professional wrestling circuit, the family act folded its tents. His mother died a couple years back, and the twins had barely exchanged two sentences with their old man at the wake. Word was that their father had developed a fever for gold. Somewhere in these mountains he'd staked a claim. Austin knew the stories of men who lived on grubs rather than leave their mine and their turn at instant riches. He was afraid his dad was one of them. Austin knew there was a risk of getting shot at, but someone had to tell the old guy the details about Laredo's demise. And it was only right that the telling be told, face-to-face, by his sole remaining kin.

The western sun was in his rearview mirror as he gained speed. A blonde woman blasted by him in a vintage yellow Mustang. Her miniature Australian Labradoodle was in the passenger seat with its face in the breeze, smiling ear to windswept ear, sporting a gleaming set of braces on its canine teeth. The vanity plate on the car read, BUCKS BABY.

Austin thought again about the lovely bartender left behind, another face in a storyline of wistful memories of what might have been. Just for the hell of it, Austin blew the Eldorado's dual-trumpet horn, sounding like one of those locomotives that opened the West and drowned out the vast, untamed loneliness.

CHAPTER 14

IT WAS NOW well after one o'clock at Number 10 Beverly Canyon. Buck had changed out of his tennis whites into a pair of slacks and collared shirt and still wore the mangled toupee atop his head. He stood in his driveway holding a long drink short of ice. Like a cat ready to pounce, he followed the progress of his Chinese cook, Jimmy Chan, as the man hurried up the pavement with a plastic bag of groceries in each hand. Chan was dressed in a black zippered hoodie that was two sizes too big for him, along with matching loose-fitting sweatpants. Buck checked his watch.

"Where have you been?"

Jimmy Chan smiled as he approached, out of breath. "Most sorry for unforeseen delay. Jimmy Chan go to market. Very busy day! Chinese holiday!" Chan answered everything as if all things in life were a big adventure.

BunnyLee thought so highly of the cook that Buck had no reason to doubt him. Chan apparently spoke five languages, all self-taught, and was currently adding English. He'd mastered the intricacies of a whole swath of Eastern cuisines and was up on the latest Asian fusion trends—Buck would need to take BunnyLee's word on that one, too. The guy was jovial to a fault. He wore his forthright nature like a Teflon coating impervious to criticism.

Chan tried to scoot by. Buck blocked his way. Chan stepped back and smiled.

"Didn't I tell you I wanted you to shop here in Beverly Hills? Didn't we already have this conversation?"

"Right!"

"Why do those bags have Chinese writing on them?"

"Oh, Jimmy Chan bicycle ride to super Beverly Hills food market late in the A.M. just like Mr. Buck insist. Ask store boss concerning ingredient of favorite dish. Many item hard to discover. Chan ask where you find rice wine and red sugar. He not know. Big man talk fast, not too swift. Chan open jar, see inside. Store man order Chan out. How you buy food without first touch, smell, taste, deciding foodstuffs carefully, avoiding misadventure?"

He bounced up and down when he spoke. It's harder to hit a moving target.

"Listen, Chan, we need to reach an understanding here," Buck said. He took a healthy drink from his glass for emphasis. "Three things..."

Chan pointed at Buck's drink. "Bar open early."

Buck put his hand gently on Jimmy Chan's shoulder. He was not one to allow an employee the upper hand. Chan continued to hold the groceries.

"Yes, Jimmy, the bar opened early. When lunch was nowhere on the horizon, I helped myself to a drink. At one-fifteen, when it became clear that lunch was not in the offing, I made myself another. That's the first thing we need to reach an understanding about. The time of the midday meal: one o'clock. This is a time carefully chosen to afford me the luxury of freshening up after tennis and, at the same time, insuring that my afternoon nap doesn't extend into the cocktail hour."

Buck didn't really mean this. He wasn't much of a slacker or a drinker, maybe a glass of wine with dinner if the event was social. After tennis he usually eschewed alcohol in favor of an energy drink. Otherwise he rarely imbibed. But he wanted to make a point.

"When you are working for someone here in America, the agreement is, you actually have to do the work that you are paid to do. On time. If lunch is scheduled for one p.m., for example, I expect that it will be ready at one p.m. A couple of minutes, give or take, usually not a problem. But twenty minutes and counting? I already have enough anxiety about what you're going to make, I don't need to be wondering about when you are going to serve it."

Chan appeared to be following Buck's words closely. He chose words with deliberation.

"Jimmy Chan most apologies, but..."

"Which brings me to the second issue: The tenor of the midday meal. I am in the habit of eating meals with names. I don't know what surprises you've got hidden in those bags, but I happen to believe that the main ingredient of the meal should have a name, an English name. Take steak, for instance. Steak is a one-word name to describe a type of dinner. Now you can get fancy and call it steak *au poivre* or steak amandine or New York Strip. On occasion, I am happy with the terms brisket of beef or prime rib for, as they say, variety is the spice… Are you following the gist of our conversation? American names, American meals. If you can cook a steak for a dog, then you can cook one for me. And, another thing, I do not require that my food be chopped up into tiny pieces beforehand. I prefer to do it myself." Buck was feeling better for having gotten that off his chest.

"Miss BunnyLee say steak too yang without enough yin on the eating table. She say steak make Mr. Buck grouchy and… something else…"

Buck would have interrupted the man if he hadn't been so ravenous for insight into what BunnyLee currently thought of him. Chan seemed to be taking the time to choose the best words for their utmost precision.

"…meat make Mr. Buck centered-on-self!"

"I'm self-centered? Really? Let me ask you something, Jimmy Chan. Who hired you?"

"Miss BunnyLee."

Buck could see why the cook thought that. Technically BunnyLee was the one who hired him.

"No," Buck said. "BunnyLee did hire you. But she is not the one responsible for filling your pocket with cash. No, the money comes from my bank account."

"Money you allow her," Chan added.

"The money is mine. BunnyLee is the middleman."

Chan said, "Middle man?" He smiled broadly. "Nice knockers for a man!"

Buck studied the cook. He weighed the intent of this indiscretion. "Yes, as I'm sure you noticed this morning, BunnyLee can really promote a bikini style, but having nice 'knockers,' as you say, does not make her the boss. Despite what you might think, I'm the boss. I don't want you siding with her."

"Yes, sir. Jimmy Chan too smart to fall into foolish. Mr. Buck

American Chairman Mao. He Mister Big. Top Dog."

"Top Dog. I like that," Buck said. "Wait a minute. That's the term in this phone message!" Buck pulled the Post-it from his back pocket.

Jimmy Chan recognized the paper immediately. "Oh, yes. Very important."

"Really? What does it mean?"

"Mr. Morris call. Number One pick. Top Dog. Urgent to call back."

"Yes, I know that's what it says, but what does it mean?"

"Cast Top Dog in new television hit show!"

"Top Dog, eh? I read something about that in Variety. The show's green-lighted. This could be big. This Mr. Morris, he say who he's with?"

"Famous casting agent. Talk mile a minute."

"Are you saying William Morris called?"

"He friend to you?"

Buck had to laugh at that one. "I'm not that old." He explained that William Morris was the world's largest talent agency: literally hundreds of agents representing thousands of actors. "If I were to call back, I'd sound pretty silly if I didn't know which one it was I was supposed to talk to. I don't suppose you happen to know the name of the actual agent who you spoke with?" He waited for a reply, then continued sarcastically, "Great. Terrific. That's just swell, because until very recently, the William Morris agency represented me. I really don't want to be cold-calling an agency a year after I fired them, you know what I mean?"

Apparently sarcasm was lost on Jimmy Chan.

Buck continued, "Now, I know that BunnyLee throws money at that dog. I mean, who puts braces on a dog? So you might think there was an endless reservoir, but if I don't work, the well goes dry. I'll let it go this one time because you didn't know any better, but from now on... Don't answer the phone! That's what the answering machine is for."

"Phone ring six time. Machine not answer when power not on."

This was an epiphany. A curtain had been raised from Buck's eyes.

"The electricity was off! Now I get it! It's that goddamn dog again!" He had flushed out the enemy, and it was Puddles. Buck bristled, then composed himself. "Okay, so we'll let it go. But on the subject of food, I'm putting my foot down. I'm not standing for any more Mickey Mouse meals around here." Buck was finished with their little *tête-à-tête* and was ready to go back to his drink when Chan interrupted.

"Jimmy Chan like Mickey Mouse. Mickey Mouse make Jimmy Chan laugh."

Buck was annoyed at this childishness. He knew that a lot of grown men liked Mickey Mouse, but he had used the term derisively. "I don't mean the cartoon, I mean the food. I want my food left in big pieces. I don't want to face any more chopped-up dishes with mystery ingredients."

"Got it. Mr. Buck no like food Jimmy Chan cook," Chan stated succinctly.

"No, Jimmy Chan no cook food Mr. Buck like. I know you people eat funny things. I just want to ensure that I'm not being fed cockroaches or some other such thing. You understand?"

Chan nodded. "Jimmy Chan from Canton. Canton people all what called omnivorous? Cook all manner of thing: ears, eyes, toes, inside stuff. Eat snake, mouse, candied scorpion... Other Chinese say Canton people eat everything but dining table and chairs. Not entirely true. American cock-a-roach too...crunchy."

"That's what's got me worried. On your own time, if you want to eat grasshoppers, that's okay by me. Serve it to BunnyLee, too, if she likes. No problem. Just not on my plate."

Chan set the groceries down on the blacktop and saluted his boss. "Yes, sir, Mr. Buck. No Mickey Mouse, no Jiminy Cricket..."

"Good," Buck responded, feeling like the conversation was finally over. He was turning to walk away when Chan stopped him in his tracks.

"No Daffy Duck?"

At first he thought the cook was pulling his leg or possibly mocking him.

"What?" The man was serious. Buck reconsidered the meaning of Chan's statement. "Duck? Yeah, I'd eat duck."

"What about Porky Pig?"

Buck brightened at the thought of pork. "Now we're getting somewhere. Daffy Duck, Porky Pig, Big Bird...but no Mr. Ed! I am not about to eat horsemeat."

"Got it! What about Kermit?"

"Kermit?" Buck studied the cook to see what he knew. "That obnoxious little frog? Sure, why not. Bring him on! I guest-starred on *Sesame Street* years ago, although I suppose you've seen that outtake. Everybody has. What you don't know is that they had me sing a duet with that whiny twit. Kermit? Hell, yes. The mood I'm in right now, I'd enjoy eating that Miniature Labradoodle in the guest cabana. In fact, that's not such a bad idea. I bet Puddles would make a pretty good stew, wouldn't she, Jimmy?"

"Tiny little dog like that? Wasted in stew. Taste better braised. Taste like braised pork."

"Really? I'm getting hungry just thinking about it."

Jimmy Chan smiled at his boss. "Mr. Buck same as Chairman Mao. Mao insisted everything. Very hard to listen to other. He insisted braised pork. During Chinese Revolution, every time big battle begin, Mao shout, 'Give me bowl braised pork, Chan!' After winning battle, Mao always excited to say, 'I win because I eat braised pork. Give me braised pork every day, I win every day.' This A-number one dish Mao loved."

"You cooked for Mao?" Buck asked.

Jimmy Chan laughed. "No!" He continued in earnest. "Grandfather Chan. Long time ago. Mao dead. He go into history. Mr. Buck famous like Chairman Mao. Mr. Buck equal A-number one, big American cheese."

Buck toyed with a scenario. "So, you'd cook a dog?"

"Could be," Chan responded. He seemed uncomfortable with the question. "Not so easy to cook pet dog."

"What do you mean? In a kitchen as well-appointed as mine, what's standing in our way?"

"Miss BunnyLee. She take Puddles."

"What do you mean take? Where? When?" he asked.

"Today, while you are losing doubles tennis match..."

"Hey!" Buck said. "I only lost today because my mind wasn't on the game."

Jimmy Chan saluted him. "Yes, sir! No, sir!"

"Good," Buck said, returning to the subject. "Now, tell me, where'd she go?"

"Jimmy Chan drop bicycle and hop in car at end of drive. She drop Jimmy Chan with Chinatown market downtown. Miss BunnyLee say she on holiday from Hollywood. Go to Yosemite up Joaquin Valley."

"She's not in the cabana? She just snuck out?" He stroked his chin in thought. "She take a lot of luggage?"

"Not so much. But she take dog… Now Jimmy Chan and Mr. Buck need differing dinner plan."

"I don't care about the dog. Wait a minute. What car did she take? Miguel had the Wrangler."

"She take muscle car."

"She took my Mustang? *I* can barely handle that car!" He cupped his hand around his mouth yelled in the direction of the garage, "Frankie! Bring the Bentley around! We're going for a ride. And pack a bag. We may be gone a while." Then he turned back to Jimmy Chan. "You too, Chan. You could come in handy."

Chan gathered up his grocery bags, then stopped to listen to his boss.

"Yosemite, huh? Shouldn't be too hard to find a woman that everybody in the world recognizes." Buck raised his fist in a mock battle cry. "Bring me braised pork, Chan! This is war!"

Buck strode into the house.

✦

Jimmy Chan called after him, "Yes, sir, Mr. Buck. Jimmy Chan make braised pork perfect, take special care, all essential ingredient chop-up super-small. Weensy, teensy. Mr. Buck eat braised pork, win every day."

Chan picked up his grocery bags and started to follow Buck into the house when Frankie whispered to him from behind the hedge.

"Yo! Chan!" He motioned for Jimmy Chan to step over.

Chan obliged.

"What's goin' on?"

"Go on road adventure. Boss say head 'em up, move 'em out!"

"So I hear. We've never gone on a road trip before."

"First time?" he asked. Chan was jazzed at the prospect.

"Boss happen to say what we supposed to do on this trip?"

"Find Miss BunnyLee and her little dog, too."

"He knows she gone?"

"Sure thing." Chan spoke closely, in confidence. "She fly the coop. We find her, she in hot water."

"You and Mr. Buck were talkin' for a while."

"Mr. Buck like to chat."

"Yeah." Frankie said. "He say something about this new TV show?"

"Mr. Buck excited about new show."

"Yeah?" Frankie.

"Sure thing. Mr. Buck say he most interested to play Top Dog."

"Top Dog? We talkin' 'bout the same thing, here?"

"Mr. William Morris *agent* want Mr. Buck in new reality show."

"Reality show? Damn! That's who called? Buck's already got a job lined up. He doesn't need some other job. We got to do something, Chan! Mr. Buck's supposed to play Nick Derringer again."

"*Malibu Man?*" Jimmy Chan knew the show. "Nick Derringer wise-cracking tough-guy make Jimmy Chan laugh. But Mr. Buck not too old to play young stud again?"

"No! He be fine. You just have to help me make that happen. You with me, Chan?"

"Jimmy Chan work for Mr. Buck now."

"Work for? Did he ask you to do something...out of the ordinary?"

"Could be," Chan said. He reasoned that braising the owners' girlfriend's pet would be considered out of the ordinary in anybody's book.

"And what you tell him?"

"Jimmy Chan tell Mr. Buck, not so easy when she not here."

"Good answer."

"Jimmy Chan no know what what. Mr. Buck say we catch bitch, she good as cooked!"

"Whoa! Now you look here, Chan, we don't want any harm to come to her!"

"Jimmy Chan friend to Miss BunnyLee. Otherwise no big deal. Jimmy Chan from Canton." Chan thought about the markets back home, so different than here. Animals of all kinds were raised and sold for food, including dogs. Chan started into the house with the groceries. He stopped, turned, and illuminated the difference in culinary sensitivities. "Whack whack, just like braised pork!"

CHAPTER 15

A SIGN IN the office window clearly stated that Jack's Gulf was closed. The driver of the pickup wouldn't have slowed down had there not been a pink camper parked in front. On the far side of the building a woman was feeding coins into the Coca Cola machine. He caught a second glimpse of her in his side view mirror after he passed—a young woman in a sky-blue dress and red suede boots. He made a U-turn and doubled back.

When he pulled up, she was kicking the old machine with her silver-tipped toe. He left the engine running and hopped down. The clock on the dash read ten past three. He had a bunch to do today and not a lot of time to do it.

"Need a hand?" he asked.

"Machine's broke."

"How much money did you put in?"

"Enough for two Cokes, but nothin's come out."

She banged the coin slot with her fist.

"Machine's empty. And that coin eject doesn't always work. So however much money you put in there, I owe you back. I think I've got some quarters in the cab."

"Y'all work here?"

"When we're open. But we're shut."

"But when it's open, you work here?"

"When I'm short on help."

"Would that make you the owner?"

"I'm Jack."

"Of Jack's Gulf?"

"Yep."

"Seriously?"

"Third generation."

"Where are yer parents?"

"They went over to Texas to bid on John Wayne's hat."

"For real?" She walked toward him a few steps. "Do you know how to fix a muffler?"

"We're closed."

"No, I mean, when y'all are open, is that the sort of work you do?"

"That's the simple stuff."

"Like you could do it in a day..."

"Not even."

She moved closer and sniffed him.

"You smell."

"That's 'cause I ain't changed in a week..."

"...a good smell, like smoke..."

"...been fightin' the forest fire."

"...and sweat."

She stood basically eye-to-eye with him.

"That sign in the window there says something about a forest fire. Is it coming this way?"

"That fire is contained for the most part."

She looked at him over her sunglasses. He scratched himself behind the ear. She had the coolest emerald eyes.

"How tall are you?" he asked.

"I am five foot eleven and six quarters, barefoot."

"You're what my grampa calls a tall drink of water. Anyhow, that's why we're closed, on account of the fire. I was headin' home just now to get cleaned up when I saw your camper."

"You're a tall drink, too. So, you're a fireman to boot?"

"Volunteer. I was a Grizzly in high school."

"A what?"

"That's where they teach high school kids about firefighting and first responder stuff."

"You rescue people?"

"When they need rescuing." He caught a whiff of her sweet-smelling perfume. "Cal Fire does the heavy liftin'. We help out when they got their hands full, which is more often than not. The world's heatin' up and they're sayin' that ruinous fire is the new normal. Bunch of us went up, cleared brush, cleared the lines. Folks were especially concerned about the Mono Winds and things began to shift. Fire threatened the town. The county folks canceled the rodeo just to be sure and postponed the fair. That danger's past, now."

"I guess y'all are heroes."

"I don't know about that..."

"I need to know about the price of a muffler because we haven't got a lot of money, so seeming as how you can't do the job, then you haven't got cause to quote a higher price."

"The problem is I need to get somewhere. Otherwise..."

"...like if we were to go to a different filling station, they might go high on the price, assuming by our looks that we were famous."

"You're famous?"

"By association."

Jack thought her accent placed her close to Bakersfield or more likely farther afield. A glance at her license plate confirmed his guess. Nevada. She was pretty. Her dress was light cotton or maybe silk, and loose fitting up top. It tapered to her waist and then loosened up again, finishing roughly above her knees, leaving a healthy view of thigh to the whims of the wind, which was gusty. From there on down there was nothing but leg until her calves disappeared into those fancy boots. The girls around here wore Western blouses and jeans as a rule. On prom night, a dress bought specially. In Jack's experience, not all young women could pull this off, wearing cowboy boots and a dress like that.

He wasn't putting anybody down. A beauty contest was held every year at this time in Mariposa County to crown the Queen of the Rodeo, and every year the competition was robust. It required, among other skills, a high degree of horsemanship, or horsewomanship to be more precise. Jack guessed this girl knew her way around the saddle. She had a natural way of standing with her hand on her hip, her hip off to the side. It conveyed a country-bred self-assurance. That, along with her other estimable physical attributes, not to mention her striking green eyes, would give the local contestants a run for their money. Jack glanced at his watch.

"What's your name?"

"Kayla."

"Let me back the wrecker out of the bay, Kayla. I'll pull you in and take a look underneath. There's some Coke in a case inside, but it'll be warm."

"Oh, and open up the Ladies' room, too, if you don't mind!"

✦

Out on the highway, Buck's Mustang was a hoot. With the top down, it felt wild. BunnyLee either held back on the reins or risked getting a ticket. Not like Heather's Pinto, which was never a speedy car. This thing was peppy. She had to keep her eye on the gas gauge, too. Buck's Baby really lapped it up.

Puddles turned out to be a good traveling companion, someone to talk to. Talking to Puddles was like consulting Buddha. She was a good listener.

"Sometimes it's just better to say things out loud," she told her dog.

BunnyLee had started their journey telling Puddles about the dog whisperer with a dog story about a summer job she'd had working for an outfitter up near Gordon Pass. Along with horses, there were border collies assigned to every wilderness party. These were working dogs that took their responsibilities seriously—keen to what was going on around them, attentive to the sounds of the wild, careful not to let anyone wander too far from the group. Tales were swapped around the campfire of how these dogs so often saved the day. BunnyLee admired these animals. They were working dogs that had their masters. Getting to know them one-on-one was never in the cards. The point of the story was that she made a promise to herself back then that one day she would have a dog of her own. She wanted to assure Puddles that even though Puddles was unexpected and unplanned, she was wanted. It just never seemed practical to have a dog at an urban university like UCLA. BunnyLee was always in a play or auditioning, so between that and studying, everything was such an uphill battle. The uncertainty and lack of direction was all part of the actor's life—spinning her wheels and going nowhere.

"…so, when Dial-A-Denture petered out, I set out for Guam and then Southeast Asia."

BunnyLee told Puddles about the Buddhist monk at the Bayon Temple in Cambodia. He was as high up on the temple as you could climb, dressed in typical draped garb robes, a very serious guy. His chakra measuring method involved doing an elaborate calculation of her body with a bamboo stick, bending it in different ways.

"He measured my fingers and different lengths on my arm to the tips of my fingers and then broke these measurements into pieces. He laid the sticks in what looked like a stick figure and wrote what looked like words around it. Then he declared, 'You are five times lucky!' which is rare. I took my sister Lizette there last winter and we asked for readings and the priest admonished me because I wanted another reading and he remembered me and thought I was pushing it. Five times lucky is the highest you can be."

BunnyLee looked at her precious Puddles riding next to her and for the first time thought that maybe the priest was right. The evidence was right in front of her. She was five times lucky to have a dog like this. She also realized, like any parent, that Puddles' puppy days would soon be over and she would be turning the heads of the dog world.

She took a deep breath. It was good to get out of the city. Her recent experience of staying with Buck had been fun, she told herself, but it was time to get on with her life. Puddles was breathing easy. No more sneezing.

After Fresno, when she started the ascent she could almost see the gas gauge move from the right side of full to the scary side of empty. BunnyLee was four hours from L.A., which was a lot farther than it looked on the old map she pulled out of the glove box, and worlds away from the teeming Chinatown market where she dropped Jimmy Chan this morning.

It was autumn up here; things were dry. The leaves were changing. The car was sputtering, gasping for air, and coughing. She began having doubts about the advisability of taking an old car on a long trip. It also started to dawn on her that Buck might not be too pleased with her if Buck's Baby broke down. She had a vague idea of where she was headed, but Yosemite was a big place. She hadn't worried too much about the details, thinking that when she got close enough, she'd ask around. Now that she was close, there wasn't anybody around to ask.

That she was still here in Southern California when she should have been starting a new semester in Thailand this fall felt incongruous. She'd spent years exploring the great religions of the world. None of them gave her any insight into her relationship with Buck. Other than Heather, the only other person she dared tell about Buck was her sister, and BunnyLee had immediately regretted that.

"Oh, my God! Are you kidding me? Buck LeGrande? No way! Is he, like, as good in bed as everybody says?"

"I can't say."

"BunnyLee, you have to tell me!"

"I haven't slept with him, Lizette."

"Stop! Oh my God, BunnyLee! You have to!"

"I almost did. It's all just so complicated."

"Did you ask him about Kermit the Frog?"

"Lizette, I would never. I'm a guest in his house. I haven't even googled it."

"Don't!"

For such a populous state, life was pretty sparse in these parts. On the northern slopes there was dense pine forest and woody chaparral, and on the southern slopes grasslands more suited for cattle grazing than agriculture. Ancient black oaks were turning gold and dropping their leaves, and before too many days the cattle lounging in their shadows would miss the generous shade.

On the steeper inclines, black smoke billowed from the exhaust of the Mustang. Feeling the gaze of vultures on high as the Mustang sputtered through their domain, BunnyLee resolved to stop at the next gas station for a check-up. It was ages before she spotted a station on the next hill and she kept her fingers crossed to make it.

Jack's Gulf was one of those old-style stations with one pump you saw in old movies. As she pulled in, she noticed the mechanic in the only bay with a work light aimed at the underside of a pink Ford pickup with lace curtains in the camper windows. "First-things-first," BunnyLee said to herself. She went in search of the women's room.

Alongside the building, a young woman was sitting on a stack of used tires draped with a towel. She balanced pink stationery in her lap against a magazine and seemed to be engrossed in the delicate art of composing a letter. Mounted on the wall next to her was a pay phone, and next to that the door to the ladies' room. A sign for the men's room pointed around the corner.

BunnyLee allowed Puddles to roam at the limit of a retractable leash as she knocked on the women's room door. There was no answer. The young woman watched Puddles through the corner of her eye. BunnyLee tried the door handle.

"There's somebody in there."

"Has she been in there long?" BunnyLee asked. "I really gotta go."

"Yep."

"You think she's coming out any time soon?"

"There's the men's room around the corner if you're in a hurry."

BunnyLee peeked around back where the men's room door was ajar and the sight inside wasn't pretty. "I'd really prefer to use the ladies' room."

"I feel the same way," the woman said. "What type of dog is that?"

"She's a Miniature Labradoodle."

"Never heard'a that one. You sure she isn't a mutt?"

BunnyLee tried not to feel offended. In her mind, all dogs were created equal. Except of course, her dog.

"Is she a pedigree, then?"

"She's a cross between a miniature Poodle and a Labrador retriever. She's the best of her breed. And as a breed, she's brand new. She came here all the way from Australia."

"They just started making them? Like with papers that say who her papa is and all?"

"That's right, you came with papers, didn't you, Sweetie?"

Her nose to the ground, Puddles appeared to be far more interested in all the smells they have around filling stations in the foothills of the Sierras than talk of her pedigree.

"I'm a mutt," the woman said, "with no papers to prove otherwise."

BunnyLee didn't know how to respond to that. "Does that phone work?" she asked. She couldn't remember when she had last seen a pay phone. Until she'd lost her cell phone, she hadn't given their continued existence much thought.

"Jack used it to call the parts store. But you've got to put money in."

"Puddles! Honey, don't roll in that!"

Puddles tugged on her leash. BunnyLee pulled back. With a dog, BunnyLee needed to do a lot of things one-handed. She dug around in her satchel for some change.

"Does this place have a name?"

"Jack's Gulf. And he's really cute."

"No, I mean the area?"

"What's today, Thursday?"

"Saturday."

"California."

"You don't happen to know where in California?"

"I'd have to check the schedule. Must be nice havin' a dog."

"You ought to try it."

"It wouldn't be fair. That's what Momma says. What with our bein' on the road right now." She sighed again with a dramatic pause. "That's show business," she said, "Maybe after I'm settled down."

BunnyLee found the coins and loaded them one at a time into the phone. She held Frankie's number on a slip of paper and carefully dialed. She tapped her finger and waited for him to answer, speaking quickly when he did, not sure how much time was allotted, "Frankie, it's me, BunnyLee. I've got a problem... What?"

She set the receiver back on the hook, "He said he'll call me back."

"Hope he's got caller ID."

BunnyLee thought about this. She wasn't at all sure about what technologies extended back into the pre-wireless days.

The phone rang. BunnyLee quickly answered it. "Frankie?" but it wasn't Frankie. It was another man's voice. "Who? Sorry. Tell me again...? Sure, I'll tell him." BunnyLee hung up. For the first time today she was feeling lost.

A man walked out of the bay wiping grease from his hands with a soiled red cloth. The young woman was right; he was cute, an athletic guy in his early twenties, scruffy, a blue work shirt pulled on over his black t-shirt with his name, JACK, stitched over his shirt pocket. The young woman sat up and gave him her full attention.

BunnyLee said, "Billy from the parts store said to tell you they're sending your parts over...that is, if your name is Jack."

"That's me. Soon as they get here, I'll put that muffler on and we'll have this pretty lady back in business."

BunnyLee noticed that the young woman was swooning.

"How's the letter comin', Kayla?" Jack asked her, looking over her shoulder at the stationery. "I like that, how you dot your i's with little hearts..."

Kayla blushed. "Look somewhere else, why don't ya?"

"I've just never gotten a letter from a girl. You write him a lot?"

"Try to. Not sure if they get delivered. I'll write you, too, if you want."

"Sure!"

"Is this the only phone?" BunnyLee asked.

"The only one that works. So, what's this fella's name you write to?" Jack asked Kayla.

"Austin, like that town in Texas."

"Is he a cowboy?"

"The genuine article."

"The kind that wrestles bulls in rodeos?"

"Wrestlin' people on TV, mostly."

"I wrestled in high school."

"You did?" Kayla perked up at this. "Did you ever think of doin' it professional?"

"Nah, although tonight I'm gonna be--"

The telephone rang again.

"That's for me," BunnyLee interrupted. And then remembered to ask, "Oh... how far are we from Mariposa?"

"The county or the town? If you mean the county, you're smack dab at the beginning, extending to and including those mountains way over yonder. Used to be that Mariposa comprised half of California, so it's gotten a lot smaller. Or are you looking for the town?"

BunnyLee wasn't sure. She answered the phone. "Frankie?" But again it wasn't Frankie. "Who? What's a lug wrench? Then no wonder you can't change your tire. Even I know that. Do you want to talk to the man in charge? That would be Jack. Hold on." BunnyLee held the phone out for Jack, "It's for you."

Before speaking into the phone, Jack asked BunnyLee, "Didn't I see you on TV?"

"You might have." BunnyLee felt Kayla's glance.

"I thought so. When you were young, right?" Jack said. He turned his attention to the call on the payphone.

"Of course! Dial-A-Denture!" Kayla said, "One Eight Hundred, Two, Five, Five..." She continued in a Marilyn Monroe seductive tone, "Operators are standing by!" She finished with a wink. "Wow, that's been on since I was a kid!"

"I didn't realize I was that old."

"No. Only that you've been around."

"Thanks a lot."

"Do you know anything about men?"

"Less and less. One thing about men is that a lot of times you have to guess about their feelings, because they haven't a clue."

"Can I read you what I've got so far?"

"Is it long?"

"Nope! Okay, here goes."

Kayla stood up and BunnyLee took an involuntary step backward. The girl was a giant compared to her, maybe a foot taller in those boots.

"Dear Austin--"

Jack, who had been half-listening to his phone call, interrupted, "Okay, but you've got to realize I'm shorthanded today, what with the fair. And I already promised to replace a muffler...I surely will." He hung up. "Dang, I am never gonna get to the fair!"

Kayla cleared her throat and began again, "Dear Austin. Yesterday morning when we watched you eating your Taco-All-The-Way back in Vegas I knew you were lonely and in need of love. And shy. Today your jump from the second-floor balcony proved that. The palm reader in the arena parking lot before your match last night said this is a good season for strangers getting together. You show such courage when you enter the ring and take on the likes of Chief Tenaya or The Welder, or the Rug Riders way back when, even though they were so much bigger than you. You have determination to get what you want, just like me. You are mythological. You could be President of the United States one day. You need a First Lady to be the mother of your babies. My mom has your names tattooed over her heart. She is your biggest fan. P.S. She could arrange your cabinet. Or run the Franklin Mint."

BunnyLee looked at Jack for any telltale smirk.

"Is that it?" he asked.

"So far. That part about the palm reader's true, too, her sayin' that it's the right season and all for the stars to align. And about how way back when, when things were mythological, stars were people. As opposed to now, where people are stars. You think it's okay? I know it sounds dumb, but after writing a lot of letters, you run out of new things to say. I'm sure he never thought about being president, but it's suitable to tell him he could. Abe Lincoln was a wrestler in his youth, and look at all he did after."

"Have you talked to this guy about children?" BunnyLee asked.

"In my last letter I told him he should have ten."

"That's a lot," Jack said.

"Because with the men that I've known," BunnyLee continued, "having babies is not the first thing on their minds."

"I just thought he should have more'n one."

"It's your letter."

"I like the idea of having babies," Jack said.

"You do?" Kayla asked.

The telephone rang again.

"I'll get it!" BunnyLee jumped for the receiver. It was Frankie, "It's about time. What's up with this car, anyway?"

"I think it would be neat to have a bunch of kids," Jack continued with Kayla. "What would you name them all?"

"You mean if pickin' the names was up to me? Well, first off, I'd name them after my uncles..."

"What about yer dad?"

"Oh, I don't really know..."

"Because it's making noise," BunnyLee spoke into the phone. "Coughing, like it's caught cold. Yeah, uphill, and with smoke coming out. Of course I put gas in...huh? Whatever was cheapest."

"My mom won't really say," Kayla said to Jack.

"Yeah, regular," BunnyLee said into the phone, "No, I didn't put anything else...what's a valve head?"

"There's yer problem," Jack said to BunnyLee.

"Yeah, I know," Kayla said to Jack.

"No, I just meant with her car's engine."

"But you're right," Kayla said.

"How the heck was I supposed to know you have to put some special additive in there?" BunnyLee asked Frankie.

"It's a definite source of friction," Kayla went on.

"I'll say," Jack said. "And it messes with the timing."

"That's funny, because like I said, the palm reader said that the stars were in alignment for things to come together tonight. It's all in the timing, she said those exact words."

"So he found out I took it, huh?" BunnyLee asked Frankie on the phone. "Tell me what he said. He did? What do you mean, 'in hot water?'" BunnyLee listened to Frankie's story. "How does he even know which way I went? Chan?" BunnyLee winced. "I'm as good as cooked?" BunnyLee shared a worried look with Jack.

"What's that supposed to mean? That doesn't sound like Buck! 'Bitch?' He used that word? That's what Chan said?"

BunnyLee was beginning to feel like she really was in hot water with Buck. But she was sticking to her guns. "Well...what's Monday, again? Oh, yeah, Warner Brothers. So I'll lay low 'til then...no, but I've got credit cards. Okay, you too." BunnyLee hung up the phone.

Kayla and Jack stared at BunnyLee.

"Are you in some kind of trouble?" Jack asked.

BunnyLee tried to recover her composure. "That's just Buck, I guess." The truth was, she wanted to cry.

"Did you guys have a fight?" Kayla asked.

"I think I offended him about his hair. He's an actor."

"A famous one?" Kayla asked.

BunnyLee nodded.

"Your husband didn't know you took the car?" Jack asked.

"Actually, he's just a friend. Oh, God, he's going to kill me," BunnyLee answered, covering her eyes.

Kayla and Jack asked if she was in any kind of physical danger.

"No! His bark is worse than his bite. He's really a nice guy. And besides, this is an emergency. My dog has been having these sneezing fits." BunnyLee added, "Anyway, he can't do anything if he can't find me."

"So you're fixin' to hide out someplace?" Kayla asked.

"Actually, I've been trying to find this spa near Yosemite where they cure dogs of all kinds of maladies. Cheyanna told me about it. A man who teaches there is like a guru for dogs. They call him a dog whisperer."

"You're friends with Cheyanna, the singer?" Kayla asked. "*The* Cheyanna?"

"She says everybody's going there. And nobody has ever heard of it."

"The Reservation?" Jack asked.

"That's it!"

"I hadn't heard about that dog thing."

"They just started it."

"It used to be a campground until some Japanese monks took it over. It's pretty expensive."

"I've got plastic. You wouldn't happen to have any of that additive they put in with the gas, would you?"

"I sure don't. How many times have you filled her up?"

"Three."

"That'll do it! The way you sounded pulling in here, I'd say you already lost compression. And what with this high altitude..."

"Can you fix it?"

"Now that's a tall order. And I'm closed Sundays."

"What are my chances of getting to The Reservation?"

"It's mostly downhill, so you could get there. You'd likely need to get towed back out. That guy on the phone with the flat tire is down that way, too, so I'll be along later and I could check to see you made it all right. It's on the far side of my ranch. I'll get you my card."

"You've got a ranch?" Kayla asked.

"You're standin' on it."

"You mean here? But this is just a fillin' station."

"Yep. Along with all that grazing land over there, as far as you can see," Jack pointed across the valley. "And all that standing timber over there." Jack pointed across the road at an alpine forest. "I'll be right back."

A man driving an official-looking green State of California SUV beeped his horn at Jack, and Jack waved back. "See ya tonight!" Jack called to the passing car before he disappeared into the garage bay.

The women's room door opened and a woman about ten years older than BunnyLee stepped out. She was dressed extravagantly, like a country-western singer, with tassels and sequins and dryer-blown big hair.

"Momma, this here is an actress who knows Cheyanna and her boyfriend is a famous actor, too!"

"Pleased to meet ya. M'name's Tammy." She held up a pocket mirror, licked her finger and smoothed her eyebrows.

"And he wants to kill her."

"That's nice. Now run along and put yer dress on!" Tammy said, tapping her wristwatch.

Kayla snagged the bathroom before BunnyLee could react.

"Hey!" BunnyLee yelled, but she was too late.

"Sorry! But I was next!" Kayla closed the door and bolted it.

"Ain't she somethin'?" Tammy asked.

"She could have told me she was waiting in line."

"Stage fright. Don't pay it any mind. Pretty as she is, even

Kayla gets nervous before an event. A simple thing like what color dress to change into or how to do up her hair all figure in."

"But, I need to go!"

"There's the men's room 'round that corner if yer in a hurry."

BunnyLee sized up the men's room a second time.

Tammy teased her hair and sighed with the tone of a martyr. "Show bizness. Ain't nuthin' like it. It is in her blood is what it is, the noise, the excitement, lights beaming down! Yes sir, it is exhileratin'! And the power! I cannot begin to tell you, when that specimen of a man enters the squared circle, his name echoing over the coliseum loudspeakers, and him larger than life, tearing off his shirt, holding it up high, chest bare for all to see, those faces of swooning women, the children dancing in the aisles waving foam fingers and chanting 'Yer Number One! Yer Number One!' it is like the Power and the Glory rainin' down from The Heavens Above!"

BunnyLee, who was thinking more seriously about using the men's room, paused at the sordid subject of fame. "My Puddles wants to be an actress, too. When she sees a camera, she just lights up!"

"My Kayla's been on TV. More'n once. No matter where we go, no matter what city we are in, when they pan across the audience, the one calm face in that sea of adulation is Kayla's, like she is a part of it and at the same time above it all, blissful and reposed, like those pictures of the Virgin Mary when a miracle's about to happen? That's Kayla!"

"That's like my Puddles! Yesterday, I took her to an audition, and you know, when people aren't interested, they just kind of steer you towards the door? Not so with Puddles. Everybody was like, 'Omigod, can I hold her?' As if all her training just suddenly kicked in! She was a sensation! Weren't you, sweetie?"

"Puddles is yer...dog? That's a new one."

"I feel so lucky!" BunnyLee said.

Jack came back around the corner and handed BunnyLee his card. Tammy slipped in the last word. "My Kayla is a sure shot if I ever did see one. Everybody loves her!"

"I'd marry her, no question," Jack said.

Tammy laughed. "Oh, bless yer heart! Well, get in line!"

"Yeah, I know. It would be like hitting the lottery. Her dad is famous, too...what's his name?"

"Has she been goin' on about him? Well, it's no secret. Her

papa was one half of a famous tag-team wrestling duo. Double Trouble. Twin brothers who held the title longer than any team up to date."

"I remember them. Which one was her dad?"

"I can't really say. They wrestled tag-team," Tammy said, as if that answered everything. "Kayla, honey, don't dally! Tick-tock!" she hollered at the women's room door.

"Because they looked so much alike you couldn't tell them apart?"

"Oh, I could tell them apart. It's just that they did everything together. Kayla!" Tammy turned to BunnyLee. "Is yer boyfriend really out to kill you?

"No!"

"'Cause you never know these days, judging by what you see on *Entertainment Tonight*, what with yer O.J.s and yer Robert Blakes..."

"And your Phil Spectors," Jack added.

"Him, too. Seems like every time you stand in line at the grocery store you read about another VIP accused of whacking his significant other."

"I assure you, Buck..."

"You really got to keep your eye on them men, 'cause for every one who's done it, there's another ten waiting in the wings. Has he got a gun?"

"A gun? No! Buck would never..."

"Not that there ain't oodles of ways to do it. I don't know what it is with them Hollywood-actor-types. On TV they seem like the nicest fellas, but when they ain't working, which is most of the time, they get to drinkin' and stewin'. They got nothin' better to do than to shoot the missus, or pop some poison in her soup, or push 'er off a cliff, or pay some goon to whack 'er upside the head!"

"Or tamper with her brakes," Jack added.

"Right. Or cut 'er up into little pieces with the chipper shredder..."

"You're starting to really scare me."

"...or drown her in the pool..."

"Come on, Puddles! We gotta go!"

BunnyLee headed around the corner to use the men's room. Tammy followed her.

"Or strangle her. Wait a minute! This Buck of yours wouldn't be Buck LeGrande is it? It is a wonder there ain't a warrant out for that man's arrest after what he done to Kermit the Frog."

BunnyLee closed the bathroom door and locked it.

Tammy gave the door a quick knock.

"Sorry to bother you, but was that you on the cover of *American Celebrity* this week? The reason I ask was because I was wondering, was that an operation that gave you yer single dimple smile? Or was it that you had the other dimple removed? I read the whole article from beginning to end and they never did tell."

CHAPTER 16

BUCK AND FRANKIE and Jimmy Chan were just outside of Bakersfield, back on the highway after a pit stop, when there came the faint ring of a phone.

"You gonna answer that?" Buck asked his driver on the third ring.

"I was gonna ask you the same thing, Boss," Frankie answered, making eye contact with Buck in the rear-view mirror.

"It's not my phone," Buck answered.

"Not mine, either."

"Is that your phone, Chan?" Buck asked his cook, who was riding shotgun.

"No phone."

The ringing stopped.

Buck reached into the leather pocket of his door to find out whether the ringing had come from there and he pulled out a flask.

"What have we here?" Buck took a sip. "Hmm, vodka." Buck took a swig. "You're going under the speed limit again," Buck told Frankie.

"Can't be too cautious around Bakersfield."

"It's gonna be dark before we get there if you don't step on it."

Frankie eased the speed up to fifty-five.

"Hey, Chan, you drive?"

"Sure thing, Mr. Buck!"

"I don't mean a bicycle. I mean a twelve-cylinder Bentley T1."

"Giddy-up!"

"These cars top out at 185 miles per hour, why do you suppose that is?"

"Get there fast."

"Exactly right, Chan, so we can get there fast. You hear that, Frankie? If they'd meant for us to go the speed limit, why do you suppose they put a 400-horsepower engine under the hood?"

"Never wanna get pulled over in Bakersfield, Boss. Nothing but trouble. Then we'll never get to Warner Brothers."

"If I didn't know better, I'd think you had some financial interest in getting me to that meeting. Is somebody paying you to get me there, Frankie?"

"Just looking out for the boss."

"You're lying and I can tell. You forget. I played the world's greatest private eye. A veritable Sherlock Holmes is what I was, Chan. I know when someone's lying."

Frankie didn't say anything.

"You know me as a thinking man, Chan. But I'm a man of action. Ever heard of René Descartes? I think, therefore I am? That's me, only part way. I figure things out. But that's only the half of it. I'm equal parts Descartes and David Hume. Ever hear of Hume? He saw things differently. Disagreed with Descartes. Said, basically, 'I feel, therefore I am.' That's the other part. Left brain, right brain. You have a feeling, a hunch, you shoot from the hip. They're opposites: thinking and feeling. BunnyLee knows all about this stuff."

Buck held up both hands like he had just pulled two six-shooters from their holster.

"Left brain, right brain. Like matching pistols. Pow! Pow!"

Buck feigned shooting with his fingers. Smiling at his own *savoir-faire*, he sat looking out the window, trying to recover the thread of his thesis. Boy, had they ever ruined Bakersfield.

"Oh yeah, action. I act, therefore I am. You haven't heard that one before, but that's me. Don't judge a man by his words, Chan. Watch his actions. Pow! Pow!"

All this pow-powing was good for demonstration purposes, but every time he said it he lost his train of thought. Buck watched the oil wells go by. Where was this lecture headed?

"Oh, yeah. Two schools of thought on acting, Chan. The Method actors, you've heard of them? Stanislavsky Method? Emotional. You feel the script. You look for the emotion in the script. Your actions are determined by the emotional subtext in the script. Some great actors came out of the Method." He took a nip from the flask. "But then people act on their desires, that's free will, isn't it?"

BunnyLee had filled him in on all these method-acting matters, and he wasn't entirely sure whether he was covering the high points.

"Then there are the improvisers," Buck continued, "They make it up as they go along. No script. They feel; they act. That's my point." He and BunnyLee had talked at length about improvisation as an acting form. He hadn't realized that it came with so many rules. Not as many as in life, but more than the layperson might think. He thought back about the night of BunnyLee's birthday when she told him about the rule of always saying yes.

"Nope, I should never have bought her that dog," Buck said.

He watched the action of the oilrigs like mosquitoes slowly sucking the earth dry. The landscape looked like how he felt: drained. He wasn't used to drinking, and looking out the window was like looking into his own mind. His feelings were an emotional wasteland of derricks pumping black ooze to the surface. But it was either look out the window or look at Chan who was hanging on his every word. The words weren't coming. "Pow, pow," he thought to himself, trying to jog his memory.

"Oh, yeah, action. I'm a risk taker."

"You want I should drive?" Chan asked.

"You have a license?"

"Nope."

"Nope."

They sat in silence. Buck ached inside. He also felt anger, abandonment, resentment, to name but a few. Emotions were like drugs; one needed to be careful mixing them. He slipped the flask back into the door sleeve.

"Enough's enough."

Buck attempted to steady himself with a stiff dose of self-evaluation. He could count his good qualities on two hands. He stared at his hands. Starting with the thumb on his left hand and moving left to right, he assessed his attributes. Nothing jumped to mind. He was stuck on number one. He closed his eyes and reviewed the sad state of his heart. There was only one person on his mind and her name was BunnyLee. Had he failed so miserably to make her happy?

When BunnyLee was a kid she told her mom that what she wanted most in the world was a dog. There were so many things in life that a person might want most in the world and from Buck's perspective, a dog wasn't it. At great risk to himself and against all practical reason, he had fulfilled her wish.

"Big mistake," Buck said out loud.

"What's that, Boss?" Frankie asked.

"I should never have bought her that dog."

The Bentley purred along at an even fifty-five. Buck leaned his head on the backseat headrest. He pondered BunnyLee's rendition of Baudelaire's rant about being drunk 'on wine, poetry or virtue.' Life was flying by: the wind, the wave, the star, the bird, the clock. Everything was taunting him. He was a lightweight when it came to drinking. He had never tried his hand at poetry. And virtue? Virtue was the character trait in Nick Derringer that people most loved. So he had the capacity for virtue; he'd played a virtuous guy on TV!

In real life, there was room for improvement. Case in point: Jadé. He shouldn't have slept with Jadé. That was a blunder. One evening with Jadé had wiped out a month of virtuous behavior alongside BunnyLee, proving among other things that BunnyLee was too good for him. Up until then, she had as much as admitted, he'd been in the running.

The ring of a cell phone roused Buck from his reverie. The Bentley was in a construction zone. The dull rumble of the rough pavement filled the backseat and Buck needed to listen closely to identify the recurring sound. Maybe it was his imagination.

"Are those clouds up ahead?" he asked Frankie.

"Those are the Sierra there, Boss."

Even from this distance they looked big. Finding BunnyLee in that vast mountain kingdom seemed outlandish. He sat lower in his seat, trying to glean some insight into the events of the previous week. Like a one-two punch, his one night spent with Jadé added a notch to his life tally of one-night stands but it had knocked him for a loop in his relationship with BunnyLee. Finding BunnyLee in the company of another man had knocked him to the mat.

Like Socrates's allegory of the cave, Buck was a prisoner tortured by his own active imagination, a captive who was free to describe reality based only upon his interpretation of a moving shadow on a wall. He tried to reconcile that shadow with the person to whom it might belong: a giant of a man moving freely in the company of the Greek Goddess BunnyLee. He was in the dark as to what was going on with her in that light-filled room, and he abhorred his best guess.

For a man accustomed to being in control of his life, Buck had never felt such despair. He had never before pursued a woman and here he was, chasing BunnyLee halfway to Nevada.

The muffled sound of a phone rang again. Buck reached into the leather pocket in the backseat door. He pulled out a small macramé purse. In the purse was an iPhone. He answered it.

"Hello?"

"BunnyLee?"

Buck looked at the name on the caller ID.

"Archie?"

"Oh. Hey, Buck."

"What the hell?"

"I was just calling BunnyLee about Puddles. About her braces. I just wanted her to know that if there is any problem, bleeding, any pain whatsoever, she should bring her back in immediately to see me."

"Since when do you have pets for patients?" Buck asked. Truth be told, Buck had never liked Archie. He tolerated him because he was Sidney's younger brother. It was confirmed: the man was a worm. "So your specialty is now porn stars and pets. And you're working on a Saturday. I didn't realize business was so bad."

"Business is booming. I just wanted BunnyLee to know."

"Know what?"

"If there's a problem, I'm here to help."

"Never mind BunnyLee, it's a comfort to *me* knowing the level of your concern for Puddle's malocclusion." On the list of available suspects, Buck had to admit he had never considered Archie a threat. But the jury was in. Buck was right to be paranoid. Even Paradise had its vipers.

Buck hung up. Few men could better appreciate Odysseus' rage when the hero finally returned from Troy only to find his house swarming with Penelope's suitors. And Buck hadn't even been away.

"She definitely wasn't alone in her cabana when I got back last night," Buck said out loud.

Frankie looked at his boss in the rearview mirror.

"Boss, BunnyLee wasn't with anyone or I'd have known," Frankie said.

"Evidence to the contrary," Buck said, waving BunnyLee's phone at Frankie's reflection in the mirror. "I found BunnyLee's phone. All this time it was tucked in the upholstery of the Bentley. Heard it ringing, thought I was hearing things. Somebody by the name of Archibald Newman called. Does that ring a bell? No? My friend, Sidney Newman's younger brother, Archie, the dentist? It's quite unexpected, don't you think, that Archie would be calling BunnyLee?"

"Archie did Puddles' braces."

"Really. You never mentioned it."

"Trust me, BunnyLee's got nothing going on with Archie."

"What other trysts have you been taking her to?"

"Boss…"

"Watch out, Frankie, I'm going to get to the bottom of this," Buck said.

Buck thought again about the shadow on the wall in the cabana last night, and he shook his head at the idea of Archie in a ten-gallon hat. The shadow was too big for such a little guy. Clearly, Archie was just one of many men in pursuit of BunnyLee.

There were credit card receipts in with BunnyLee's phone. With his own phone, sleuth Buck called the eight-hundred numbers to ask where and when the cards were last used. This was not information that any one of the companies was willing to divulge.

CHAPTER 17

"DAMN!"

AUSTIN DIDN'T need to see it to know that his rear tire had gone flat, or to go looking in the trunk to know that his tire iron was in the company of an attractive barkeep somewhere in the last county, or to look around at his surroundings to surmise that he was shit-out-of-luck with a slow leak on a quiet mountain road. He knew all this before he pulled over. And it was with no real surprise that he found a lead bullet lodged in the sidewall. Guns were weapons. Bullets had no moral conscience. Even a round deployed as friendly fire by the "Mechanic" could do its mischief.

Austin took a deep breath and adjusted his hat.

"Dammit!"

It was with guns that the West was won...or lost, depending upon your viewpoint. The ghosts of the Ahwanee tribe who haunted the high chaparral of the central California Sierras would attest to this: a poor defenseless clan in this wonderment of creation whose only crime, if you could call it that, was living here atop the mother lode.

It was just like men (and the Forty-Niners were mostly men) to arrive without provisions and without much thought as to where the next meal was coming from. They had their guns and shot everything that moved. The natives took a futile stand against the relentless influx, and then in retreat they made a fatal error in judgment. They assumed they wouldn't be followed to their haven: Yosemite Valley, the most exquisite valley on the planet.

In the back of his mind, Yosemite was Austin's destination of choice, but his chances now of getting there tonight were nonexistent.

It was off-season, there was very little traffic on the road. Austin was stranded. The few who stopped weren't much help; their lug wrenches didn't fit his lugs. A Good Samaritan gave Austin the number of Jack's Gulf, but Jack was non-committal as to when he might swing by.

A number of cars coming from the other direction turned off about a quarter mile before they got to him, hitting a long dirt drive that disappeared into a redwood grove. Smoke hung in the trees below. It was hard to see any life through the vegetation, but it looked promising enough to check it out. Where there was smoke, there was very likely food.

As he closed the lid of his trunk, the glint of a silver canister containing Laredo's ashes caught his attention, and the sight of it stopped him cold. He could no longer lock his trunk. That meant everything in it was vulnerable.

He surveyed the majestic surroundings. It was coming on golden hour, that period of evening that photographers prized, when the shadows crept longer, the shade grew mysterious, and the illuminated world was filled with the warm glow of sunset. The sky above was deep blue. Wisps of clouds were tinged with orange.

Above the trees, Austin watched a pair of brightly lit red-tailed hawks yawing on an updraft and saw that as a sign. Austin reckoned a man's soul could soar there just as readily. It was truly beautiful and, by the looks of things, tranquil. He knew the Sierras were at their grandest a few miles down the road near the likes of El Capitan and Bridalveil Fall, but Yosemite Valley was overrun and a far cry from tranquil in summer.

What had felt before like an act of free will, driving up into these mountains, now felt fateful; that he had a flat tire here in this primordial place felt like it was meant to be. He was retreating to the womb of determinism, yielding to a guiding force: that this was what today was all about. The time drew nigh.

His only hesitation was whether the winters would be too much to bear. The snow here was legendary. He imagined with resolve that death would be cold no matter where, that it came with the territory. And besides, snowmelt was the source of life. It formed the headwaters of the San Joaquin river valley, the breadbasket of the country. It formed the vernal pools from which sprang the orgy of life. This was the realm of the giant sequoias, the largest creatures on earth; if it was good enough for them, he reckoned, then this was about the best place on the planet to spend eternity, the closest to heaven a garrulous cowboy could hope to climb.

Austin grabbed the canister from the wheel well, stepped back and held it high. He said a prayer aloud to any gods who cared to listen. "What are we here for but to bear witness?" he questioned them. "What more is there to life but to see and to have been seen?" he asked.

Austin unscrewed the lid of the canister and set his brother's ashes free.

Then he resealed the canister and chucked it as far as he could throw it. The cursed thing had dogged him for a year.

As he made his way down the dirt lane, his phone rang. Austin looked at the caller ID. It was Big Eddie, his producer. Austin had been ignoring his calls all afternoon.

"It takes you until now to call me back?" Austin asked as he walked, taking the offensive in a conversation he felt a need to dominate. "I texted you hours ago! That's funny, maybe I just don't know how to work this new phone. Where you at? What's its name? No, the arena tomorrow, I know it's in the schedule, just tell me again."

As he talked, Austin left the lane and followed a footpath marked with an arrow and sign that read 'To The Reservation.' He ducked in behind the trunk of a giant oak to relieve himself. Supporting the phone between his neck brace and his ear, he peed against the ancient tree.

"Yeah, I'm writing it down," he lied. "Fresno Coliseum and Convention Center, that's easy enough...no, I am not in the car right now."

Austin finished, shook off, zipped and stepped back. He had splattered a brass plaque that read: Vespers Tree, Oldest Black Oak in Mariposa County.

"Huh," Austin said after glancing at it. He didn't have time to read the short history. He needed his full attention to sidestep anything that Big Eddie had to serve up on the phone. "No, I am not...'cause a fella needs to stop for dinner, for heaven sakes! What time do I go on tomorrow? Listen to me, Ed, I need you to do me a favor. I want you to tell Vic that I've got this thing with my neck..."

The sandy trail was neatly tended. Austin paused to puzzle over it. It had recently been raked. Someone had gone to lot of trouble to keep it looking pristine.

"Eddie, would you calm down a second? Did I say I wasn't performing? All I said was I got this pull, that's all. No! Gosh darn it, would you let me explain..."

The path took an interesting turn into a dense bamboo thicket and then passed under a pergola with vines of blooming hydrangea.

"...no, I have not been drinking. Listen, Eddie, this is yer ol' pal, Austin, 'member me? I got a flat tire and I got to change it, okay?"

Austin came to a steep step. He changed hands with the phone so that his closer arm could grip the limb of an ornamental cherry tree. He carefully lowered his stiff body down onto a larger field of immaculate sand. The path immediately widened as it wrapped around rather good-sized stones, some so large as to be classified as small boulders. Each was separated one from the next by those undulating waves of sand. Given the orderliness with which these granite specimens were displayed, Austin had the brief thought that he had stumbled into the showroom of a quarrying business. A simple carved teak sign read: *Serenity Garden®: the registered trademark of the Kyoto Corporation Yosemite Reservation.*

On the immediate periphery, closely tended patches of lawn were adorned with simple stone benches on which robed women sat cross-legged. Their breathing was rhythmic and they were making ominous sounds.

✦

A Japanese woman sitting on a grass mat at the far end of the Serenity Garden opened her eyes. The sight of a large man disturbing the pristine sand was hard to ignore. So was his voice.

"I no longer have a lug wrench so I had to flag down a car with the right sized...yeah, well, it sounds easy to me, too, but suddenly everybody's driving those little Japanese cars and the lug wrenches don't fit! Lug nuts...I'm not makin' it up, Eddie, it's a fact: Japanese nuts are smaller."

She gave the tall man with the Texas accent a withering look. He pulled the phone away from his ear and explained. "Not the men! The cars!"

She looked around for support. She'd paid good money and driven up from the Bay Area for this weekend respite. The brochure specifically stated that talking wasn't allowed in the Serenity Garden.

"Don't start with me, Eddie," the man continued into the phone. "I know as well as you do that Vic is going to be steamed... would you listen?"

It was a pleasant alpine evening, the occasion of the Autumnal equinox. The full moon was rising, and it was a Saturday evening, to boot. In the fading light, candles were placed in strategic positions to illuminate the contemplative energy and quietude of this carefully tended oasis. The Serenity Garden was a kind of theatre in which the audience was playing a part in a performance, both witness to and partaking of the experience. Everyone who journeyed here was in effect participating in a metaphor. They were part of the picture, part of the scenery, sitting in quiet peacefulness as if they themselves had grown here, their roots firmly planted in the soil, their faces like ripening flowers in the rare mountain air. The goal to be attained was to be *of* the moment.

Maybe this man was a test? She didn't think so.

The intruder paused to ask another woman, "Hey, little lady, is there any place around here where a hungry fella could find a meal? Hello? Hello!"

✦

Austin waved his hand in front of her open eyes and shrugged. Earlier in the day it had been the Deaf Bikers who couldn't *hear*.

"No, I am not shacked up with some cute little number," Austin continued. "Those days are over, Ed. Trust me, I'm ridin' solo here...All you got to do is tell Vic... Wha...? Who's there...? No, I don't want to talk to..." Austin shook his head. Big Ed had apparently handed his phone over to Vic. "Vic, that you? How's it goin', man? Great...uh huh... great! Listen, I've been practicing those new moves we went over together? Killer moves, man, dynamite...uh huh. Yeah. No. I was just thinking that, maybe, that flip off the third rope, you know, when I go in for the full body slam from so high up?" It wasn't like his boss had trouble hearing, but everyone tended to talk emphatically whenever Vic was on the line.

Austin indicated the fluidity of his proposed wrestling maneuver with his arm. "I was thinking that it would work better if I did it from the second rope, you know, not so high, and... no, uh-huh, yeah, I see what you're sayin'... more dramatic from higher up. Yeah. And that part where I flip over in mid-air before I crunch him? Keep that, too? Okay, well, that's why you're the boss, Vic. Yeah, I'm psyched, too! I feel great. Just one little thing while I got you on the phone...Tonight? What about tonight...Vic? You there?" As quickly as his boss had materialized at the other end of the call, he had just as quickly vanished.

"What happened to Vic, Eddie?" Austin yelled. "And what's he talking about tonight? What celebrity appearance? No, I wasn't at that meeting. No. I am not at all sure where I am."

Austin looked around at the strange assemblage of people. "I'm surrounded by zombies."

✢

In their brochure, Zen was described as a variety of Buddhism that concentrated on introspection and enlightenment: that elusive mental state achieved through deep meditation. This was what a Zen garden ambiance was designed to enhance. The brochure contained a brief history of the thirteenth century when this symbolic depiction of water and islands was first introduced to create a tranquil environment. If one were to let one's imagination take a metaphorical voyage, these stones were the islands of the Japanese Archipelago and the raked sand was waves in the Sea of Japan.

"All right, so tell me where this thing is tonight. Yeah, I'm writin' it down. Mariposa. What? Really? That's the direction I was headin' anyway. Okay, so I'll show up there tonight. And listen, from now on, don't call me 'brother.' If you were my 'brother,' you'd have my back."

On this particular evening, those in the audience around him represented a fair cross section of persons at all levels of enlightenment, from novices to initiates to pros. It was safe to say that, given the reaction to Austin's appearance onstage in this arena, the introduction of his footprints to this sand was antithetic to all levels of the introspective journey. That he then sat against the Mount Fuji of stone islands to brush the sand from his boots was doubly troubling. To pursue the metaphor of the Serenity Garden even further, his boots were an invading armada in the Sea of Japan, not unlike the ships commanded by Field Marshal Douglas MacArthur, another well-known cowboy with west Texas roots.

✛

"One other thing, just between me and you. Can I trust you, Big Eddie? There is no way I can perform those moves. Never could. He's got me mixed up with Laredo. No. And besides, my neck is stiffer than a board and that's not the half of it. You wouldn't believe. I'm not just talkin' pain, I'm talking stiff all over. I think it's these new steroids, man. This new cycle, the D-ball from Mexico? Yeah, well, it's the wrong dose or something...I'm serious. Why do I know that it's the steroids? Because the only thing that isn't stiff is my dick!"

There, he had said it. Austin's secret pact with the devil was now public knowledge. Contraband. He'd pawned his virility for a few uninterrupted months under the bright lights.

It was apparent from their withering expressions that everyone in the vicinity could now hear and see him just fine. It wasn't like him to employ rough language in mixed company. And his words had woken everyone from their trance.

Austin tipped his hat. "Pardon me, ladies, name's Austin Sway, and I am one hungry fella."

CHAPTER 18

ON THE EAST side of Fresno, with the sunset-drenched mountains looming, Frankie popped into a Starbucks and returned with a Venti Americano.

"Better drink this, boss," Frankie said. "You know how you feel about heights."

Buck tasted it.

Frankie knew that if they were going to venture into those taunting mountains, turn by ever-steepening turn, Buck would need something to blunt the dizziness that a man unused to drinking alcohol would inevitably feel.

Buck was no fan of coffee. He didn't like the way coffee made him feel. His hands shook on their own; they didn't need extra help. The moment of clarity that coffee brought was rarely worth the inevitable unease it produced. He took a couple sips to try to establish a balance between his dizziness and the jitters.

Back on the road, as the elevation increased, so did his sense of gravity. He wasn't afraid of heights *per se*. It was the depths surrounding them that gave him pause—gravity being the one law you should never tempt breaking. He sipped some more.

BunnyLee had been filling him in on the French existentialists who hung out in Parisian coffee shops after the war, each with their own well-worn translations of Kierkegaard's *Concept of Anxiety* along with everyone's favorite, *Fear and Trembling*. Those guys made a commodity of despair, coining loneliness for its virtue value.

BunnyLee was big on the father of existentialism, and Buck wished he'd paid closer attention to the central theme, especially to that part about straying into the void. Kierkegaard likened anxiety to dizziness. "He whose eye happens to look down into the yawning abyss becomes dizzy" were some of her exact words.

Well, duh!

Nietzsche weighed in on mountain climbing, too. He called it the pathos of distance. This, BunnyLee read, was a "craving for ever new widening of distances within the soul itself...the development of ever higher, rarer, more remote, further stretching more comprehensive states." Buck begged to differ. These mountain roads were full of ever higher vistas alongside ever more yawning abysses. One was no sooner behind them when another gaping chasm of even greater magnitude taunted him around the bend. The Danish Doctor of Dread postulated that the gulf was "as much in his own eyes as in the abyss."

She had a point. Because when he closed his eyes, the abyss was not only still there in his imagination, but bigger, deeper, wider. Peaks and valleys, cliffs and chasms, in this muddle of fatal distractions his head was still spinning with dizziness.

One of the coffeehouse guys that BunnyLee talked a lot about named Sartre wrote a book about nausea which he cleverly titled: *Nausea*. Sartre's thesis somehow fit in with the theorem that "anxiety is the dizziness of freedom." Who would have thought that nausea was a heightened state of mind rather than just an affliction? Moreover, Buck had growing evidence to the contrary what with his gut currently sending distress signals. The coffee and booze were sloshing around in his gullet, one liquid clear as water and the other thick as mud, comingling like adulterous neighbors on a bed of Poppycock that he'd fished out of the backseat pouch. Together they were really whooping it up. He realized that he had better dump the dregs of his cup out the window, only to find on closer inspection that he'd already drunk the dreadful dregs.

The sudden twists and turns in the road were making him sweat. He slouched back into his seat, nursing his malaise. In a note-to-self he forcefully decreed: in the future, avoid coffee shops at any cost!

Buck compared himself again to Odysseus. Had the wayfarer

in his years-long journey home ever encountered such frightening terrain? Hill and dale, mountain and valley, peak and precipice, such were the highs and lows of his career, his life, his love for BunnyLee. All seemed likely to be dashed on the rocks below.

The ancient mariner had the help of gods to slay the obstacles he encountered. Not Buck. Not tonight. Apollo was packing it in for the night, surrendering his dominion to his sister, Artemis, who, as often as not, covered the night shift. Meanwhile she was slow to rise above the eastern ridge. Neither god was paying Buck any mind. He sat alone in the backseat of his Bentley. All those little abysses Frankie miraculously skirted along the route were nothing compared to the giant yawning abyss of nighttime blanketing the mountain wilderness.

✦

"You okay, boss?" Frankie could see Buck slumped down in the back seat. Buck didn't answer. Frankie steered the Bentley off the two-lane road onto a ramp leading to a scenic text stop. They entered a stark, rocky setting, illuminated by a full moon rising through a dip in the ridge. Their headlights panned the foreground and came to rest on a wooden sign: "Mariposa County Scenic Overlook." The back door of the limo opened and Buck doddered out. He looked dizzy. He steadied himself against a picnic table.

Frankie got out of the car but kept a safe distance.

"You all right there?" Frankie asked. There was no answer. "I only ask 'cuz…"

"I'm all right. Never better," Buck answered.

The fact that Buck hid a tube of wet wipes under his arm gave his objective away. The man was carsick and he didn't want the world to know.

"FYI, that sign says they're closed."

"What sign?" Buck turned and read it out loud, "Closed Dusk Until Dawn. Hmm! Well, can't be helped."

"Boss, we got to steer clear of trouble 'til Monday. Just sayin'."

"What's Monday again?"

"When you sign that deal."

"Not likely." Buck raised his forefinger in a hold-that-thought kind of gesture. "'Excuse me." He jogged unsteadily in search of a more private place, then quickly returned. "What was that?"

"Look like mama deer and baby deer," Chan said.

"You sure?" Buck retreated as far as the picnic table. "Do you think they'll charge us? It's not safe out here without a gun."

"A gun?" Frankie asked.

"Protection," Chan said.

"Can't help but feel a little vulnerable, can we, Chan?" Buck focused on his navigator, the one with the map, who was doing Tai Chi exercises beside the Bentley. "Meanwhile, it feels like we're going in circles."

"Stomach go in circle, car go straight," Chan answered in that non-judgmental tone that Frankie knew would stoke the flames of Buck's ire.

"I say we're lost," Buck said.

"When time of essence, you stick by Jimmy Chan."

"Yeah?" Buck held up his cell phone to see if there was reception. "Damn. And how old is that map?" Buck asked Chan. "You don't suppose there's not some Interstate that goes across these mountains?"

"No road 'cross Sierras here, big or small," Frankie said.

"Beside," Chan added, "pretty girl like BunnyLee, blonde hair, blue eye, tight short, drive yellow four-barrel muscle car? Girl like BunnyLee take scenic route."

"He's got a point there, boss."

"Who's the private eye here, him or me? This road is suicide. Every bend is a hairpin. What makes you think BunnyLee's any great shakes of a driver, either? With these cliffs along here, how do we know she hasn't just gone off the road and is now knee-deep in rattlesnakes? I imagine there are a few snakes around *here*, too."

"Expect BunnyLee can take care of herself," Frankie said.

"I'll be right back."

Frankie watched Buck lope away. He turned back to Chan, and he saw the cook slipping away in the other direction.

"And where you goin'?"

"Jimmy Chan patrol 'area of operation,'" Chan answered in his animated tone. He disappeared into the night.

Frankie sighed. He was alone—nothing to do but wait. He rubbed the picnic table with his finger to see whether it was clean, then sat. Truth be told, he was no more comfortable in the great outdoors than Buck. If there were deer around, what were the chances of mountain lions? What about bears? Aside from an occasional car passing on the road, they were alone in the wild. A picnic table seemed like an island of civilization in the primal gloom. There was a nice view of the waning light in the western sky, too far gone to give much comfort. The sun had set behind the coastal range and the colors of the sunset faded to gray. In the east, the light of the moon was backlighting the teeth of the intimidating Sierra.

He took a deep breath and collected his thoughts. He'd spent the last six years steering the famous Buck LeGrande clear of trouble and he was weary of it. Frankie was just hours away from Buck signing that contract, hours away from taking a giant step forward in his life, but he wasn't there yet. Whenever Buck was out in public there was potential for trouble. Even if the man himself was predictable, the public was not. Celebrity sightings brought out the worst in people. Women got giddy. Men got envious. Proximity to fame made people ask stupid things. "Are you in a movie right now? Is there a part in it for me?"

There was a widespread conception in America that you were only one chance encounter away from fame. As if fame was an American birthright. Factor into that uncertainty the detail that Buck was inebriated—he was liable to say or do impulsive things. With all that in mind, Frankie was content to sit here the whole night, mountain lions and bears be damned.

A green SUV pulled off the road into the parking lot. Its headlights came to rest on Frankie's back. He turned to see. A flashing red police light startled him.

"Freeze!" came the voice from a loudspeaker. "Put your hands up where I can see them!"

Years of harassment by the L.A.P.D. influenced Frankie's decision to follow these simple instructions unambiguously. He raised his hands high. As a Black man living in Los Angeles, Frankie had been stopped many times for DWB. The same officers who had cheered him on football Saturdays while playing with the UCLA Bruins would just as readily pull him over on his way home for Driving While Black.

A tall well-built Native American wearing the bright green uniform of the California State Fish and Game Commission got out of his truck.

"Is that your car?" he shouted.

"Yes, sir. No! That's my boss's car."

"Does your boss know you took it?"

"No! I mean yes! No! I didn't take it. We're together. He's with me."

"We don't get too many Bentleys around here. So when we do, the odds are it's a stolen car."

"He's over there by the scenic lookout."

"Scenic Overlook's closed, says so on the sign. Closes at dusk." The officer advanced to a safe distance. He rested his right hand on the butt of a holstered gun. "People don't drive up into these hills at night just to sightsee. Illegal marijuana growers, game poachers, meth cookers come in all shapes and colors, and they're wreaking havoc with the fragile alpine environment. So we can't be taking any chances."

Frankie knew that it wasn't going to do him much good to quibble with the officer, but when a man was carsick, you had to stop. He tried the voice of reason. "Road pretty narrow. No place to pull off. Lookin' for maybe a washroom…"

"You put a washroom in up here, next thing you know all kind of folks will stop, the kind of folks who don't give a damn about scenic overlooks, people who don't see beauty when it's staring them in the face…"

"Soon as he comes back, we'll be on our way."

"…the kind of folks who are in too much of a hurry."

"Yes, sir."

"Takes millions of years to form all this beauty, but not nearly so long to mess it up. You put in a restroom up here, then you just have people stopping to take a dump, swipe a roll of toilet paper, maybe scrawl some graffiti. Disrespectful is what it is. And who's going clean it up?"

"Shouldn't be too long, now…" Frankie assured the officer. He called to Buck, "Hey, boss!"

"This boss of yours, he wouldn't be doing anything disrespectful out there, would he?"

"No, sir. What with this twisty road, boss feelin' a bit woozy. We stop for some fresh air is all."

"Woozy is not a good thing."

"No, sir."

"Means you want to puke."

"You sure got a nice view here," Frankie said.

"You like it?" He pointed off into the distance. "See that

ridge silhouetted there? Those geologic domes are a classic form of granite exfoliation. The same phenomenon that formed Half Dome, Yosemite's most famous landmark."

"It's really somethin'," Frankie said. The sooner they got away from him, the better.

"My people are born from this granite. These mountains were their domain. They built sweat lodges up here. Butterflies come back here every year at this time! Mariposa in Spanish. They're said to be the spirits of my forebears. We hold a festival to honor them."

"Sounds real nice…"

"We get our share of pukers up here, too," the game warden added, coming back around to the order of business. "This boss of yours, he's not high on peyote is he?"

"No, sir. We're just an actor and his chauffeur out for a drive."

"It's no picnic arresting people high on peyote. Every year you find them up here, after dusk, running around howling at the moon. Guys, gals, you tell them you've got to bring them into the Ranger Station, and they can't find their clothes. Can't even remember if they were wearing any. You put them in the squad car and they're liable to start puking. Not what I'd call a religious experience."

"No, sir. And who's gonna clean it up?" Frankie said.

"Exactly right."

Jimmy Chan came trotting back to the clearing. He held the front of his loose-fitting sweatshirt out as a sling. It was full of acorns. The startled officer unsnapped his holster and held onto the butt of the gun.

"Lucky, lucky day. Jimmy Chan find bushel-full. Perfect ripe."

"Is this your boss?"

"No, sir. Chan. He's the cook."

"How many more you got running around?"

"Only us three. Jimmy Chan, Mr. LeGrande, me."

"Jimmy Chan ride shotgun."

"Oh, yeah? Stand over there next to him," the officer said to Chan "This boss of yours, he coming back soon?"

"Mr. Buck? He at scenic overlook. Tough time for Mr. Buck. He lost dog."

"He lost his dog or he's a lost dog?" The officer asked.

✦

Precision. This was what Jimmy Chan liked most about American officers of the law. Whether their uniforms were blue or bright green as in the case of a game warden. They pursued accuracy.

"Yes." Chan answered, highlighting the dualism of the question. "Which one?"

"Both. Boss lost dog and boss, lost dog." Chan explained, "Mr. Buck Top Dog!" he added for clarity.

"Lost his dog. What is that, some kind of euphemism?"

"No. Labradoodle." Chan had never heard of a euphemism. But then again, he had never heard of a Labradoodle before hooking up with Buck and BunnyLee.

"What do you have in your shirt?" the officer asked.

"Acorn."

"This is a protected wilderness. We've got laws against picking anything that's growing here. California preservation statutes."

"Jimmy Chan no pick. Acorns in trees too green. Better to choose from ground."

"You're saying you found them on the ground."

"Perfect ripe. Snap open, mash up, form acorn paste. Calm stomach. Grandfather Chan say happy general fight best with peaceful tummy."

"Interesting you should know that. There is a rock over here with hollows worn in it." He pointed at a large flat rock surface that appeared to be pockmarked. "You find them around these parts. My people carved these cavities out as a mortar. Then, using a stone in their hand as a pestle, they would pound the acorns into flour. What to a layperson is a pockmarked granite surface, to a Native American is a prep kitchen. My grandmother put acorn in her pheasant stuffing. Called it her secret ingredient. 'The seed of the oak, which touch the sky.' The problem we have here is...this area is a wildlife preserve. Like that sign up there says, 'Take only pictures. Leave only footprints.' So if you were to drive off with those acorns that would be a breach of the wildlife statute. I'd have to run you in."

"No, no, no, we eat right here. You want try?"

The California Fish and Game Warden shook his head.

+

Frankie saw Buck running back. As he ran his boss waved his hands frantically about his head.

"Yikes! The little bastards are everywhere!" Buck yelled.

"Mosquitoes?' Frankie asked.

"No! Bigger than mosquitoes! Jeezus!" Buck answered, swatting at tangible shadows.

"Bats?" the officer asked.

"No! Smaller than bats!" Buck yelled. "They're colored!"

"Colored?" Frankie asked. He had never liked that word.

"Butterflies." Jimmy Chan informed Buck.

"Damn!" Buck answered in a panic. "Do they bite? What am I saying? Of course they bite. Everything bites."

"Nuthin' to fear in butterflies, Boss," Frankie assured him.

"No? You sure? Phew. Thought I was seeing things. I haven't felt like this since I was a kid sneaking hooch on the back lot of Warner Brothers--"

"Boss, this here's an officer of the law," Frankie interrupted, recognizing that Buck was launching into a story while oblivious to the danger at hand.

Buck acknowledged the officer with a cursory wave. "Hey, how are you doin'?" And then back to Chan, Buck continued, "John Hough was directing this picture with me in a minor role as a hot-headed little kid who doesn't answer to nobody...It was my first picture with a leading part--"

Frankie interrupted again. "I was just explainin' to this *Officer* of the *Law* ..."

Buck held up a finger. "In a minute."

"...how we were leavin' on account of the fact that it's after dusk..."

"But I haven't finished my story, Frankie. Rex West and I scored a bottle of booze from one of the rigging grips and we started chug-a-lugging it behind the makeup trailer. Sidney was there, too. Anyway, Hough's on to us. Doesn't say anything, just quietly 'sidles' around back and busts the three of us red-handed. Then what do I go and do? I puke all over his boots. One of those thousand-dollar-a-pair hand-stitched lizard-skin types. The kind English blokes buy when they first come over. I think it was Hough. Might have been the assistant director. Doesn't matter. All

I remember was his boots were made of one of those endangered species. Anyway, it looked like we were going to be thrown off the picture, the three of us. But Rex, he turned things around. Told them we were doing sensory work to better understand our parts. Hough knew he was full of it, but he liked Rex's swagger. Taught me the ropes, Rex West did—opened my eyes to the bad-boy parts. Funny the things you remember." Buck paused while he ruminated over the memory. "That movie opened the door to me becoming a star. Anyway, lucky thing we pulled off the road when we did, Frankie. I was about to redecorate the Bentley."

"Lucky thing you don't get sick, eh boss?" Frankie said, making light of a situation that was causing the hair on the back of his neck to stand up. "Well, sir, end of story. Guess we gotta shove off. Nice to meet you, officer."

"Oh, I got sick, all right." Buck laughed. "All over those swarmin' butterflies!"

There was an awkward silence. Jimmy Chan looked at Frankie; Frankie looked at the officer, who stood stone-faced. Frankie wondered whether the man had heard Buck correctly.

"Which is nothing compared to the power of that Starbucks coffee," Buck continued. "Shame they don't have public toilets up here because I really stunk up the place. Glad I had those wet-wipes. Anyway, I feel a whole lot better now."

"Okay, that's it. Everybody into the squad car! Now!" the officer ordered.

"Wait a minute. Who are you?" Buck asked.

The officer flashed his six-point silver-and-gold State of California Department of Fish and Game Warden's badge. "Officer Brokenclaw, Fish and Game Commission," he stated succinctly. "You're busted."

Buck laughed "Fish and game?" Apparently the green uniform had him confused. "What are you, like, Ranger Smith from Yogi Bear?"

Frankie winced. In his experience, men with badges in the line of duty did not take kindly to being laughed at.

"And besides, I'm sorry, but what laws have we broken?" Buck asked.

"Desecrating a Native American monument. Two counts. Now move! Either you come peacefully, or I cuff you."

"Whoa! Wait a minute. I'm on your side. The L.A.P.D. even

gave me an honorary badge. Where is that thing, Frankie?"

"You had it framed."

"I thought we were going to leave it in the Bentley."

"It's on the wall in the den."

"Wardens are sworn California peace officers with the same law enforcement authority and general public safety responsibilities as the California Highway Patrol, police, and sheriff. And as a Native American myself, I also answer to my ancestors. Now hop to it!"

Jimmy Chan launched into his own brand of reason. "Mr. Buck world famous private eye, known all over prime time, a.k.a. Nick Derringer." Chan paused to let the gravity of this information sink in. "Nick Derringer solve all kind crime spree, keep world safe for Democracy. Has handprint in concrete sidewalk outside of Mann Chinese Theatre. Named All-American hero: baloney and cheese... foot long! Top sandwich on Cantor Deli menu. Is best buddies to Captain Kirk...Kermit the Frog..."

"Kermit the Frog?" The officer asked.

"Okay, enough of this, Chan!" Frankie said.

The officer pointed his finger at Buck. "Wait a minute! You were on *Sesame Street*."

"Here we go," Frankie said under his breath.

"Only that one time. That was my agent's idea. I assure you..."

"Man, I love that little green guy. What's he like?" the game warden asked.

Buck looked at Frankie as if to ask, is this guy joking?

"Kermit the Frog?" Buck asked. "He's a... puppet."

"Yeah, but is he nice?"

"Compared with other...puppets, I guess he was all right."

"Did you get his autograph?"

"Yeah, I think I've got that someplace." Buck said. "It's with that plaque in the den, isn't it Frankie. When was that, years ago? Didn't he die?"

"Kermit?! That was the voice of Kermit who died. Kermit didn't die!" the officer said, "Kermit's immortal."

"Thank you!" Buck said.

"Not like actors. They get old," Brokenclaw said.

"Somethin' to that, boss," Frankie said.

"Enough with the levity, Frankie," Buck said.

"Kermit the best," Chan said. "He and Mr. Buck sing duet," Chan added, broaching what Frankie knew to be one of Buck's sorest subjects.

Buck gave Chan a withering look.

"That's all water under the bridge, Chan," Frankie said.

He knew where this story was headed. He was with Buck the day it happened. Frankie had been hired by the studio to diffuse situations like this, but it was a tricky business when the cameras were rolling. An experience that famous people knew all too well and non-famous people were all too ignorant about was that the media treated its celebrities as fair game. Any day that the media could embarrass a celebrity in front of its voracious public was a pretty good day. Not that the good people of *Sesame Street* were aware of how humiliating it was for Buck to sing in public. Indeed, Buck's manager had actually agreed to the skit without consulting him. That decision, not coincidentally, coincided with his manager's last day on the job.

"They sprang that little stunt on me after the tape was rolling," Buck said. "Once the cameras are on, you've got no choice but to sing." Then he added, sarcastically, "Can't disappoint all the little kids out there in TV land."

"Has Anybody Seen My Gal?" Jimmy Chan said. He was a cultural sieve. Like it or not, the beauty of the internet was that all this stuff was out there, forever. Chan sang in the voice of Kermit, "Five foot two, eyes of blue, oh what those five feet could do--"

"Yeah, that's it," Frankie said, trying to make him stop. "That's the song."

"I remember that!" the officer said.

"You do?"

"Cootchie, cootchie, cootchie, coo... Has anybody seen my gal?" Chan sang.

"Yeah, we got it, Chan..." Buck said.

"Now you!" the officer ordered.

Buck gave the officer an astonished look. "Me what?"

"This is where you came in," the game warden said. He held his finger out like it was a gun.

"I'm not gonna...With all due respect, I make it a rule not to perform in public unless I'm under contract."

The officer tapped the butt of his pistol. Buck looked at the gun.

"You don't want to disappoint," the officer said.

"Maybe you want to make an exception just this one time, boss," Frankie said.

His heart clearly wasn't in it because Buck spoke the words. "Turned up nose, turned down hose. Never had another beau. Has anybody seen my gal?"

Jimmy Chan was really getting into it. He bounced as he sang, like Kermit, "Now if you run…into a…five-foot-two…covered with fur. Diamond ring…all those thing… Bet your life it not her…"

"Then you!" the officer directed Buck.

Buck sang, "Could she love, could she coo. Cootchie, cootchie, cootchie, coo…" Together, Buck and Jimmy Chan sang the finale. "Has anybody seen my gaaaaaal?"

Frankie clapped.

Jimmy Chan took a bow.

"Okay, not bad. Not like with Kermit, but not bad."

Frankie was waiting for Officer Brokenclaw to mention what happened next that day on the set with Kermit when, between takes, Buck was videotaped strangling the little green guy. The bootleg shot had been anonymously posted on YouTube earlier this year and the outrage it stirred up had derailed Buck's career. If the officer knew about the incident and had seen the outtake, he didn't bring it up.

Jimmy Chan filled the officer in on the noble purpose of their current outing. "Right now we on official business. Locate disappearing woman with little dog, very important to find. All evidence suggest she in this neck of woods. You see her?"

"My responsibility is conservation, but if she's in trouble…"

"She blonde hair, blue eye, maybe over five-two, nice bazoombas, girlfriend to Mr. Buck."

"You say she's a girlfriend. Has there been some sort of fight?"

"No, no, no. She girlfriend to Mr. Buck. We find her, make dinner plan."

"Oh, so you're traveling together."

"That's it. We just got a late start, didn't we Frankie?" Buck added.

"That's right, boss."

"We form a posse," Chan added.

"She lost her cell phone, otherwise we'd call," Frankie said.

"What kind of car was she driving?" the game warden asked.

"Yellow antique Mustang car," Chan said.

"That I might remember. I saw a car matching that description earlier this evening stopped at Jack's Gulf south of Mariposa…"

"Bingo!" Chan exclaimed.

"Filling the car with unleaded?" Buck asked.

"Which way we go?" Chan asked the officer.

"North."

"Pleased to be excused to find her?" Chan asked the officer.

"Not so fast. You're not getting out of here without filling out a ticket." The officer pulled a book of tickets from inside his uniform jacket. "You folks like professional wrestling?"

"Oh, yes, very much, big fan," Chan answered for all of them.

"What I have here is a book of tickets which not only get you into the stands, but give you a chance to win an autographed picture of Chief Tenaya from the Worldwide Wrestling League. Not too many Native Americans make it to primetime television, and Tenaya is a local hero, so we feel honored to get him. It's in lieu of the rodeo that was canceled this year on account of the fires. So now the County Fair and the Autumnal Pow Wow overlap the same night. Should be interesting. One night only, starts tonight at ten, at the Mariposa Fair Fairgrounds. It's for a good cause. They're twenty bucks apiece. I recommend you buy three, one each, for a total of sixty dollars." The officer nonchalantly indicated with his gun that this would be a bargain at twice the price.

"Autograph picture look real nice over the bar, Boss," Frankie said.

Buck was not about to get arrested in a dispute over sixty dollars. He pulled out three twenties and took the raffle tickets in exchange.

Chan tugged at Buck's sleeve.

"Jimmy Chan return acorn to ground. Mr. Buck to come help. Come now!"

"What?" Buck asked. "Frankie, you fill these raffles things out." Buck followed his cook. "What are you doing? Where are we going?"

+

Chan pushed Buck a safe distance away from the picnic table where the officer directed Frankie in the correct way to fill out the raffle tickets. Chan made a big show of spilling the acorns out onto the ground, then pulled Buck further into the shadows. He was anxious to show him the gun he had been hiding under the nuts.

"Tada! Model one nine zero dash B. Single action pistol!"

"Whoa! What the hell? Where'd you get that?"

Chan answered in his own version of a conspiratorial whisper. "Officer hide under front seat inside SUV. Jimmy Chan help himself, say, 'Whoa, lookie here. Just what doctor order to finish operation! You want to hold?"

"No! Not here! You could get us arrested!"

"You say you wish to have a gun."

"I did?"

"No? I put back?"

"Back? It's a little late for that. Just keep it hidden! And don't let Frankie see that thing, either!"

Jimmy Chan saluted his superior officer. "Jimmy Chan play supporting role to Nick Derringer."

CHAPTER 19

"ARE YOU SURE?" BunnyLee asked. "I always keep my credit cards paid up."

"I ran them both through twice. Look!" The desk clerk pointed at the flashing display with her index finger. "Transaction Denied. Sometimes they do that when there's unusual activity on the card."

"Hmm, okay, well hold on, I know I've got another one."

The desk clerk wore a silver ring inscribed with roan symbols on a hand that extended from the plush sleeve of a burgundy Buddhist monk's robe. Her gold nametag identified her as Shirley—a member of the spa staff whose team uniforms set the standard for new-age secular corporate piety. Her knowing smile reflected the contemplative tone of the establishment, which at the moment, BunnyLee found quite trying.

"Just to let you know, my shift was over ten minutes ago," Shirley said.

"Wait, wait! There is a third credit card in here somewhere."

BunnyLee was beginning to panic. It was dark in the open-air courtyard of the Reservation Spa. She was having trouble seeing under her dog into the recesses of her shoulder bag. She placed the bag on the sisal rug and bent over to look more carefully.

BunnyLee was sympathetic to the fact that Shirley had already logged out of the computer at the end of her shift and twice had to re-enter her security code. The charge card reader was uncommonly slow to reboot.

"Or you could pay cash."

"When I lost my phone the other day, I guess I lost my purse, too. It had all my money, receipts, everything."

"Maybe somebody found it and reported the cards missing."

"Why would somebody do that?"

"As a way to find you and return them to you."

"I guess that's possible. There is somebody looking for me. I'm pretty sure I don't want to see him right now. Wait a minute, hold on! I think I see it!"

A tall, stiff cowboy wearing a neck brace entered the courtyard from the interior of the resort. He approached the U-shaped kiosk from the opposite side of BunnyLee. He knocked on the counter to get the desk clerk's attention.

"Now what?" Shirley asked herself before recovering her composure. "Are you here for the Howling Workshop?"

"No, ma'am, but I'll certainly remember it for next time. Fact is, I should be in Mariposa, were it not for an unfortunate happenstance with my front wheel coming up lame and a lack of lug wrench to change it. In the meantime, if you could please direct me to a restaurant where a hungry cowboy can tie on the feedbag, I'd be much obliged. I figure that as long as I'm waiting for the wrecker, I might as well eat."

BunnyLee stood up. "Hey, did you call Jack's Gulf, before?" she asked.

The cowboy swung around. "Ouch!" He grabbed his neck.

"That was me that answered at the gas station," BunnyLee said, "Sorry if I startled you."

"No need for apologies. Happens all the time. People recognize me, think because they know me, I should know them. It's usually a simple case of misconception. Makes a fella jumpy, though."

"Why do you think we should know you?" the desk clerk asked.

"On account of me being readily recognizable."

"I've never seen you before."

"Lotta times it'll be your boyfriend that knows me first."

"Strike two, I don't have a 'boy' friend."

"Really?" the man asked. "A pretty lady like you?"

Judging from the grimace that followed his remark Bunny could see that this was not a desk clerk easily seduced by pedestrian flatteries.

"I meant no disrespect," the cowboy added. He reached into his pants pocket and pulled out a small plastic toy. He stood it on the counter. "Some folks'll be more apt to know me because of this."

"What is it?" the desk clerk asked.

"That's me. Austin Sway, The Dust Devil, rumored to have wrestled a twelve-hundred-pound bull to the ground with his bare hands. It's what we in the trade call a collectible Action Figure."

"That's you?" BunnyLee asked.

"People collect them?" the desk clerk asked.

"It's like some people collect stamps. Or girls collect dolls. Some people collect action figures. I carry them to give out as mementos. This one's particularly valuable because they only released a few of them."

"So you're not that famous," the desk clerk said.

"You could look at it that way, relatively speaking, but how many official action figures have you met in the flesh?"

"Good point!" BunnyLee said.

"You don't have a reservation?" the woman asked.

"No, ma'am, I don't. Just need to rustle up some grub..."

"Our kitchen's not set up to take cash. You need a voucher. Nobody gets served without a voucher. And you only get a voucher when you register." Shirley shrugged, looked at her computer with that calculated stoic smile. "I don't make the rules."

"How do I register?"

"You don't. Not without a reservation, and we're full up."

"I just took the last opening," BunnyLee said. "Oh, here, try this one."

BunnyLee handed her last credit card to the desk clerk who fed it into the card reader. BunnyLee studied the action figure. "What's with the big belt around its waist?" she asked.

"That belt signifies that I, along with my brother, were the Intra-Continental Middleweight Tag-Team Champions of the World," Austin explained, returning the figure to his pocket. "Which was a very high honor indeed."

"How come you're not wearing it now?" BunnyLee asked.

"First of all, it's not something you would wear in your everyday attire. And secondly," his tone darkened, "we lost that belt under grave circumstances."

"Is that how you hurt your neck?"

"No, that was a different incident entirely. See, a fella like me has got to be on the constant lookout. Can't even go into a bar without some guy trying to prove himself. And as for the gals..."

Austin turned his body around and scanned the room. "The gals are after something a little more personal than an autograph, if you catch my drift. Some gals stalk wrestlers the way men hunt big game. This here pulled muscle, this happened yesterday afternoon in Las Vegas as I was having lunch. One, or possibly two, ambushed me. They appeared to be working together. Let's just say that's why I stick to the back roads."

"Women," the desk clerk said.

"I'll say," Austin said.

"No, the word is women. We don't use a pejorative term like 'gal' to describe the female gender. We say women."

"Yes, ma'am."

"I'll give you one of my food vouchers if you want, just as soon as I get this credit card thing worked out," BunnyLee said.

"I'm afraid that's not going to happen either. This card just came back 'not activated.' It's a Puppy Passport. Have you never used it?"

"No. I wasn't planning to."

"So activate it. You just need to do it from your cell phone."

"But I don't have my phone. It's with my…this is like a nightmare!"

"Or, if you'd like to pay cash…"

"Four hundred dollars? I don't have that kind of money. Like I said, I lost my purse."

"You could try the Miner's Inn Motel in Mariposa."

"So what you're saying is, if she were to pay you the nominal sum of four hundred dollars, she'd get the vouchers and the room?" Austin asked.

"Teepee," the desk clerk said.

"Teepee?"

"People don't stay in rooms here. Just teepees," BunnyLee said, realizing as she said it how silly the idea might sound to anyone who wasn't familiar with the brochure.

"Okay, but anybody holding a voucher would get a meal?" Austin asked the desk clerk.

"Right."

"Then what do you say to me paying the full amount? I take the voucher and then this pretty gal, errr, woman, can take the room."

"Teepee."

"Teepee."

"You'd both have to register."

"Where do I sign?"

"Right there below her signature."

BunnyLee was flattered, but a bit cautious, "I don't know. I hardly know you. Did you really wrestle a twelve-hundred-pound steer to the ground?"

"No, ma'am, I did not," Austin answered as he signed the guest book. "I prefer my beef one pound at a time."

"I don't know how I can repay you."

"One, two, three, four hundred. There you go." Austin counted out his money in hundred-dollar bills and handed it over. "Givin' me a lift into town after dinner would go a long way," he said to BunnyLee.

"But my car..."

"That will be five hundred for a couple," the desk clerk said.

"Five hundred? People spend five hundred dollars to stay in a teepee?"

"It's the deluxe model."

"That's an expensive meal!" BunnyLee said.

"I'm sure it will be worth it," Austin answered. "Some problems you just need to throw money at." He handed Shirley another hundred. Now if you could direct me to that restaurant."

"You'll find it past the hot stone massage room across from the reflecting pool. They open at five a.m. sharp."

"A.M? What about tonight?"

"Tonight, we fast. Nobody enters the sweat lodge with food in their stomach. It's all in the brochure." The desk clerk handed Austin a tri-color pamphlet that underlined the highlights of the Howling Workshop Weekend, then turned to leave via an inside office.

"Wait a minute!" BunnyLee said, "What about the dog whisperer? Is he around tonight? My dog is sick."

"Most everybody's at the Mariposa Fair. I was due there half an hour ago."

An elderly Japanese man with a shaved head, dressed in a burgundy monk's robe similar to the desk clerk's robe, glided through the lobby area and stopped to show the desk clerk something.

"Look what I found on the Tranquility Trail!" He held out a silver cylindrical vessel. "It's got a dent here in the side, but otherwise, pretty cool, don't you think? It's like some sort of urn."

The monk turned to Austin for an opinion. "Do you think it's made on this planet or maybe it fell from outer space?"

Austin was not sure how to reply. The truth was, when he chucked Laredo's urn away, he never expected to see it again.

The monk pointed his roan-ringed index finger at him.

"Hey, I know you!"

"You do? Really?" the desk clerk asked.

"I certainly do. This is the guy who trampled the Serenity Garden," the monk said, adding, "after I spent all day raking it. And before that, I saw him take a leak on the Vesper Oak!"

"Pleased to make your acquaintance." Austin tipped his hat, then turned his body to address BunnyLee. "What do you say to me buying you dinner at the Mariposa Fair in exchange for a ride out of here?"

The monk and the desk clerk disappeared in a huff, possibly to find backup.

"But my car isn't running. I had to coast the last mile."

"What kind are you drivin'?"

"An old Mustang."

"What year?"

"'64 and a half. It stalled out by the road."

"Has it got a lug wrench?"

BunnyLee brightened. "Now you're talkin'!" She gathered up her unusable credit cards. She heard men approaching.

"I'm gonna check over here, Boss," came Frankie's distinctive voice.

"Uh, oh!" BunnyLee said to Austin.

Buck's chauffeur appeared out of the darkness and spotted her. "You might want to hide, BunnyLee."

"How'd you find me?"

"Car out by the road. Tried to drive by, but Chan, he saw it."

"I've got to find the dog whisperer!"

"BunnyLee, Buck, he's miffed. Says he stopped by your cabana last night. I'm not sure you owe him an apology, but…"

"For what?"

"He insists he saw the shadow of a man wearin' a Stetson."

"Frankie, there is no way…"

"Not sayin' it's any of my business." Frankie was looking straight at Austin's Stetson. "I don't know what to believe."

"You need to understand. My puppy is sick and she needs help.

I know I shouldn't have taken his car. I'll pay to have it repaired, whatever it takes, I'll make it right. But first, I have to find this dog whisperer!"

"Thought we had a deal. I give you the keys to Buck's Baby and in turn you say you'll put in a good word for me concerning his doing my TV pilot."

"And I will! I'll come back right away and straighten things out."

"We supposed to sign the deal on Monday!"

"I promise! But you have to believe me. This thing about there being a man in my room, that's his imagination getting the better of him."

"Frankie!" came Buck's voice out of the darkness.

BunnyLee scurried for cover behind the kiosk.

"I was not with some man!" she whispered.

BunnyLee crept into the shadows of the spa courtyard and made a run for it.

✢

"What's that? Who are you talking to?" Buck asked, as he entered the outdoor reception which was basically just a clearing in a redwood grove. Jimmy Chan was close behind. "What is this place?"

"Boss, you found your Mustang safe and sound. What say we head back and…"

"I don't care about the car."

Frankie studied his famous boss.

"Evening, gentlemen," the man in the Stetson said.

"The Dust Devil!" Jimmy Chan declared.

"What's that, Chan?" Buck asked.

"World famous wrestler!"

Frankie recognized Austin. "Oh, yeah."

Buck looked around. "Any sign of a desk clerk around this hotel?"

"She just stepped away," Austin said.

Buck looked Austin up and down. Frankie did too. Being of the same size and age, Frankie and Austin could have been teammates in the same defensive backfield.

"What's with your neck?" Buck asked.

"Strained it a bit. Must be getting old."

"Old? You've got to be ten years younger than me."

"What say I look around a bit, Boss?" Frankie said.

"You stay where you are! I don't want you tipping her off. You say the desk clerk's a gal?" Buck asked Austin.

"I wouldn't say 'gal'."

"I'm not checking in, just looking for one of the guests." Buck tapped the bell. "Could I get some service here?" Buck looked down at the guest register. "Hmm, what have we here? Aha! Frankie, come over here! I want you to see this!"

"What's that, boss?"

"Proof!" He pointed at the signatures. "Bunny Lee Welles and Puddles."

Frankie looked at the register and nodded. "I guess that's BunnyLee, all right."

"Yeah, but what about this other signature? 'Austin Sway.' I told you she's hooked up with some guy!"

Frankie looked at the signature and at the miniature figurine of The Dust Devil that stood on the counter next to it. He looked up at Austin who shook his head.

"I'm sure there's some other explanation. BunnyLee, she's a straight shooter." Frankie said.

"Can't ask for clearer evidence than this." Buck said.

"How is that, again?" Frankie asked.

"That she had a man over last night."

"Oh, golly, that's a tough one. Like I said before, I don't know what to believe."

"When did you say that?" Buck asked.

"Before, when I…I guess maybe I just thought it. Anyway, she sure took me in!"

"Damn! I really liked her," Buck said.

"Everybody did," Frankie said.

"Love her smile," Chan said to Austin. "Nice teeth!"

"The thing is, I really liked having her around," Buck said. "We had fun together. I don't want her to go."

"I had no problem drivin' her to auditions and whatnot. Easy company. She was just so nice. And up front."

"Well rounded up front," Chan said to Austin.

"I mean, I am certainly not in the position to dictate what she does or who she does it with," Buck said.

"Truth is, we don't rightly know who she is," Frankie said.

"Dial-a-Denture girl!" Chan said to Austin.

"Don't none of it add up.," Frankie said. "I mean, how can BunnyLee show up for tennis that first day unless somebody tip her off? Like how'd she know you needed a fourth? Maybe we just be happy we get the car back, Boss. Chalk BunnyLee up to experience. You go back to bein' yer old even-tempered self."

"Even-tempered. You mean like, sanguine?"

"That's a good word."

"But not an everyday word. I had to look it up. You went to college. Is that a word they tossed around in college, Frankie?"

"I suppose they did."

"Exactly! The point is, how does a fella like me know who to trust?"

"Is what I'm sayin'," Frankie said.

"Not like I have any claim to say what she should do with her life. But all this sneaking around behind my back...With Jadé, at least I was open about it. I feel like BunnyLee owes me an explanation."

"You and me both," Frankie said.

"A man in my position has got to be very careful. I really liked her, no question. Maybe even loved her."

Frankie glanced at Buck. Love was not a word his boss had ever used in reference to a lady friend. Buck stood there, arms folded across his chest, eyes cast at the ground, looking lost.

"Well liked all around," Chan said to Austin.

"Sounds like quite a lady," Austin said. "Now if you gentlemen will excuse me, I have a dinner engagement." He politely tipped his Stetson and walked out the same direction BunnyLee had fled.

"Very pleased to meet famous man!" Chan called after him.

"Okay, Frankie, give me the car keys!"

"Sure, Boss. Right here."

"Not to the Bentley, the Mustang."

"The keys to the Mustang? I must've left 'em..."

"You keep them on the same ring," Buck said. For Frankie to say otherwise would be to lie, and they both knew it.

"Well, I'll be damned!" was all that Frankie could muster.

"And you'd have me think she lifted the keys from Miguel. Four seasons I played the private eye. You take me for a novice? You're in cahoots with her! That's sedition, you know!"

"Boss, I swear I don't know nothin' 'bout all this."

"You're telling me you don't know the guy she's with?"

"Austin Sway, the Dust Devil!" Chan said.

"What? What did you say, Chan?" Buck asked. "Wait a minute! That's the guy?" Buck pointed at the colorful toy wrestler and took an involuntary step back. "The guy who just left? Whoa, he's big!"

"Wrestle twelve-hundred-pound bull to the ground with single hand!"

"Yikes!" Buck pointed a finger at Frankie. "I deserve some answers, here! I'm not going back without answers."

The desk clerk reappeared from her inner office. She had changed into a white paramedic's uniform.

"Are you here for the Howling Workshop?" she asked.

✦

Austin doubled back the way he'd come through the torch-lit Serenity Garden, ignoring the angry looks. He left a trail in the sand that any television sleuth could see. Austin continued back along the path to the entry road and caught up with BunnyLee. He took one handle of her shoulder bag with Puddles in it and together they raced to the abandoned Mustang.

They found the tire iron in the trunk and ran to Austin's Eldorado.

Austin untied the rope holding the mangled trunk closed. He fished around in the dark cavity for the jack. With the tire iron from Buck's Baby, they went at loosening the lugs. They were no pit crew. Between Austin's stiff neck and BunnyLee's lack of heft, it was some time before the car was standing on all fours again.

After the last lug was taut, Austin threw everything into the trunk and tied the lid down to the bumper. He paused to look at the moonlit landscape where he'd recently spread his brother's ashes. He shook his head and smiled because Laredo would have been rolling his eyes just about now at the looks of his current traveling companion and the jam Austin was sauntering into.

"My apologies for the fact that the top doesn't close," Austin said, once they were underway.

✦

BunnyLee wasn't about to say anything; another ragtop that didn't close was just another of today's many complications. But the more she studied the beat-up vehicle, the more she had to wonder. There was a suspicious looking hole in the center of the windshield and a second one in the glove box door.

"Those wouldn't be bullet holes, would they?" BunnyLee asked.

"Most likely, yes."

"There's another one embedded in the clock."

"Not to worry, it didn't work, anyway."

"Was it those women who are stalking you?"

"Oh no, friendly fire. Earlier in the day when I couldn't get the trunk latch to open a mechanic came along and shot it open. Shot this hole here in my neck brace, too. Fortunately, I wasn't wearing it at the time."

"My grandfather used to say there is more than one way to skin a rabbit."

"Mine would have been more crude."

"What about that big dent in the trunk?" she asked.

"That there," Austin said with an eye to the rearview mirror, "couldn't be helped."

BunnyLee hadn't felt the chill of the night air until they were safely under way. She held Puddles in her lap to stay warm. It was a day for traveling in antique convertibles, fun while the sun shone but cold on a September evening in the Sierra. The crisp air swirled around her exposed legs. She tied her sarong around her shoulders and head.

Austin fiddled with the climate control. He slid the lever from auto to bi-level to defrost with minimal effect.

"It's unlike me. I didn't think to bring a sweater," BunnyLee said. "After all the hot weather we've been having, I never thought about being cold."

"It's worse when it rains. There's a sweatshirt in the trunk, but what with those headlights behind us, I'd say it's not advisable to stop."

BunnyLee looked over her shoulder at the twisting road and saw the occasional bright lights of a car a few curves back.

"There is a very good chance that's your friends."

They drove for a moment in silence. Austin glanced over at her from time to time. BunnyLee tried to put on a brave face, but she was shivering.

He said, "You're welcome to sit closer if you'd like."

Austin lifted the center armrest to make room. She looked him over with her single-dimple smile.

"I don't bite." Austin assured her.

BunnyLee checked again to see whether they were being followed. "In for a dime, in for a dollar." She slid across the carmine leather seat, under his arm, and nestled into the warmth of his body. She felt like a rebel in a teen movie from her grandparents' generation.

"What's with this guy? He's an actor?"

"Buck? You didn't recognize him?"

"He wouldn't be that guy who embarrassed himself so bad on *Sesame Street?*"

"You saw that?'

"Who didn't?"

"I couldn't bring myself to download it. I mean, the guy's been so nice."

"After that duet they sang together, Kermit went to kiss him on the forehead and your buddy went for the jugular. The video was in slow motion, so that probably made it look more violent than it was."

"It's just so strange. I've known Buck a while and I haven't detected an ounce of a temper. I know he's steaming mad at me right now. I mean I feel bad for the guy. He worked his whole life to build a career and then one little thing like that changed everything. It's been months since that clip surfaced, and he still hasn't lived it down. He hasn't worked a day since."

"How long have you guys been dating?"

"We're not. I've been staying at his place for the last month."

"You're not dating, you're living together."

"Not with him." BunnyLee smiled. "In his guest cabana."

"Looks a bit more serious than you let on," Austin teased.

"Who are you, my dad?"

"Actually, I stuck around to listen. I think he used the term love, if I'm not mistaken."

"What? Referring to me?" BunnyLee stroked the top of her dog's head. Puddles raised her eyes and they shared a look of understanding.

"And I think you oughta know, he saw our signatures together on that guest register."

"That's not good."

"I was feelin' as antsy as a whore in church, if you'll pardon the expression. After what you and that other fella were sayin' about your being with a man in a Stetson, and what with me wearin' a Stetson."

"I had no right dragging you into this. I mean, I heard stories about out-of-work actors turning on people and it does make you think. Not that there is anything in his personality to accuse him of that! I guess I've just been so focused on my dog that I haven't considered his feelings, too."

"'Hell hath no fury like an actor scorned,' Wasn't that the line from Shakespeare?" Austin asked.

"I think the term is 'woman scorned!' and that would describe me. I hate the way I feel! My sister Lizette screamed at me over the phone when I finally admitted where I was. She was like, 'He's like the most eligible bachelor in Hollywood! I'd have jumped his bones so fast…' This from a devout Christian mother of three. My parents are super-conservative. Bad enough that I studied acting and then traveled the world alone. They would never condone me staying with a single man. I've been avoiding even being seen with him. I mean, in Hollywood? It's all so tawdry. Didn't help. I'm on the cover of *American Celebrity* this week despite my efforts to avoid the press."

In BunnyLee's experience while traveling abroad, strangers become confidantes in a matter of minutes. Spilling her heart out to Austin seemed natural, whereas it can take weeks in other instances when people are more guarded. Case in point: Buck LeGrande. It had taken him dating Jadé before BunnyLee stated anything close to her feelings for him.

"I mean he's been really great. The perfect host. He's just so much more experienced than I am. Maybe I should be okay with that. But it's just not me."

BunnyLee was getting sleepy after the long drive. She'd stayed up pretty late last night taking pictures of Puddles to upload. The fresh night air, the warmth of Austin's body, she was getting dreamy.

"My friends call me a serial monogamist. I can't be with more than one guy at a time. Basically, if you want to get technical, I've only had a couple of boyfriends, one sloppy relationship in high school, and the other I met in college. He's a stand-up comedian now. We hung with a crowd of actors trying to make it in 'The Biz.' Ted. I saw him at a wedding recently and he was okay but I kind of felt like I dodged a bullet. He's actually starting to make it, though. That's not to say that in four years I've been on the road I haven't had my share of passing fancies. Girls like me grow up with this notion that they are going to meet a great guy and settle down. In my mother's day, she had a choice between the boy next door and the boy down the street. And I think she would have been happy either way. Nowadays, relationships are a lot more complicated. There is a world of men to choose from. Or not. I could just as easily continue going it alone. I'm not good with decisions. Part of me just likes the idea of being part of a family. Part of me wants to be free."

BunnyLee looked up at Austin, who was busy watching the road. He smiled. "When it comes to settlin' down, I'm not the guy to consult."

"Don't get me wrong. I like men. I like being with them. And I really like Buck. A lot. It's just so improbable. Why me? The first thing I thought when he offered his guest cabana was that it was a ploy. You know Hollywood: the casting couch. Many a young actress has met plenty of those guys, myself included. But why would he go to all that trouble? Women throw themselves at him. Why waste a month on me?"

"Why not?"

"Because he's famous! Oh, man, I feel so bad. I've been really punishing him. I mean, the guy's been eating health food because of me and not complaining. What is wrong with me? He'd be so much better off if he'd never met me." She sat in silence for a while. "Meanwhile, it is really nice to be out on the road again." A coyote trotted across the road, its red eyes flaring in their headlights.

"It has its advantages and disadvantages."

"You meet the best people when you're traveling alone, so you're never alone, even trekking in the Himalayas and mountain biking through Myanmar to Cambodia. Everywhere you go people have their own beliefs and philosophies. They have their favorite deities. I never encountered any trouble. In India, the men would always assure me 'you are safe in my village, but you mustn't trust the men in the next village. I know them, they are not good men.' In the next village, it was the same story. 'Me you can trust, but in the next town, those men, I know them. They are not to be trusted.' On and on from town to town, country to country. In my experience, once a man becomes your protector, you're safe with him."

"You think you're safe with me?"

"Unless my radar's broken. And that neck brace is a ruse."

"No. The truth is, I'm in worse shape than my car."

"I'm sorry to hear that."

"It happens to the best of us. I'm in a business better suited to youngsters. Cute dog!"

"Thanks. Buck gave her to me."

"Nice. I guess. Who gives someone a dog?"

"Yeah, I know, right? Out of the blue, such an odd gift. It was so *not* me! I'm the girl who pulled up the tent stakes and headed off to Asia. I mean, hello! It was my birthday. He offered to take me out, but like I said to him, it's just so much easier to dine in. He planned this nice evening, just the two of us, candlelight, the most expensive bubbly. I was thinking that some simple earrings would have been a nice gift. Even a tasteful undergarment would have at least signaled his intentions. Then I thought I heard a dog yelp. I was totally surprised. It was love at first sight. I got so emotional. It was like Buck knew something about me that I didn't know. That's what's so amazing about this guy. Somehow he knew I would love this dog. And strange. A dog is about commitment. A dog is about settling down. A dog is about being in one place. Meanwhile, I know people who hitchhiked through Southeast Asia with their dogs. I met a Canadian girl who adopted a young pup when she was riding her bike through Thailand. He rode in a basket clamped to the handlebars. You'd think that having an animal would be such an encumbrance, but it didn't cramp her style."

"And here you are, hitching a ride with your dog."

"Exactly. I'd actually begun to think he wasn't interested in me. The night he gave me Puddles, I was his for the taking. I was like, 'Here I am, come and get me.' but something stopped him. He's been with women younger than me, so that wasn't it."

"I get it. I recently met a woman, a bartender in a backwater establishment. Kat. There was something about that woman where you know that if you hang your hat on her four-poster bed, that hat is going to hang there for many a night to come. Like being offered a ride home. You long for it."

"A ride home. I like that."

"Unfortunately, show business does not permit such

indulgences of the heart. You arrive at forks in the trail and never know whether you're taking the right turn. But on you trudge seeking further fame and glory. It gets old."

"That's it!" BunnyLee sat up and looked Austin in the eye. "We were long past the one-night stand. Crossing the line for us would mean a long-term commitment. Neither of us was prepared to make the move. We're at a standoff." BunnyLee sat back and thought for a moment. "One thing is for darned sure, there is no way I can stay in that cabana any longer; it's either cross the yard into the main house or hit the road, Jack."

"And don't come back."

BunnyLee watched the road as Austin carefully navigated the steep winding decline.

"So, do you love him?" Austin asked.

"Yeah. I mean, I don't know. It's just so darned complicated. I'm not sure what I feel."

He gave her a look. "But yeah means yeah."

"Yeah, I know."

Crossing a bridge across a steep gully, they approached a desolate intersection. A pickup truck with a camper was stopped. Austin had to steer around it. A cellphone illuminated the faces of two women who were studying it.

"Damn!" Austin uttered under his breath.

"Oh my God, it's the women from the gas station!" BunnyLee said as they slowed to make the turn. BunnyLee waved, "Hi!"

"No, don't!" Austin warned, but it was too late.

The driver looked up and yelled in surprise, "Hey!"

Austin floored it. Six of the eight cylinders answered the call to action. The rear tires burned the pavement as they spun through the turn. He grabbed the wheel with both hands.

BunnyLee sat up. She put Puddles on the floor between her legs, then felt around in the dark to clip her seat belt. She looked at Austin.

Austin shrugged. "I guess we're even."

"How so?"

"Those are the women who are stalking me," he said. "Now we've got two carloads of people behind us, each thinking you and I have hooked up. Strange how they always seem to know where I am."

+

Frankie slowed the Bentley and yielded for the pink Ford Ranger as it pulled out in front of them. Frankie wasn't about to pass on this steep winding road descending toward Mariposa even though the man in the back seat was prodding him to do just that.

A few miles further down the road, a colorful Ferris wheel appeared as a beacon of trouble in the valley ahead amid the lights of the Mariposa Fair. Cars were parked along the road for a mile. Frankie didn't feel in any hurry to get to that fair and was wary when they pulled up to the parking lot behind the pink camper.

"You're in luck. There are just two spots left," the attendant said.

Buck lowered his tinted window and spoke from the backseat. "Excuse me. Where is the VIP parking?"

The man was slow to answer, then laughed at what he apparently took to be a joke.

To Frankie's way of thinking, Buck was arriving at a small-town county fair in a Bentley with his Black bodyguard at the wheel and his private Chinese cook riding shotgun. It seemed unwise to draw further attention by asking for preferential parking.

"What's with the badge?" Buck asked the octogenarian attendant.

"I'm a deputy sheriff, if you can believe that. The young folks are all out at the fire."

In his *The Return of Malibu Man* script Frankie had changed the character of Nick Derringer. The way he'd written him, the newly reconceived private eye had an over-abundance of self-importance; he was a legend in his own mind, forever over-stepping, like an arrogant poker player showing his hand. He was the lame gunslinger who shoots from the hip and rarely hits his mark. What Frankie was witnessing before his very eyes was Buck LeGrande emulating this new character.

No sooner had Buck rolled down his window than the driver of the pink Ford Ranger pickup jumped out of her truck and confronted him.

As Buck's longtime bodyguard, Frankie should have been quicker to respond to the woman's aggressiveness. But the author in him held back.

"Hey, yer Buck LeGrande, ain't you?" was the first question the woman asked, and as first questions go, it was a softball. Not so the second.

"Is it true yer aimin' at whackin' yer two-timin' girlfriend BunnyLee? She's hooked up with Austin Sway, y'know. Are you here to even the score?"

"What?" Buck LeGrande stammered.

From Frankie's perspective a simple 'no' would have sufficed. Buck was clearly caught off guard.

"None of your business," was Buck's answer.

The man was clearly shooting from the hip.

The deputy sheriff seemed taken aback. Frankie was out of the car and stepping between the woman and the car, but the damage was already done; the seeds of doubt were sown.

"All right now, we don't want any trouble here tonight," the deputy sheriff said.

"Mr. LeGrande is just here to enjoy the festivities, Officer."

"Don't pay her any mind," a younger woman yelled from the truck. "We're just a couple of fans, officer, comin' to a country fair."

CHAPTER 20

THE MIDWAY WAS in full swing. Lines had formed for the Tunnel of Love and the Rocket. Smaller tykes tugged their parents toward the Tea Cups. Young lovers plied their skills at Ring Toss and pitched ping-pong balls into empty fish bowls in pursuit of plush toys and glory.

A news crew from Los Angeles interviewed a paramedic in front of one of the carnival rides. Jack knew a lot of these men and women from the firehouse, and he was rooting for them in their attempt to set a world record for revolutions on the Tilt-a-Whirl.

As the featured hometown contestant in tonight's celebrity wrestling match, Jack was distressed about being late. After he'd tightened the last clamp on Kayla and Tammy's muffler, he raced home to shower and change. The parking lot at the fairgrounds was full, further delaying his arrival. Then his friend Brokenclaw texted to say that their headlining performer, Chief Tenaya, had not shown up.

Jack zigzagged through the crowd. He had an eye out for the famous Native American chief, but everywhere he looked there were Native Americans dressed in full ceremonial dress.

He only glanced into the 4-H Pavilion; there was no time to socialize with the young bakers, needlepoint contestants, and dog trainers who would be offended if he didn't pause to admire their blue ribbons. He even took a jog around the animal pavilions where prized livestock were displayed.

Up the hill the entrance to the rodeo arena was decorated

with a totem and prayer sticks. The insistent sound of percussive drums emanated from the arena where the Autumnal Pow Wow was building to its climax. For a moment Jack didn't recognize Brokenclaw because he, too, was wearing a headdress. It was his body language that gave him away. The fish and game warden paced nervously. Theirs was the main event. Much was riding on the success of tonight's upcoming festivities. He'd sold a good number of tickets for a noble cause, and the thought of having to refund the ticket price was something that neither of them wanted to think about. "No good deed goes unpunished," Jack muttered to himself.

"Any sign of Tenaya?" the officer asked.

"I looked everywhere! How much time do we have?"

"There's the opening ceremony and open-saddle tribute, the barrel race, then the crowning of the Queen. That buys us some time. All I can do is stall things as long as I can. Check the food concessions again, maybe he stopped for a snack. I'll meet you around by the rodeo holding area."

Jack jogged back into the thick of things toward the cotton candy and zeppole wagons. He looked in the beer tent where he was met by jeers and catcalls. "Good luck, Jack!" and "Better you than us!" were some of the printable statements of encouragement yelled his way. There was so much going on he hadn't given it much thought, but the reality was sobering. His name was on the ticket below Chief Tenaya; within the hour he was to appear center stage with a real pro. While he had finished All State in high school wrestling and held a letter for gymnastics, taking on a professional like Chief Tenaya was beginning to feel like he was way out of his league.

Jack checked out the line at the sausage and pepper stand. He spotted BunnyLee standing in the shadows talking with a man in colorful wrestling tights, silver cowboy boots, and a western shirt. The man's cowboy hat was red, white and blue, as was his multicolored cape, tied delicately around a neck brace. On any other day, the man would have looked out of place dressed as he was, but in this carnival setting he blended right in.

The two were eating acorn dogs, a new cuisine choice introduced this year in commemoration of this being the first time the county fair shared a double-billing with an Indian powwow. A common hotdog on a stick was battered with indigenous acorn flour and dipped in boiling oil. Jack was dying to try one.

BunnyLee waved to him.

"Now I owe you for dinner, too," she was saying to the man as Jack approached.

"Don't mention it," was the man's reply. He fed a small bite of his acorn dog to Puddles, and BunnyLee's dog responded in kind with a lick to the man's face.

"Did you get to The Reservation all right?" Jack asked BunnyLee.

"Yeah. It was just where you said."

"I passed your car on my way over, back there at the turnoff. How are those? Good?" Jack asked, pointing at the food.

"Yeah, very good," BunnyLee said.

"Long line to get one," Jack observed.

"You want a taste?" BunnyLee asked.

"Sure!"

"Here, you can have the rest of mine," her acquaintance said, handing his stick to Jack. "I already ate two."

"Oh, sorry, this is Austin. Austin, this is Jack. I got to The Reservation okay, but the dog whisperer wasn't in. They said he's somewhere here tonight. So I've just got to hope that I can find him. Oh, and Austin is the guy who called about the flat tire this afternoon. Isn't that a coincidence?"

"Pleased to meet you. When I went by, only BunnyLee's car was there. I figured you got the tire changed."

"Yep, thanks to my rescuer, here."

"You haven't by any chance seen an Indian in full headdress?" Jack asked.

"You mean like half the people here?" BunnyLee asked.

"Yeah, I know, right? But this one in particular is supposed to be performing with me in the arena, tonight."

"Oh, yeah? Are you going up to the arena?" Austin asked. "I'll walk with you."

"Sure, I could show you the way."

"Oh, I know the way. I used to perform here in my rodeo days."

"You did? But the rodeo's cancelled this year."

"Shame about that." Austin pulled his cell phone from his shirt pocket and checked his texts. "I need to find the Master of Ceremonies, name of Officer Brokenclaw."

"He's a friend of mine. I guess I can take you there. I don't know what else to do."

BunnyLee held back.

"I think I'll just ask around in that animal pavilion and see if anybody knows the dog whisperer."

"The 4-H Club has an exhibition on dog training. You should check that out, too," Jack said.

"Thanks, I will. I guess this is where we go our separate ways. I wish I could repay you somehow," BunnyLee told Austin.

"You got me here in time, so I get to keep my job a little bit longer. I have you to thank for that. Come by the arena after the show and I'll give you a ride back to The Reservation."

BunnyLee stood on her tiptoes to kiss Austin goodbye.

+

From across the Midway, a concession stand had a window on both sides where the curious could watch a deep-fat cauldron turn liquid dough into funnel cakes. Buck and his posse peered through the display. They watched as BunnyLee conversed with her two athletic friends.

"The Dust Devil!" Jimmy Chan said at the sight of this television hero.

"This is his idea of a date?" was all that Buck had to say.

Frankie just shook his head.

The simple fact that Buck had been watching BunnyLee and Austin through the window of a funnel cake machine might have explained his sudden relapse into nausea. The overwhelming smell of sugar and dough oozing in a bubbling vat of lard could turn anyone's stomach, especially one who had already been sick once today. But that wasn't what had Buck upset. No. The cause of Buck's torment was clear and undeniable. What Buck saw through the funnel cake glass was BunnyLee kissing another man, and the sight of it made him suffer. It was a feeling brought on by self-doubt and metaphysical anguish. He realized what Sartre had been talking about. Nausea was indeed an emotion, and it should be given its right and proper place at the bottom of any compendium of loathsome emotions. In a word, the overriding feeling Buck felt was Despair.

In all fairness, the kiss had only landed on the wrestler's cheek, which, all in all, was a rather benign location for a kiss of any kind to land. It could have been worse. Given the alternative kiss locations, say on the neck or on the ear or on the mouth, to a neutral observer a kiss on the cheek could have been hailed as being as bland a location as one could have hoped for.

The world-famous wrestler was wearing a ten-gallon hat. Sure, the man's cowboy hat was red, white and blue, but the one he had worn earlier was standard issue. Austin appeared to have cornered the market on Stetsons. Buck's worst fears about the shadow on the cabana wall the night before had been realized. In his quest to unmask the man in the ten-gallon hat, Buck had encountered the archetypical cowboy.

Buck felt chastened. His ego was as malleable as uncooked dough just before it entered the bubbling cauldron. His hunch had led him to the truth and the truth wasn't pretty. The fact that BunnyLee was enjoying such a simple date spoke for itself. All this time he had been attempting to wow her with his fame and celebrity, the finest this, the grandest that. The evidence unfolding before him was that BunnyLee was just a simple girl with simple tastes. Self-doubt was consuming him. The possibility that she was a grifter trying to charm him out of his money now seemed a polar opposite of the truth. She was standing with a real man, the one thing at this moment Buck felt least capable of being. His deepest fear was on display before him, that BunnyLee had not been attracted to him at all, but rather to the television character he had played. In essence, BunnyLee was the one who had been duped. His celebrity had duped her. He was not a good actor. He was not an artist. The evidence was right before his eyes. BunnyLee had chosen a man of action over him.

The character Nick Derringer would have stepped out of his hiding place and confronted the secret lovers with one of his trademark quips, but Buck felt diminished by the whole affair. He was a mere shell of the man he wanted to be. The last thing he wanted was to be found lurking in the shadows, spying on BunnyLee. He would sooner walk away, defeated, than step into the light and confront her now. As an old cowboy stuntman had once told him, "No sense in digging for water under the outhouse."

"Okay, we follow him!" Buck said to his cohorts as Austin and Jack headed off together in the direction of the rodeo ring.

"But, Boss, we come all this way. What say we say hello to her?"

"Fat chance, Frankie boy," Buck answered in as strong a tone as he could muster. "We're following the wrestler. I want to know what he's up to," he said, making his best effort to save face.

The three men followed Austin and Jack as they made their way to the arena.

+

A few steps behind Buck LeGrande and his comrades, Kayla and Tammy followed the crowd up the midway toward the arena.

"You're sure the schedule said Austin?" Kayla asked her mother. "'Cause there ain't nuthin' 'bout him here on this ticket."

Kayla looked like a million bucks. A lot of men noticed her as she passed. She returned no one's gaze. Kayla had her eye focused intently on the immediate future.

"If Chief Tenaya is here," her mother said, "then Austin Sway cannot be far behind. You know that they are mortal enemies. We may be seein' history in the makin'."

"Mama, I don't think you should have told that actor about our havin' seen his girl with Austin."

"I had to say somethin'!"

"There is no tellin' what he might do."

"Meeting him there in the flesh, I mean, how often do you get to talk to someone of his caliber? That's just what come out."

CHAPTER 21

"HEY, ISN'T THAT the Fish and Game Officer?" Buck asked.

Buck, Chan and Frankie crouched low behind a hay wagon outside the holding area. They watched Officer Brokenclaw in a heated discussion with an extremely short man in a striped referee's shirt.

Austin and Jack stopped at a safe distance so as not to interfere in the dispute.

"Jeezus! I can't frickin' believe it!" Officer Brokenclaw said to the referee. "I ordered an Indian to wrestle and you sent us a cowboy?"

Austin joined the conversation. "I'm going to make a wild guess here and say that I fit that description."

The officer was incredulous. He was clearly at the boiling point.

"Hey, Brother," the striped-shirted man said to Austin.

✦

"I didn't expect to see you here, Eddie."

"Didn't you read the email?"

"Just tell me what's going on!"

"I come up with the equipment truck. Vic asked me to sort things out."

"Sort what out?"

"Since Tenaya couldn't make it, he sent you."

"He told me I was to make a celebrity appearance. He didn't say a thing about a performance."

"You ain't read none of my emails, did you? That's all right. You're here," Big Eddie said in a tone of underappreciated martyrdom. "I figgered you got lost on some back road on yer way."

"How would you figure that?"

"Figger what?"

"About what route I was taking."

"It's called pairing."

Big Eddie was a short drink of water. More like a sip. He had been recruited years before as comic relief to manage the career of Andre the Giant, one of the largest men to ever walk this earth and one of the most beloved wrestlers to ever enter the ring. The two even wrestled tag team on occasion. Andre's legs were like giant tree trunks that the nimble Eddie would dart between for cover. When Andre's health problems interceded with fate and after his untimely death, Big Eddie's career languished backstage. He filled in as a scout in the WWL and from time to time as a referee. He was the one who discovered the Sway Boys.

"Do you have some technology wherein you happen to know where I am at any given moment?" Austin asked his producer.

"It's free. Comes with your smart phone. You just gotta know what app to download. So when you lose your phone, somebody can find it."

"I didn't lose my phone."

"You could have. I'm just lookin' out for you, Austin. This is what family does."

"This is not family. Don't call me brother!"

Big Eddie shrugged.

Austin eased closer to where Eddie stood and stared down at the short referee, about three feet down.

"You wouldn't happened to have 'paired' me with somebody else, now would you, 'brother?'"

"You mean with Vic? You know I would never..."

"No, I don't mean with Vic. I mean with a particular pair of ladies who have been tailing me ever since you got me this phone."

"I'm sure I wouldn't know anything about that."

"Yeah? You're sure? It's a coincidence that these women happen to know where I am at any given hour of the day?"

Officer Brokenclaw stepped between the two. "Gentlemen, we have a show to put on. And I have some of my own questions I'd like answered."

"Fair enough, but this discussion isn't over, Eddie," Austin warned. He turned his attention to the man wearing the feather headdress. "How do you do? Austin Sway at your service."

The officer was slow to respond. "We paid for an Indian."

"Hey, wait a minute! I just figured out who you are!" Jack said to Austin.

Austin took a step back and sized Jack up.

"I met some folks today who are looking for you!" Jack said.

"Three men?"

"Two women."

"I don't know which is worse. And my producer, Big Eddie, claims to know nothing about that."

Austin looked around. He felt vulnerable. If this had been a normal venue, he would have disappeared into the bowels of the arena by now, protected by security personnel stationed at all backstage entrances. Security at a country rodeo ring was far more porous, verging on leaky.

"Listen," Brokenclaw said, "this is a big problem. I've got a full house in there expecting to see a wrestling match between the most famous Indian wrestler of our day and a cowboy. Having two cowboys wrestling misses the point of the evening entirely. Chief Tenaya is something of a local favorite in these parts. My friend Jack has been good enough to volunteer to go a few rounds with him. He was State Champ in his weight class back in High School..."

"Professional wrestling differs from your varsity type," Austin cautioned.

"He's up to the task."

"Of that I am sure. Let's just get one thing clear," Austin said. "There is the big difference between professional wrestling and the garden variety of which you and Jack here are familiar. I know they say the wrestler named Chief Tenaya and I are mortal enemies. As Big Eddie here can attest, nothing could be farther from the truth. We travel together. We work out together. The last thing either one of us wants to see is the other one get hurt. It is paramount.

"Guys like me are on the road three hundred and sixty days a year," Austin went on. "We have got to be on our guard every second. A little injury can be a career-ender. When a knee goes south, you can still favor the other leg. Same thing with the elbow. But with the neck, the good Lord only gave me the one. Which is a round-about way of saying that I am feeling a little too frail to be going around with anybody, especially someone in as good condition as our friend Jack here, no matter what the cause."

"It's a benefit for retired rodeo performers down on their luck."

"My dad was a rodeo announcer...since retired," Austin said.

"We've sold over nine hundred tickets. It would be a shame to give it back," Brokenclaw said.

"They all could use our help," Jack said.

"Well, you've got me there."

"Unfortunately, this was billed as a match between a cowboy and an Indian." Brokenclaw continued. "It's all in good fun, political satire if you will, but the folks here want to see the Indian win one for a change."

"I see the problem. The truth of the matter is that from time to time I am asked to make a celebrity appearance. And I am usually happy to oblige for a good cause. So when Big Eddie informed me of this booking today, I drove straight up. Luckily I was in these parts anyway on a matter of personal business."

"But what am I going to do with two cowboys?"

"Allow me to fill you in on a little-known fact about Chief Tenaya. Contrary to popular belief. Chief Tenaya is neither an Indian nor a chief.

"His real name is Alan, even though everyone knows him as Max. He's a Jew from Sheepshead Bay, Brooklyn. He trained as a social worker until he discovered his calling. I happen to know for a fact that at this very moment Chief Tenaya is back in New York for a wedding of the shotgun variety." Austin held up his hand to discourage interruption. "Now I know that this trickery might come as a surprise, but believe you me, in the world of show business, not unlike politics, very little that meets the eye is truthful. Long story short, for every problem there is a solution. I propose that if you would lend Jack your ceremonial headdress, with the help of a little makeup no one will be any the wiser."

"You want me to play Chief Tenaya?" Jack asked.

"Then when I enter the arena, it will be like getting two for the price of one."

"I don't know about that," Jack said.

"The crowd gets what they paid for with a little added surprise. Everybody likes a surprise."

"SURPRISE!" a woman yelled from right behind him.

Austin spun around, re-pulling his neck for what seemed like the umpteenth time today.

"Bet you didn't expect to see us!" the older one said.

"Ow! You again! Please stay away from me!"

"You remember us?" she asked.

"You are stalking me!"

"Now, Austin, I have never been no trouble. I have left you alone..."

"I don't know who you are, but..."

"I'm Tammy and this here is Kayla. Ain't she somethin'?"

"I'm the one been sending Christmas greetings, and birthday greetings, and postcard greetings." Kayla said. "Not sure if you ever got the chance to read any of 'em."

"I've been receiving letters asking me about making babies, if that's what you mean. Letters with little hearts dotting the 'i's?"

"I just thought you might want more than one, that's all," Kayla said. "I never meant disrespect..."

"Hi, Kayla."

"Jack!"

"Just look at her!" Tammy said to Austin, "Ain't she the cat's meow?"

"Now, lady..."

"Tammy."

"If you are implying that there is some past history between us..."

"The National Finals Rodeo, Las Vegas, eighteen years ago. I discovered you."

"If I remember correctly, it was Big Eddie here who..."

"You and yer twin lost at blackjack."

"That, I might remember."

"It was me, Tammy James, the blackjack dealer, who come to the rescue."

"There is a lot about that evening I don't recall."

"It was a whole weekend, Austin. I hold no grudge."

"*You* hold no grudge?" Austin stared at her. "I don't know what shenanigans you concocted..."

"There was no funny business," Tammy said, "Hardly any. But when the Lord deals you a pair of aces, you double down. I told my mama, to hell with them sperm banks, I want to know the specimen in action. And look what become of you! You two became stars!"

"What, you used us like some kind of 4H project?"

"No!" Tammy looked around. All eyes were on her. "Okay, but that bein' said, I never ever woulda asked two teenage boys to man-up and do that fatherly thing. I never asked you for nuthin' after. I got everything I ever wanted."

"And what about her?" Austin asked, referring to Kayla.

"Well, now, with Kayla, that's a different story. She got every right to want somethin'. She's yer kin."

"Okay, I think this has gone far enough!"

"She's your spittin' image, Austin. Just look at them eyes. Ain't she somethin'?"

Austin looked into Kayla's green eyes. He had to admit that they did look like Laredo's, which, by default, meant they looked like his.

"She might be Laredo's."

"The odds is fifty-fifty. But now that Laredo is gone, any way you slice it, Kayla's the only kin you got."

"The good Lord willing, I have still got my papa. I'll admit when we were young we were full of spunk, messing with trouble. But I never did want a child. I mean, this is no life for raising kids. What do you want?"

Kayla waved to Big Eddie, who was busy ignoring everything that was going on.

"Hi, Uncle Eddie!"

Austin turned and stared at the world's shortest referee. "*Uncle* Eddie?"

"That's yer uncle?" Jack asked.

"Uh huh." Eddie turned to address Austin, "Which makes me your brother-in-law, brother."

"Oh, sweet Jesus, this just keeps getting worse and worse."

"She wants to be on TV!" Tammy said, "She wants people to know her name. Like when she walks down the street, or into the Golden Nugget where we first spied you yesterday. Or not just Golden Nugget, but all the fancy places. She wants folks to nudge each other and say, 'Hey, we seen that girl on Worldwide Wrestling.' to stop and stare and say she's ever' bit as purdy in real life as on her show. And twice as nice! And not only that, but Austin Sway is her dad. Plain and simple, she wants to be Kayla Sway!"

Austin looked at the girl. Damned if she didn't look like his dearly departed mother.

"Kayla, I have got to tell you. This wrestling game, it is a tough row to hoe. I am on my last days with the circuit. Just look at me, I am a mess. I am hanging on by a thread. There is no way that you can appear beside me, daughter or not. No wrestler in my position would appear with a daughter full grown. Look, I feel terrible. But those are the hard facts."

Kayla stepped away from Jack and looked Austin straight in the eye. Father and daughter, they were nearly the same height.

"It's okay, I'm just glad to meet you."

Kayla held out her hand.

Austin awkwardly took it.

"I just want you to know you aren't alone in this world. Yer brother was the greatest of the greats. I am sorry for yer loss."

That was below the belt. It caught Austin off guard. He could go many rounds with many a wily acrobat, but a kind word toward Laredo was enough to knock him down for the count. Austin was a man of many words, and he had coined many a long-winded statement about his twin brother in his head, but he would choke on those words if he tried to put voice to them. One lone tear fell to his cheek. He was truly half a man without his mirror twin.

"In the meantime, I have got to go into that arena and make a celebrity appearance," he said. "If you wait around until after the show, I would be happy to know you better. I do feel honored to make your acquaintance, young lady. But whether you are Laredo's or mine, the cold reality is that I have no more right to call you my daughter than a stranger. It is your mother that made you what you are."

"Well, sure, but not wholly. You've always been there for me. You've been standing up for all that is right in this world for as long as I know. All I had do when I was sad or low or felt no one in this world got me, all I had do was turn on wrestling and you were there. Even after you went from baby-face to a heel, I always knew in my heart of hearts you were on the side of good."

"Then I would ask you to come in as my guests and root for me now."

"She can do more'n that," Big Eddie piped in. "She can help me get this fella into costume. I've got a show to stage-manage here!"

Brokenclaw closed the gate to the holding area with a clang and joined the others as they made their way down to the rodeo performer entrance where Big Eddie's equipment truck was parked.

"All this time you had me thinking Austin was your boyfriend," Jack said to Kayla.

"I never had time for a boyfriend."

CHAPTER 22

WITH AUSTIN OUT of his sight, Buck's confidence recovered.

"Not that I could hear everything that was said, but that cowboy friend of BunnyLee's looks like a deadbeat dad! She's too good for him!"

"Not sure that's any of our business, Boss."

"We could give him a stern talking to and do BunnyLee a huge favor. I think we'd be able to take this guy. It's three against one. All we'd need to do is when he comes out, Frankie, you grab him from behind and hold him. Then Chan and I..."

"I never go lookin' for no trouble, Boss. That's my job...to steer you clear, so it's no good yer askin' me 'cuz it ain't in my job description."

"Your job description?"

"I've got to see that you get to that producer's meeting, Monday. That's my job. Always has been."

"You sayin' you're back on their payroll?"

"Not yet."

"Aha!"

"Aha, what?"

"I sign that deal, you get your old job back."

"Somethin' like that."

"It's all beginning to come together. All the pieces of the puzzle."

"Afraid this is your battle, Boss."

"Just like that?"

"Just like that."

"Every week Nick Derringer take on tough guy," Jimmy Chan said. "Nick Derringer scared of nothing."

"What's that, Chan?"

"Nick Derringer need no help from other. Nick Derringer show him who the boss."

"Chan, this guy is the real deal," Buck said. "He beats people up for a living. Real people. Audiences pay big bucks to see him win."

"Chairman Mao say, 'When dark cloud appear in blue sky, they only temporary darkness.' Mr. Buck equal Mr. Big Cheese. You Top Dog!"

"I just played a tough guy on TV."

"Same as Austin Sway."

"Not exactly."

"Season one, episode twelve. Bank robber escape in Honda Element. Nick Derringer jump on SUV roof, reach through driver window. Don't think twice."

"Chan, that was a stunt double," Frankie said.

"Stunt double?" Apparently he hadn't heard of that. "Season four, episode twenty, Nick Derringer on surf board, ride big wave, shark all around, blood thirsty."

"That was our last show."

"Nick Derringer jump the shark, see bad guy on next wave. Bad guy now yesterday's news."

"Stunt doubles, Chan," Buck said. "That's what these guys do for a living. When you're the star of a show, there is no way that they are going to let you do your own stunts."

"Even if you'd wanted to."

"What are you saying, Frankie?"

"Nothing, Boss."

"Sounded like maybe you were saying I wasn't up to the task."

"Just the voice of reason, Boss."

"First thing first," Chan said. "Every great general on the side of right. Right?"

"Okay, I'll buy that. You could say I've been wronged."

"Right. Right now, General beside his Self. Not acceptable place to be. Great General must get hold of Self. When General beside his Self, risk getting ahead of his Self. Adversary sneak up from behind."

"What do you mean, get a hold of myself?"

"Act like everything hunky-dory. Act like not so hard to beat.

Enemy think, maybe he not so hard to beat. He no know what what. He think he swat you away like small fly."

"So, you're saying I should act small. How do I do that?"

"Not stand so straight."

Chan demonstrated walking bent over. He hunched his shoulder and lowered his center of gravity by bending his knees.

Buck mimicked the action.

"Act like not so strong."

Chan loosened his arms and led with his chin.

Buck followed, then straightened, "But I'm in great shape, everybody can see that." He pounded his stomach to demonstrate its firmness.

"Best that enemy not know this. Best to act tired, like leaf blown by autumn breeze. Dried out, partly crumpled."

Then Chan hit on an idea.

"Carry big stick!"

"I am not going to walk with a cane!"

"No cane. Need big staff!"

"A big staff? I like the sound of that."

Chan pulled a prayer stick from the display on the horse trailer and handed it to Buck.

Something about the feathers reminded him of Jadé. The staff was like a giant version of her accoutrement, her jewelry, her bling. He took hold of the stick and hefted it. It was something symbolic to hold onto, something to give him confidence.

Chan said, "Hmm, almost right. Now take animal off of head!"

"What are you talking about?"

"Dead animal. Take off from head!"

"Now see here, Chan..."

"Look like drown rat."

"There is a limit."

"Even for heart of beautiful princess?"

"Nobody knows I wear a toupee."

"Miss BunnyLee not know?"

"Well, sure, she knows. But she's the only one."

"She and Puddles."

"What's your point, Chan?"

"Everybody know."

"I didn't know," Frankie said.

"Would you get the hell out of here! Chan and I are talking."

And then to Chan, "And the toupee stays!"

One thing he had learned from playing Nick Derringer was how to talk tough.

"Come on, Chan, you and me!"

Chan saluted him. He followed Buck alongside the chain link fence where it eventually led to the ticketholder's entrance. Frankie hung back a safe distance. He crossed his arms as Buck walked up the ramp towards the deputy sheriff who was checking tickets. Buck saw the man taking tickets, stopped, turned around. He walked back down the ramp to Frankie. He held out his hand.

"You've got the tickets."

"You ain't goin' in there without me."

Buck sized Frankie up. "Okay, the least you can do is make sure I don't get killed. In the meantime, Chan and I have a plan. Come on, Chan, you and me!"

Frankie warily handed the tickets to Buck.

Buck walked back and handed the tickets to the ticket taker.

"You, again!"

Buck hadn't recognized the man. He was the guard from the parking lot.

"I've got my eyes on you fellas," the elderly deputy warned. His eyes looked huge behind the thick lenses of his glasses. "I have an ear for trouble."

Buck looked at the man's ears. They contained the largest hearing devices he had ever seen.

CHAPTER 23

"HOW CAN I wrestle with this darned thing on my head?" Jack asked.

"It was designed to wear into battle," Austin said.

"I know, but still…"

Jack tightened the leather laces of Brokenclaw's ceremonial headdress. The cultural artifact was embroidered with thousands of tiny white shells that clung to his brow. Black magpie feathers rose from the weaving and stood in a row above his forehead. Jack and Austin were rehearsing some simple wrestling moves. With much to learn and precious little time to learn it, Austin showed him how to lock up arms when they were in the ring together so that he could whisper in Jack's ear what the next series of moves should be.

Three women on spirited horses were congregating by the arena's gate. They were the remaining contestants vying to be crowned Miss Mariposa, Queen of the Rodeo, and the title would be decided by a barrel race. Jack knew all of the young ladies and waved.

"Be careful out there, Jack!" one of them yelled from her saddle.

He could sense the excitement in the behavior of their horses. They all seemed jazzed about their impending entrances. None showed behavior close to the way Jack felt. Not one seemed at all concerned about making an ass of himself.

"Here, try these on!" Kayla called to him from the back of the equipment truck. She held up a pair of black tights.

"You sure I can't just wear my old high school uniform?"

"Chief Tenaya don't wear no singlet, Jack," Big Eddie said. The short referee nimbly disembarked from the truck, leaving Kayla to make sure she found a costume suitable for Jack to wear.

"The Chief pounds his bare chest when he's riled, so your chest has got to be bare," Kayla explained. "Isn't that a fact, Uncle Eddie?"

Jack looked to Austin for support. His sparring partner's nod only confirmed what the others were telling him.

"Kayla is good with the makeup and she knows her wrestlers," Big Eddie said, "so she's gonna do yer war paint. I gotta run. Just paint the broad strokes, ain't no time for detail!" He opened the chain link gate and entered the rodeo ring.

Jack could see across the open expanse to the bleachers filled with people. Every year since he was a kid he'd looked out from those seats. Never once had he seen it from the perspective of the arena looking back. His stomach tightened at the sight of the restive crowd.

"You comin', Tammy?" Big Eddie asked.

"You go on ahead. I got things to say to this gentleman." She aimed a finger at Austin.

"Alright then, I need to go find Vic," Big Eddie said.

"Huh? Wait a darned minute! Vic is here?" Austin asked.

"Meantime," Tammy said to Kayla, "you pull that door down part way! That boy don't need the whole darn stadium watchin' 'im change. And you don't need to hear what I got to say to yer father, neither."

Jack used the lift gate as a step up into the truck where Kayla was waiting.

"You don't realize how big some of these wrestlers are 'till you hold up their tights," Kayla told Jack. "They've got costumes in those rollin' hampers goin' back to the days of Earthquake and Typhoon, tights big enough to fit the both of us together! But these here are a lot smaller. They should be just the ticket. And they don't smell too bad." She held up the tights for Jack to admire. "And look! I just noticed. There are red and gold lightning bolts on the thighs! That's somethin' an Indian chief might wear!"

"You sure they're big enough?"

"They stretch!" Kayla pulled the truck's rolling gate down all the way with them inside.

✦

"Go ahead and be mad," Tammy said to Austin. "All I got to say on the matter is that I was happy lettin' bygones be bygones. It was Kayla always goin' on about who her papa was that started things along this path. I had to tell her. I offered her the moon and the stars for graduatin', but that girl stuck to her guns. 'All I want is to meet my dad' is what she said. That girl worships you."

"Stop! Do you realize how young Laredo and I were?"

"Old enough to lose yer shirts in a gamblin' casino."

"With borrowed ID."

"I was a blackjack dealer, not a truant officer. You two were stars!"

"Was Big Eddie in on it?"

"Only to the point where he scouted you for Vic. The part about you two bein' like brothers-in-law he figgered later."

"Tell me what you put in those drinks."

"Nuthin.' Nuthin' but free alcohol that you ordered yourselves. You were young and willin' and able. And of course I was quite somethin' myself. I swear there was no hanky-panky; except later, 'a course, when there was a whole lot of it."

"Our papa never did forgive us for that, losing our prize money and the rest. When he met Big Eddie and Laredo told him that we signed up for wrestling, my old man turned his back on us for good."

"That's all water over the bridge, Austin. What you need to know is that girl in there is the pure light of day, as pure and bright as they come. She thinks the world of you, so don't go breakin' her heart!"

Austin looked away and said no more. Long ago his father cautioned him that there were only two ways to argue with a woman, and neither of them worked.

✦

Alone in the cube truck, Jack and Kayla had a solitary dome light for illumination. The portable wrestling ring along with all the lighting and sound equipment had been unloaded and set up in the arena. The shelves were bare. The empty truck echoed their voices.

"We all wore compression briefs back when we wrestled in

high school," Jack told Kayla. "Coach insisted on it because the normal briefs, they ride up."

"That's good, a lotta guys wrestle with those, I expect."

"That's the thing, I looked everywhere…"

"Go on now, you've gotta get changed!"

Jack took the garment to the middle of the truck where a group of mostly empty hampers afforded him a bit of privacy. Kayla held a clear zippered bag full of makeup and did a quick inventory.

"A whole lot of nuthin' here and a lot of it's dried up."

"Like I was in sayin'," Jack said. His voice echoed. "I was in such a hurry when I got home, havin' done yer muffler and all…"

Jack stopped talking when he realized Kayla had followed him to the middle of the truck.

"Don't worry, those will be fine," she assured him.

Jack hesitated. He held up the tights. He was not at all sure about anything. "This is the damnedest thing I ever got myself roped into."

"No turnin' back now. Go on!"

Jack unbuttoned his shirt and took it off. Underneath was his sleeveless green and gold high school uniform and under that, nothing at all.

Kayla said, "I am not at all sure I have enough brown color."

"The thing is, Kayla…I'll be damned if I could find those briefs…"

"I was gonna paint yer face white and then add the black lines of the skeleton, but Uncle Eddie says to draw the dark outlines first, then fill in. Says that's faster…"

"Kayla."

"Hold still!" She was coming at him with an eyebrow pencil. "I was hoping for burnt umber for your chest which there ain't enough of. So I got to mix the terracotta with the charcoal grey. That should look like war paint, but first I got to paint these lines here while you change."

Jack unbuckled his belt while Kayla attended to his face. He expected Kayla to turn around at some point during these proceedings. She didn't appear to feel the need.

"And then there are the ribs on your chest. People don't realize it, but if you were to look close at those fan pictures, there is a lot of blue between those brown and red lines formin' your rib skeleton. Good thing we got plenty of blue."

Jack thought about turning his back to her, but really, what difference would it make? If she didn't care, why should he? He didn't want to appear modest if the moment didn't call for modesty; he had nothing to be ashamed about. This was show business, after all. Practicality must often trump modesty.

"I guess it's all right, right...?" He dropped his jeans and stepped out of them. He pulled down the shoulder straps of his singlet uniform. "I mean, this is show business, right?"

"I know! Isn't it great?"

Jack could feel her gaze on him while she spoke. She was studying the muscular structure of his chest area. He wasn't too self-conscious about that. After working the fire line, he was feeling rather buff.

"Then we got to do the third eye on your stomach, which a lot of folks know is a real tattoo, so that can't get rubbed off."

Kayla was taking such a professional approach to the proceedings that Jack shrugged and decided he should, too. Soon he would be appearing as an imposter in front of people he had known his whole life. It was dawning on him just how important the makeup would be: the more makeup he had on, the better his disguise.

He shrugged again. He lowered his high school wrestling uniform and stepped out of it, rendering himself naked from the embroidered Indian headband down to his black Nike wrestling shoes.

Like so many icons afoot these days in the pantheon of emerging American heroes, Chief Tenaya was a confluence of mixed metaphors. He was an icon in search of a meaning. Along with the headdress and skeletal makeup, the tattoo on his stomach was his signature motif. When he entered the ring, Chief Tenaya's most fearsome move was to fold his stomach muscles over his navel in a weight lifter's stance to make the eye tattoo close and open. That was a real crowd pleaser. Nobody seemed to be bothered by the meaning of the tattoo or realize that the tattoo was a holdover from the days when the same man wrestled under the moniker of The IRS, which stood for The I-Ranian Swami. Jack wouldn't look like Chief Tanaya without it.

"Uncle Eddie found a Sharpie up front in the glove box to do the tattoo, so..."

Kayla paused momentarily from her strategizing. She looked Jack up and down, head to toe.

"Oh my gosh!" Kayla turned away and let out a nervous

laugh. "Now, I see what y'mean about not havin' briefs. That's okay. Everything's fine. Now, I forgot what I was doin'. You got me all flustered," Kayla said.

"You were telling me how you were going to do my makeup."

"Right, and I guess now would be a good time for you to put on them tights."

+

"I don't know what you want from me," Austin said to Tammy a few paces from the truck. "Whatever money Laredo and I had, we pissed it away. And as for fame, that's run its course. Last thing I need is to have Vic here tonight."

"I should think that's a good thing, that the man drove all the way up here to see you perform."

"It's only a matter of time before he's on to me, if he isn't already. Vic is a promoter. Vic calls the shots. The man is running footage in every local market promoting a video of me doing a back flip off of the third rope…"

"We saw that!"

"I don't have to tell you that is about the most dangerous move in all of sports."

"You're amazin'. Like I keep tellin' Kayla…"

"Tammy, it is not like that. Never was. What Vic doesn't know is that footage he's airing is of Laredo. It was Laredo who did those stunts. Vic is promoting a dead man. I met people today who placed bets on whether I'd finish with that flip last night in Vegas and they lost."

"But you and Laredo was twins."

"On the outside. We might have shared the same type body, but deep down it was Laredo had the courage to try those acrobatics. It was Laredo could laugh in the face of an oncoming bull."

"You can't do that back flip?"

"Not for years. Being identical, nobody knew which one of us did what."

"You looked pretty swell jumpin' off that railing this mornin'."

"Even if I wasn't hurt, it's a mental thing. I've got the Angel of Death breathing down my neck as it is."

+

"No time for dilly-dallying! Your makeup is gonna take a fair amount of work."

Kayla stood with her back to Jack. She was naturally inclined to do the right thing by giving him his privacy. But she was beginning to worry. The success of tonight's show weighed on her shoulders, and she didn't have enough time as it was.

"I've never put on tights before," Jack said.

"Well, it ain't rocket science."

Kayla could hear him struggling. Even for a person of her gender with a lifetime of practice, it would have taken finesse. For a guy like Jack, it was hopeless. In his defense, he was naked and in a hurry, and more than a bit flummoxed.

"You need to put your toes in line with the front." Kayla said, her back still to him.

"I just need to figure out which side is front. These things don't have a fly! I've got a fifty-fifty chance of getting it right and I got it right on the third try. Don't laugh!"

"I'm tryin' not to."

"These things are jammed up around my ankles and are refusin' to budge."

Jack fell against a hamper. Kayla turned to look as the cloth vehicle rolled away with him holding onto the metal rim for support. Jack hopped along and flailed to stay up while the hamper gained speed. He crashed against the back wall with a resounding boom.

"Everything okay in there?" Tammy called from outside the truck.

"We're fine!" Kayla called back.

"Oh, god, this is embarrassing!" Jack said. "I'm stuck."

"Do you need help?"

"I'm afraid so."

Kayla hurried to his aid and diagnosed his problem right away. "I think maybe you needed to take your shoes off first."

"I feel faint."

"Stage fright," Kayla said. It was her job to get Jack ready for his entrance, and she took her responsibility seriously. Show business was just as new to her as it was to Jack, but one thing she knew for sure was the show had to go on. "Let's start over! I'm gonna help."

Kayla stooped down by his feet and helped Jack free himself from the tangled mess. She unlaced his shoes and helped pulled them off.

"Now you best stand up!"

Kayla kept her eyes trained on the floor. She straightened the tights and guided one foot in while he put his weight on the other. This time Jack had Kayla's shoulder for support. She steered his second foot into the tights. She was trying her darnedest to maintain a professional attitude, but really, there was no polite way to steady the naked man stooped over her while wrestling a spirited pair of spandex tights.

The equipment truck hadn't been swept out in years. The floor was strewn with bits of rope, slippery pieces of discarded theatrical gel, empty tape rolls, and cigarette butts.

"Ow, ow, ow!" Jack yelled, having stepped on a broken clothespin with a bare foot. He fell over onto the wooden deck and took Kayla with him.

✦

Austin and Tammy looked at the closed roll-up door of the truck.

"Do you think it's okay that they're in there together?" Austin asked Tammy.

"I suppose so. Kayla's a grown girl."

"Which is my point."

✦

"I am so sorry, I truly am," Jack said as he tried to get his weight off of Kayla, his left arm in the neighborhood of her legs. His right thigh was in the vicinity of her neck. "It's just that they're so tight."

"They're supposed to be tight," Kayla said from underneath. "That's why they call 'em tights."

"Like puttin' on a straightjacket."

"They're just old and stiff. Give-em a chance to warm up. Roll over!"

"I can't. I'm jammed up against this hamper."

Kayla wiggled out from under him and helped Jack stand.

As counter-intuitive as it might have seemed to the athlete whose feet were hogtied by the tights, Kayla insisted that he couldn't raise one leg of the costume completely in deference to the other. She directed him in the delicate art of raising the fabric on each leg incrementally. First one foot, then the other, then one ankle, then the other, then each calf one at a time and so on upward. While Jack pulled from above, Kayla pushed from below, alternating legs. They were in a race against the clock, but once they passed the knees the progress slowed to a crawl. Jack's thighs were muscular and the fabric clung to every contour. Kayla pushed and Jack pulled. It was hard work, and they were both breathing heavily.

"What's going on in there?" Tammy asked.

"Almost done!" Kayla called between breaths. "It's probably not a good idea for my mom to see us in here like this," she said to Jack. She was working his left thigh, "Oh, man, would you look at that? That is nice!" She was referring to the lightning bolt that was slowly unfolding on the outside of Jack's thigh.

At a snail's pace, Kayla coaxed the bunched-up garment onward toward the finish line. She smoothed the fabric upward with both hands. She encircled his thighs with her fingers and worked each small wrinkle to stretch out to its maximum coverage. They had a rhythm now, slow, then strong, alternating between Kayla's delicate pushing and Jack's insistent pulling. She was getting lost in the minutia of the moment, forgetting the big picture. They were on the home stretch, drawing near the goal line when Kayla finally looked up to gauge their progress. It was right there, the goal line. She had known it was there, but from where she was kneeling, it was a lot closer than she expected. If she wasn't careful, it would have brushed against her head. Jack was doing his damnedest to cover the remaining ground.

"What's so funny?"

"I just never seen a man from this angle, bouncin' around like a hedgehog."

"I can't help it."

"I don't mean in a bad way. It's like some furry critter stickin' his face out to see what's up."

"This is the craziest thing that has ever happened to me."

Kayla was straightening the supple section where Jack's loin attached to the rest of his body when she sensed that the hedgehog was standing on its hind legs.

"Look at them lightnin' bolts!" Kayla exclaimed, drawing attention down and away from the subject. She quickly stood up and dusted herself off, leaving Jack to manage the last distance himself. There were lines you don't cross with a man you just met that day, Kayla thought, even in show business.

With one last tug, Jack pulled the waistband into position, imprisoning every contour of his swollen anatomy.

"Well, that should take care of that," Kayla said, although, without a pair of compression shorts underneath, Kayla wasn't altogether sure.

"Can a person die of embarrassment?"

"You look awesome! You're like some super hero from the League of Superheroes."

"Are you sure these aren't your Uncle Eddie's tights?"

"You mean from when he wrestled with Andre? I guess it's possible. Uncle Eddie was bigger back then from all his workin' out."

"Bigger than what? The man's a dwarf!"

"His kind prefer you say Little Person."

"I think my voice just went up an octave!"

Jack's voice did seem higher, and it worried her. "Jack, you gotta get into character! You're a wrestler and you're going in the ring with one of the greatest of the greats."

"It was one thing when I was going as myself. Everybody knew I was gonna lose. But to be playing a famous Indian Chief who they're expecting to see win... I'm not an actor."

"You don't have to be an actor. You just have to act like a famous Indian Chief who's come back from the dead. You got to pound your chest like you mean it! I read about this Tenaya fella online, the real Tenaya. He was Chief of the Ahwanee back in the Gold Rush days. He told the American army where to go. Said he was comin' back as a ghost to torment the White man."

"Yeah, I know who he was."

"Did you know he killed a grizzly bear with his bare hands?"

"My high school team was nicknamed the Grizzlies, I think on account of him."

"Hand-to-hand combat with a grizzly and he won. I mean, how cool is that? Not for the grizzly of course, but for him to have done that. That's what you got to do, play a guy who can pin a grizzly bear. What if I was to come at you like this, all crazy and mean like a grizzly bear, growling like *errrrrrr*, what do you do?"

Kayla stared at him with feral grizzly-like eyes and growled again. Jack growled back. Kayla growled even harder and Jack growled even harder back. Kayla jockeyed around Jack, her arms out high like a bear. She tried to look formidable in her high-heeled boots. She knew Jack had the advantage of agility being barefoot. He just had to be wary not to step on something.

"Don't look at the ground! Look at me!"

Kayla gave him a warning shot across his cheek with her fingertips. Her hands were quick and her fingernails were sharp.

"Ow!"

Jack dodged her next advance, but she grazed him on the arm. With the side of his foot, he swept the area around him clear. She stood taller than him in her boots and acted like a wild animal.

Jack was athletically inclined. Brokenclaw had said he was All State. She just needed to awaken his confidence. He took a swipe at her wrist and she slapped his hand away. His tights were taut like stretched rubber bands. There was a springiness to his legs. The tights seemed to lift his legs from the ground against the laws of gravity. She watched him test their buoyancy and was surprised by his nimbleness. He faded to the left, then spun around her to his right. He grabbed her below the rib cage from behind. She tried to wiggle free. He held her close.

Kayla twisted to face him, her expression fierce and confrontational. She could feel her own heartbeat against his wrist. She bared her teeth and growled again. He growled back. She pinned her lips to his and kissed him hard. That hadn't been her plan, but it seemed the thing to at the moment. Not something that a wild grizzly would do, of course, but she was improvising and it definitely felt wild. Jack pursued her tongue with his and she bit it.

"Ow!"

Kayla pulled away.

"Now, *that* is the confidence you need when you enter the wrestlin' ring!" she said. She wiped her mouth with her forearm.

Austin banged at the truck door. "What's going on in there?"

"Just rehearsing!"

"Rehearsing for what?"

"For tonight!"

"That didn't take long," Jack whispered. "He's your dad for ten minutes and he's already watching you like a hawk!"

"Wow, I know, ain't this great?"

CHAPTER 24

HOGS, GOATS, COWS, poultry, and rabbits: these were the local stars up the hill in the livestock and farm animal exhibitions. Among their breeders were experts on every imaginable domestic animal, but nobody in any of the barns knew anything about a dog whisperer. BunnyLee started to feel funny just asking. It was dawning on her that she'd made a fool of herself, driving up here on a whim. It was an act of desperation. And now, with Buck mad at her, she'd made a real mess of things. The bottom line was she wasn't anywhere closer to solving the mystery of Puddles' sneezing. And on the subject of Puddles' sneezing, the incidence of these fits was only getting worse. Puddles began sneezing uncontrollably the minute BunnyLee started asking around the livestock areas and she didn't stop until they were in front of the 4-H pavilion. There was no rhyme or reason why she had these sneezing fits sometimes and at other times not. All BunnyLee knew was that it was terrifying to watch.

Outside the pavilion she spotted a brightly colored fortuneteller trailer decorated with symbols from the Tarot. The psychic was set up in an out-of-the-way place off the midway and was clearly lacking in clients. BunnyLee walked over to say hello.

"I'm sorry I don't have any money with me but I was wondering whether you knew anything about dog whisperers. Not that I have the faintest idea of what dog whisperers do, but my puppy could sure use some help. I mean, do you guys travel in the same circles?"

A voice from behind pre-empted the psychic's response.

"Could you turn your head a little bit to the left so that we could get you in profile?"

BunnyLee turned to see who had spoken and was shocked to realize that she was on camera. She instinctively turned away from the news crew. The longer she extended her stay in America, the more awkward it had become trying to stay out of the limelight.

"BunnyLee?" the reporter yelled.

BunnyLee was afraid to look.

"It's me, Rebekah. Heather's maid of honor. From the wedding?"

"Omigod, Rebekah!"

"What are you doing here? I thought you were supposed to be in Thailand."

"That's what everybody thinks. Please, you cannot show that footage of me!" BunnyLee said, pointing at the lens. "My parents are such news junkies. If they saw me on camera, they'd freak."

"Not to worry, there's no story line, anyway. We were just getting cut-away shots," Rebekah said as she approached and they embraced. "Although maybe I should run it just to get even with you."

"What do you mean? What did I do?"

"It's what you didn't do. You stood us up on that tennis date."

"No, I didn't."

"Yes, you did."

"No way."

"Way!"

"I showed up. But there wasn't anyone there who you said would be there."

"That's not what I heard. Gwendolyn had to go to Guam as a last-minute dance replacement. So she texted Heather, who was on her honeymoon and she called me and then when I couldn't do it, I recommended you."

"Right. And I went."

"You did?"

"Yeah, and I want to thank you because I've had kind of this thing going with Buck LeGrande…wait a minute, is that camera really off?"

"LeGrande was there?"

"Well, yeah…"

"I did an on-camera with him the other day at a protest rally. I didn't know he was going to be there."

"Well, it's his house."

"No, it wasn't. You were supposed to be at the Shpielman's. Did you go to the wrong house?"

"Maybe. You never told me whose house it was. So I really did crash Buck's tennis game? That explains a lot. But when you say Shpielman, do you mean the director?"

"Yeah, and I'm so mad. He was looking for somebody our type."

"Get out!"

"Jane Baker got the part and she doesn't hold a candle to me as far as talent goes. That girl, every time I think of her I go ballistic. The woman has no range. She has no...Did you see her in that national spot? All she does is hold a taco chip! I mean, she told me she's making ten grand a month in residuals!"

"Stop! I don't want to hear this."

"So, Buck LeGrande, huh? I could see that. I mean, say what you will about the guy, and after that *Sesame Street* YouTube, but I thought he was charming."

"Promise me you won't tell anyone! I don't want it to get out that I'm actually staying with a movie star. The whole business is so intrusive."

"You don't have to tell me. Intrusion is how I make my living. Listen, gotta run. We need to shoot this wrestling match thing and make a report at eleven. Are you going?"

"I don't have a ticket."

"I'll tell them you're with the news crew."

"You will? But there's one more place I need to check first. Maybe I'll see you there after."

"Okay, catch you later. Cute dog."

"Thanks. Buck gave her to me."

Rebekah spun around. "Buck LeGrande gave you a dog?"

"Yeah. For my birthday."

"Really. When was your birthday?"

"A couple of weeks ago."

"Did he say where he got it?"

"Rodeo Pets."

"You have got to be kidding me! I interviewed him in front of that store! Oh, man, that was smooth. I can't believe it! Boy, has that man got a set of brass!"

"What are you talking about? Did he do something wrong?"

"Wrong? I guess you could say it was wrong. He came out as

the poster boy for shutting down the puppy mills and then jumped the picket line! We were covering the boycott story and there was a big demonstration in front of that store. I got him on camera signing a petition! I can't effing believe it! We figured he snuck out the back, but damn, I never thought he bought a dog! All that time we're waiting out front, thinking he's coming back and I'm like, 'Oh my gosh, he smiled at me!' Did I ever fall for that one!"

Rebekah's cameraman joined the conversation, speaking from behind the eyepiece. "Like what George Burns used to say, 'The most important thing about acting is honesty; if you can fake that, you've got it made.'" He was aiming the long barrel of his Ikegami on Puddles.

"But he is honest! Besides, who asked you? And don't you dare point that camera at my dog! I don't care how he got her, she doesn't need to be dragged into this!"

"BunnyLee, listen to me!"

Rebekah grabbed BunnyLee by the wrist and looked her straight in the eye.

"Ow!" BunnyLee yelled and Puddles growled, but Rebekah held on tight.

"Not for nothing, my dear, but Buck LeGrande must really like you, because that was some stunt he pulled!"

"Why shouldn't he like me?" BunnyLee asked. She pulled her wrist free and covered Puddles' face. "I gotta go!"

Protecting her dog was the central motivating issue in BunnyLee's universe, and as a consequence the rest of her life was spinning out of control. She was so mad she was shaking. She didn't know what to do. She wasn't mad at Rebekah; that would be shooting the messenger. She was mad at herself for ignoring the truth. She'd come up with a whole list of reasons why Buck wouldn't like her, but no reasons why he shouldn't. Maybe the holy man at the Bayon Temple was right; maybe she was five times lucky. Was this what it meant to be lucky? She'd been so guarded of her own feelings, she'd given scant consideration to Buck's. The man had risked his reputation to get her this dog. That was huge.

BunnyLee's heart was racing. She tried to calm her nerves. She headed into the last pavilion. She hadn't attended a 4-H exhibition since she was a kid when she followed her older sister Lizette into the program. They stayed with it for a couple of years, then discovered the local community theatre and took that leap.

Tables were set up with baked goods arranged into categories, some with red ribbons, some yellow, some with blue. There was needlepoint and quilting. Young teens stood next to cages with their dogs. Puddles was in heaven. BunnyLee set her dog down and let her run from cage to cage, sniffing and wagging her tail. There was whimpering and barking that devolved into general chaos to the point where BunnyLee was getting dirty looks from the adult chaperones. She felt compelled to scoop her dog back up.

After things settled down again, BunnyLee asked a 4-H girl if she had ever heard of the dog whisperer.

"Is that like a horse whisperer for dogs?"

"Yep."

"Nope."

BunnyLee looked around for somebody else to ask.

"Is that a Labradoodle?" the girl asked.

"She sure is."

"I read about them. Is it true they can stand on their hind legs?"

"Absolutely."

"Can I see?"

"Okay, I guess." BunnyLee scanned the pavilion to see whether there were any more discouraging looks from the folding chair section. A couple of the 4-H baking mothers down the aisle were looking her way, and BunnyLee could see that the women were ambivalent about who should get up and amble over. Both were rather thick around the ankles, and their heaviness blossomed from there up. There were only two folding chairs, and the needlepoint mothers had none, so they were clearly wary about leaving those seats unattended.

Before she set Puddles down, BunnyLee gave her dog a little pep talk. She'd read that one needed to grab a poodle's attention from the outset. Puddles stood on cue, but she seemed out of character without her costume. During the housebound week of Santa Ana winds, BunnyLee had kept busy sewing a vest with an oversized sheriff's badge. She also made a pair of cowboy boots that velcroed over Puddles' back paws and a miniature holster with matching six-shooters that strapped around Puddles' hips where yesterday the tutu had been. BunnyLee took these things from her bag and put them on Puddles.

BunnyLee gave Puddles her cue and she stood on her hind

legs with her forelegs to her side— a gunslinger reaching for her holster. A group of young onlookers began to form. Even the mothers got up from their chairs. Puddles was a natural performer, and nobody wanted to miss the show.

The young girl watched with delight. "Too bad they don't have a category for dancing dogs, because yours would win hands down," she said.

BunnyLee pulled the *piece de resistance* from her bag: a miniature cowboy hat from the pet store with an elastic chinstrap. There was a shriek of glee from a younger member of the audience.

"It's a genuine Stetson," BunnyLee heard herself say. Then she froze. "Oh my God!" An incubator light in a nearby hamster cage was casting a man-sized shadow of Puddles on the nearby wall. Last night, when she took pictures of Puddles to upload to her agent, she'd set a table lamp on the floor to illuminate the dog from floor level. When Puddles stood, her shadow was cast on the wall larger than life—the same as Puddles was casting now.

"Oh my God!" BunnyLee said again. Puddles' shadow looked every bit like that of a man's, and the realization made her light-headed. That's what Buck had seen when he knocked on her door last night.

BunnyLee couldn't think of anything worse than to have her host think she was entertaining a male friend. Even if there had never been any romantic attraction between them, BunnyLee was too good a houseguest to have ever done that. And, of course, there was attraction, physical, emotional, call it what you will. The evidence of Buck's affection was dancing right in front of her-- Buck had risked the wrath of the liberal Hollywood establishment by crossing a picket line to buy her this amazing dog.

Puddles was doing her pirouettes without prompting, and the crowd in the room was growing. All BunnyLee could think about was how Buck must have felt. He'd had a one-night stand; there was nothing anyone could do about that. But much had changed in the last week. He'd been doing everything he could to make it up to her. The truth of the matter was that, against all caution to the contrary, her feelings were getting the better of her.

Another thought crossed her mind, a thought that made her want to bolt out of the pavilion: Austin was wearing a full-sized Stetson just like Puddles.

"Hey, thanks for watching, but I've really gotta run!"

She scooped up her dog and headed for the arena. She was pretty certain that Buck was not going to miss Austin's show.

And neither was she.

CHAPTER 25

KAYLA AND HER mother stayed close to the fence as they hurried along the inside of the rodeo ring toward the bleachers and ringside. The deputy sheriff waved them over as they passed his checkpoint.

"Whoa! Where do you think you're going?"

"We're with the show," Kayla said.

The two proudly held up crew tags that hung from lanyards around their necks.

"How tall are you?" the octogenarian officer asked Kayla.

"Five foot eleven and six quarters."

"There weren't women that tall when I was a lad, 'cept maybe in the freak shows."

"I know, right? And my Uncle Eddie's four foot five and he's runnin' this show. He used to wrestle with Andre the Giant."

"Would that be Big Eddie?'

"Yep."

"Thought that was him that passed before. Quite the showman. I always liked the midget wrestling."

"That was before my time."

"You can still watch their matches online."

"You can?"

"Yep. Huh. Big Eddie. They called him The World's Shortest Giant." the deputy officer said, smiling. "I liked that. Wore those tights with lightning bolts on his legs."

"Big Eddie did?" Kayla asked. "You sure?"

"Oh yeah," the deputy sheriff said, "his thing was the lightning bolts."

"Yep. Totally. For sure," Tammy said.

✦

"Do you know any Indian war dances?" Austin asked Jack. The two were hanging back by the equipment truck waiting for their entrance cues on the public address system. Jack's untamed tights were riding up and the tops of the lightning bolts were twisting.

"Huh? No. I mean we all learned a little dance in gym class as part of Native American Studies, but…"

"Because whenever Tenaya enters the ring, they play his theme song and he does a simple dance: Ha ya ya ya. Ha ya ya ya." Austin demonstrated a simple skip-dance step.

Local dignitaries on horseback were standing ready to enter. Jack was relieved to see that no one recognized him. The magnitude of Jack's responsibility was not lost on him. Chief Tenaya was the person that people had bought tickets to see and when these people looked at him in costume, Chief Tenaya was the person they saw. He stifled his fear by growling.

"What?" Austin asked.

"Nothing. Just getting into character."

The fact that he had to perform a war dance before knowledgeable critics seemed absurd. Half the audience was comprised of real Native American war dancers who had been competing all day.

"Confidence sells," Austin advised Jack. "You're Chief Tenaya to them. The only way people are going to know you're not who they think you are is if you let up on your performance. Otherwise, nobody knows. Just be thankful you have such a good disguise. It's a great part. Have fun with it!"

"I look okay?"

"Kayla did a good job. Trust me, no one will know."

"I don't want to let Kayla down, either."

"That matters to you?"

"Yeah," Jack said. "You don't mind, do you?"

Austin studied the young man. "It matters what I think?"

"Sure, her being your daughter or niece or whatever."

"Well, I appreciate that. She's written me letters. Darned shame I never caught on," Austin said. He returned to the subject at hand. "The other thing to keep in mind is that there is always a special microphone positioned dead center under the mat. Don't be startled when one of us falls. The sound is loud and it reverberates. Once you get used to it, you'll find it really helps to put an exclamation mark on the action. I always slap the mat with my hand when I go down. You'll see. It really gets the audience going."

They stopped to listen as the announcer in the booth tapped his microphone to get everyone's attention.

"Good evening Ladies and Gentlemen and welcome to the greatest venue in the world!"

His voice echoed off the surrounding hills. Austin listened closely for their cues. There was a considerable distance to cover on foot. He warned Jack not to waste any time getting to the ring. A person's entrance, when handled properly, went a long way toward firing up the crowd.

The horsemen and horsewomen carried flags. One at a time they rode at full gallop into the arena. They carried emblems from local ranches, flags from local sponsors, a flag in support of breast cancer research that read TOUGH ENOUGH to WEAR PINK, and, finally, the flag of the United States, which brought most everyone in the place to their feet for the national anthem.

+

One final rider held back. She rode a handsome palomino and led a second horse saddled up with no rider. Austin knew what that meant. They were honoring a lost comrade. Austin kept his hat over his heart.

Level ground was a commodity in short supply in the Sierra Nevada Mountains. The grounds of this arena were small by California rodeo standards. Many of the events such as calf roping and barrel racing were shortened to fit into the truncated space, but the historical significance of this venue wasn't lost on many cowboys.

Originally, Mariposa County was the largest county in the state. It was also one of the oldest, dating back to the gold rush. And although its prominence waned over the course of a century and a half, as its political authority was divvied up, the Mariposa

Fair was still a proud tradition. Its unique, quaint, down-home appeal was hard to beat. Austin was keen to the fact that their performance tonight was a substitute to that venerable tradition. He wanted things to go as smoothly as they could.

"I was seventeen when I last stood in this same holding area waiting to perform. That was just before the National Finals Rodeo in Vegas. Laredo and I were a bit of a sensation that year. That's when Big Eddie saw us and brought us to the attention of Vic. Few would remember us from those days, but my brother, Laredo, and I were rodeo clowns like none other and before that, bull riders. As kids, we had the run of this place, being the sons of the rodeo announcer. These fair grounds are about as close to native soil as I could ever hope to get."

The echo made it difficult to hear the individual words of the announcer.

"Rodeo fame is short-lived," Austin continued. "Many a cowboy feels chewed up and spit out after one season."

A bull rider has eight seconds to hold on. The time between the chute opening and the winner's buzzer is an eternity on the back of a bucking bull. Anyone who has come up short, and that would be everyone who has ever tried, knows all too well that collective groan from the bleachers and the long lonely walk back to the holding area. It is a slow walk back to anonymity.

Austin could tell from the tone of the announcer's voice that the fallen cowboy was someone dear to his heart. This cowboy was not forgotten. A wave of sadness swept over him as he contemplated his own mortality and the seeming meaninglessness of his life's choices.

They said that hindsight was twenty-twenty, and Austin would agree. He could see clearly the arc of his career: the twins had gone on to greater fame on the national stage when they moved to wrestling, but, for all their fame, they had given up so much more. Austin was an outsider looking in, a lone bystander with no place to call home. The remainder of his career would be a slow walk back to anonymity.

"So ladies and gentlemen, please join me in a moment of silence for Laredo Sway."

These words from the announcer hit Austin like a bullet. In a career where survival hinged on being prepared for the unexpected, he was dumbstruck. That empty saddle was for

Laredo! He couldn't help but tear up. In that moment, he felt that no greater honor could have been bestowed upon his brother on this, the one-year anniversary of his accident. The whole day had been an emotional roller coaster, but to have it end like this was the topper.

"You all right?" Jack asked.

Austin looked at his young co-star and nodded. "Didn't see that coming. Laredo was my brother."

"Ladies and Gentleman, approaching the ring, it is my pleasure to introduce one of the greatest wrestlers to ever enter into the squared circle, Native America's native son, Chief Tenaya!"

"Whoops! I thought they'd call me first. That's your cue, son." Austin said to Jack. "Take a deep breath; let's give 'em a show!" Austin slapped him on the backside with his hat and Jack jogged into the limelight.

✦

As this was built as a rodeo arena, the audience was seated in one set of risers in the center of the elongated field. The portable wrestling ring was set up on casters and wheeled onto the track in close proximity to the seats so that the audience could have as intimate an experience as the generic setting would allow.

Kayla held her breath as Jack passed. She started to giggle at the way his costume rode up between his legs in back and their elastic pull added bounce to his skip-step dance. It was a nervous giggle. The deputy sheriff shot her a quizzical look and so did Tammy. Judging by the catcalls from some of the ladies present, Kayla could see that his costume was well received.

"Are those Big Eddie's tights?" Tammy asked.

"Well, I didn't know!" was Kayla's weak defense.

Big Eddie welcomed Jack into the ring. He, too, shot Kayla a startled look.

✦

The crowd chanted Tenaya's name. Jack knew the exhilaration of entering an auditorium to the sound of theme music, having wrestled in Greco-Roman competitions across the state. But he had never been promoted as a sex symbol before. He danced on one foot, then on the other. The taut lightning bolts across his thighs nearly hit him on his chin. Austin was right. Everyone was so excited at seeing a television celebrity in person that they suspended their disbelief toward his bogus war dance. The fact that this wrestler depicted the spirit of their most storied Native American brought the crowd to its feet in applause.

The music ended. Jack stood in the ring with his fists held over his head like a seasoned pro. He bounced around the ring, trying out the ropes to get used to their give. He wasn't expecting the lights to be quite so bright. The place was packed. Kayla stood with her mother down front. She caught his eye. She cued him to pound his chest. When he did, the crowd went wild again. Jack was beginning to get into it.

This audience was no different than your run-of-the-mill murder trial crowd where people sat with other like-minded people because there was strength in numbers. The large contingent of Native Americans who had remained for the show sat together on the stage right side of the house, and they were among the most vocal in their enthusiasm. Jack was a little surprised to see the news cameraman down front to his left. And the reporter standing by, microphone in hand, added another layer of importance to the event.

✦

After Jack's intro as Chief Tenaya, it was Austin's turn to enter the ring. His theme music came out over the loudspeaker. But apparently Big Eddie had dropped the ball. He'd neglected to inform the announcer about the presence in the arena of another great wrestler, Austin Sway. Instead, the man read the intro for Jack.

"In the other corner, an immoveable object meeting an irresistible force, I have the great pleasure to introduce to you, Mariposa's other favorite son, All-California State wrestling champion, Mr. Jack…Wait a minute, hold on there! I have just been informed of a last minute…there has been a last-minute substitution. Oh, my! Ladies and Gentleman, it is with the greatest pleasure that I introduce a change in tonight's card. Wrestling against Chief Tenaya tonight we will all have the pleasure of watching one of the greatest wrestlers of our day, one of the greatest rodeo clowns ever to turn wrestling pro, my son, Austin Swaaaay, The Duuuuust

Deviiilllll!"

Austin started his jog into the arena at the start of the intro. The sound of cheers and jeers drowned out much of what he could hear. He paused before climbing in under the ropes.

"Dad?"

Austin held his hand over his eyes to block the harsh lights from washing out his view of the man in the booth.

"Dad?"

The only familiar face that he could pick out was the dour mug of Vic. Austin released the two straps that held his neck straight and tossed the contraption away. He did not care to be seen by Vic in a neck brace.

It had been a long day for Austin Sway, with many twists and turns, emotional and otherwise. Never in his wildest dreams had Austin expected to be introduced by his father. He resolved that from this moment on he would read all his texts and email, even the spam. He climbed into the ring and stood for a second, center stage, taking it all in.

For an entire year he'd been traversing the West with the memory of his brother bottled up in his car. A heavy heart will weigh on you. It will wear you down. This event, an annoyance from the moment he heard about it, was now anything but. What had felt like a side trip was in fact a homecoming. He was honored to be there in front of a packed house.

As a rule, Austin would rather talk than wrestle. Nursing a neck injury made him a tad more loquacious than normal and normally he was quite content to address an audience at length. This audience was all on one side in a proscenium setting as opposed to being all around. The row of lights hung from a box-truss above the seats was closer than usual and more theatrical. He couldn't have asked for a setting more conducive to addressing the audience directly. He motioned Big Eddie to reroute the microphone under the first rope so that the audio cable could take the shortest path. Austin liked to move around when he spoke.

The twins and their dad had never seen eye to eye on their decision to forsake the family business in their pursuit of the national spotlight. Talking directly to the fearsome patriarch on a good day was a venture fraught with trepidation. In no way did he savor the moment when he would have to face the old man with the events of his brother's death. So having a thousand people in the room, so to speak, helped Austin feel moderately safer.

"Mr. Tyler Sway, Ladies and Gentlemen," Austin said into the microphone. "Could I have a round of applause for the greatest rodeo announcer of all time?"

Austin started by congratulating the man on his retirement and thanked the audience for their participation in such a worthy cause. Then he told his woeful tale of Laredo's last performance:

"We were in a small venue with a low ceiling. The zip line was cabled to the grid like it always was. A riser scaffold was erected in the far corner of the arena, giving both the highest elevation and the longest possible run. It was a tag-team event. Our world championship belt was on the line. I was in the ring and, for those of you who are unfamiliar with the rules of tag-team wrestling, one member of each team initiates the match, one-on-one in the ring. When the first member is tired or is about to be pinned, if he is able to tag his teammate, he is immediately replaced. The second team member is not allowed to set foot in the ring until he is tagged. The zip line is in essence a loophole in the rules. A team member can fly into the ring on the zip line at the strategic time and dangle over the mat inside the ropes without being disqualified."

+

The evening air was turning chilly. Many in the stands carried over-shirts and jackets. Jack could see them putting them on. His thin tights did little to stave off the cold; even his feather headdress was open at the top. Truth be told, he would have happily taken the headdress off, anything to stop the incessant soreness of the tiny shells that dug into his forehead. He was sorry he'd tightened the thing.

People were listening to Austin. Some were snickering uncomfortably, probably wondering whether Austin's speech was for real. Enough in the crowd knew that it was. Some remembered the twins from their rodeo days. Others had heard the lore.

+

The ticket taker stood with his back to the entrance as BunnyLee arrived. BunnyLee caught sight of Tammy ringside and pulled up short behind the elderly officer. She waited as Tammy bought a Karmel Korn from a vender and he tossed her the box over the fence. The officer turned around. BunnyLee smiled at him while he stepped back.

"Didn't see you come in."

"Nice evening for a fair." She said. She was still out of breath.

"Do you have a ticket?"

"I'm with the news crew."

"I don't see your dog tags."

"They're on my dog."

"Huh?" he sized BunnyLee up. "Strange goings on here, tonight. Not yer usual fair. We need to be on our guard."

"Should I be nervous?"

"The men from this town you can trust. But there are others here, from the city, they're not to be trusted."

"I'll be careful," BunnyLee said. She moved quickly along the front aisle, not wanting to block anyone's view. Rebekah stood next to the cameraman, inside the fence. BunnyLee crouched down behind the newswoman and tapped her through the chain link fence. Rebekah turned and rolled her eyes at her. She was clearly bored at the prospect of covering a wrestling event. BunnyLee caught Austin's attention and she gave him a simple wave.

"Move along, you can't stay there," one of the ushers informed her.

"I'm with the camera crew," she told the woman. Rebekah nodded to the usher that this was true.

"Then go around to the far end gate over there and tell them to let you in."

Above them on the wrestling stage, Austin continued, "Laredo was on the jump tower waiting for a signal from me. The line was set at an angle that would sufficiently clear the heads of the audience. Laredo, the consummate showman, wore a colorful cape that waved majestically in the breeze. He hung on with one hand and waved his hat with the other. That brought the fans to their feet. Laredo Sway to the rescue!"

✦

Jack was getting restless. Waiting politely for Austin to finish, the energy he had felt during his entrance was draining away. His tights were so tight they were cutting off the circulation to his legs and feet. He was getting that tingly feeling that was so often an early warning sign of numbness. He danced around in his corner, trying to get the blood flowing. Jack's bouncing shook the structure of the portable wrestling stage he shared with Austin. Austin shot him a look to stop.

Austin continued, "Like I said, the stunt had been tried and retried, the elevation and the pitch of the zipline were determined to be well out of the way of even the tallest fan. It was the foam finger on the hand of the tallest man that hadn't been included in the calculation. That one outstretched foam index finger clipped Laredo's foot as he came sliding by and spun him around."

At any other time, Jack would have been happy to stand and listen to every detail Austin cared to share about his brother's untimely death. Jack felt bad for the guy, let there be no doubt about that. He also felt for his legs and found that they were asleep. All this waiting around for Austin to get to the point was having a serious effect on Jack's ability to perform. If he didn't keep his legs moving and the blood circulating, they would cease to support him. Plus, his face itched something awful under the makeup. Kayla had warned him not to scratch and smear his face paint no matter how bad it got. He was having difficulty heeding her advice. He scratched under his eye and Kayla glared at him from below.

Austin shook his head. "Spinning in itself was not the worst thing, and Laredo, as was his nature, incorporated the unexpected into his act. It was what happened when he came over the ropes that got him. His head came into contact with the corner stanchion, a metal post that is adequately padded on the inside of every wrestling arena. It is hardly ever padded on the outside. And because his head hit the post on the outside, the impact addled his brain."

✦

"Huh!" BunnyLee took in an involuntary gasp of air. The tragedy of this story was brought home by the fact that she knew Austin. Earlier she had noticed an aura of grief about the man. Not until now did she understand the tragedy he endured. She looked around at the audience to gauge their reaction.

A wrestling crowd, not unlike a rodeo crowd, tended to be on the raucous side. Where your live theater audience taking in an orchestra or a play tended to stay in their appointed seats, guarding their turf like it was a piece of Manhattan real estate, a wrestling audience tended to navigate on the other end of the spectrum. They liked to jump up and move around. They normally drank beer and bought nacho cheese products that were easily flung and stuck readily to the backs of the heads of the people in the better seats.

This audience was silent and attentive. People who had handed over hard-earned money to see and cheer the high-octane performance of a professional wrestling match were quieted to a whisper. BunnyLee marveled at the aplomb with which Austin was controlling the moment. The only person not all ears was Jack.

Frankie tapped BunnyLee on the shoulder.

"Frankie! Where's Buck?"

"With Chan."

"Is everything okay?"

"They ditched me."

"What's he planning on doing?"

"I dunno, BunnyLee. Whatever it is, it's bad."

"Oh, Frankie, this is all my fault."

"You should have told me you was meetin' a man."

"But I wasn't!"

"Evidence to the contrary, BunnyLee," Frankie said. He nodded at the man with the microphone who was currently speaking directly to her.

"Is this the lady in question?" the man standing on the other side of BunnyLee asked Frankie.

"Oh, gosh. Didn't see you there," Frankie said, "BunnyLee, this here is *Officer Brokenclaw* who I had the pleasure of meeting earlier today."

"Your husband was sorry that he lost you," Brokenclaw said to BunnyLee.

✦

Jack could see that his moving around and scratching was a distraction to Austin, so he carefully repositioned himself to an upstage corner behind where his opponent could see him. Now everything was itching, even his back. He rubbed up against the turnbuckle padding in as subtle a manner as possible.

His activity was gaining the attention of a fair number of people. Even Jack's more subtle motions were causing some laughter and finger pointing in his direction.

+

"My brother was still conscious when I unclipped him from the harness, but I could tell he was hurt somethin' bad. He knew it, too. Laredo was quick to smile whatever the occasion, and this night was no different. There is something about a person's last smile that tells the whole story. It was that kind of smile reserved for old friends at the end of a great weekend when the party is over--the voices are hoarse, the liquor has all been drunk, and the lipstick has long since worn off the ladies."

+

Jack's legs were really beginning to worry him. He tried to circulate the blood in ways that didn't vibrate the stage. He did a deep knee bend to assess the costume's tautness. His tights fought him all the way down and when he came up his feet left the ground. He came down with a bounce that was hard for Austin to ignore. Jack waved at Austin in a feeble attempt to apologize, but his constant moving about, however innocent, was having a deleterious effect on Austin's ability to control the moment. Jack had a responsibility to stay warm; he owed it to his audience. He bounced around some more.

+

"*Amor fati* was our mother's philosophy. Love your fate. You can't choose your own death, and you can't fight it either. Laredo's smile was of the knowing kind that says, what a pity it is to have to say *adieu*. He told me to tell you, Dad, that he was going to check on Mama and not to worry one minute about him. So here I am, one year later, with this sad story to tell. This was how your son, my brother, my better half, met his Maker. It was a foam finger, that iconic souvenir of sporting events countrywide, that did him in."

People were beginning to howl at what they saw as a deliberate attempt by Chief Tenaya to discredit Austin's monologue. Standing upstage of another performer while he was speaking was considered unprofessional, even among professional wrestlers. People saw Jack's behavior as a passive aggressive attempt to get Austin's goat, and the tactic was working.

✦

Jack tried to concentrate on his upcoming performance. As Chief Tenaya, he was, after all, the featured performer of the night. He was the man whom everyone had paid to see. Austin's monologue was compelling, but the cowboy was stealing the show.

✦

Death was a hard act to follow, and Austin was unsure where to go from here. He removed his hat and held it over his heart.

"I am sorry to bring you the details of this terrible news, Papa, but you have got to know that Laredo was thinking of you and of Mama when he died. That is my tale of woe, and I thank you all for listening."

Austin turned and looked at Jack, then back at the audience.

"What do you say we get on with the show?"

CHAPTER 26

"HERE'S THE PLAN." Buck said to Jimmy Chan.

The two had scaled the inside rails of the bull riding release chute and were presently climbing over the release gate. Before jumping down, Buck surveyed the landscape. The brightly lit wrestling ring was between them and the bleachers. A large open area separated them from the stage. Their position was in relative darkness. But the closer they came to the ring, the more visible they would become. Fortunately for Buck, three orange plastic barrels remained from the Miss Mariposa barrel race. Each was large enough for a crouching man to hide behind. Buck jumped to the ground. He wore Chan's hoodie and held the Native American prayer stick like a staff.

"I'm going in," Buck said in a low voice. He closed the collar around his neck and pulled the hood up over his head. "If anything bad happens, you back me up!"

"Right. I go with you," Chan said.

"No, no, you cover me!"

"Right. I cover you." Chan saluted Buck.

Buck crouched low as he moved cautiously toward the first barrel. Halfway there he became aware of his cook walking alongside.

"No! I go first."

"You go first?"

"You stay behind! The barrels are only big enough to hide one person at a time. I go first. You stay!"

"Right. I stay. You go."

Buck ran to the first barrel and ducked behind it. Chan followed close behind, then, seeing that there was only room for one, he ran ahead to the second barrel.

"What the...? Chan!"

Chan saw Buck waving at him and ran back to the first barrel.

"Chan. I go first, you cover me!"

"Right."

Buck ran to the second barrel and Chan beat him there.

"What is it about this plan that is so difficult to comprehend, Chan?"

"I cover you."

"From behind."

"Right."

Buck took off for the third barrel. As he drew nearer to the stage, the light around him grew perceptively brighter and there was increasing danger of being seen. He kept his body as low as possible as he traversed the most dangerous leg of the trip. Chan scurried along behind. Buck ducked behind the barrel and Chan plowed into him, knocking both Buck and the barrel over. The cook landed on top.

"What is your problem?"

"Jimmy Chan cover Buck LeGrande," Chan said. He stood to salute his boss and Buck pulled him down. They lay on the ground behind the tipped barrel and watched.

Chief Tenaya and The Dust Devil were in their respective corners, awaiting the bell to signal the start of their bout. Big Eddie spoke into his microphone and explained the rules of the match.

"This has been promoted as an 'I Quit!' match."

His amplified voice filled the stands and the crowd was shushed to attention.

"Both opponents have agreed beforehand that the match will last until one or the other contestant says into the microphone, 'I quit!' Those two words, and only those two words, will end the match."

✢

By now, Jack would have happily grabbed the microphone from the world's shortest referee and yelled "I quit!" He felt defeated in any number of ways: by the rawness of his forehead caused by the shells in his Indian headdress, the itching of his face under the makeup, the pins-and-needles he felt from the lack of blood flow to his lower extremities. The bottoms of his feet tingled something terrible just standing on them. And he was shivering from the cold. If it wasn't for Kayla standing ringside, the sorry fellow dressed as Chief Tenaya was ready to throw in the towel.

The clang of the bell woke him from his misery. Austin moved to the center of the ring and Jack followed suit. He figured that Austin was going to give him his first cue, so he locked up arms with the man, just as they had practiced.

"Tried to upstage me, did you?" Austin asked. Austin hooked his leg around Jack's ankle and tripped him backwards. Jack fell to the ground.

BOOM! went the sound from the microphone positioned under the platform.

"Hey!"

"Nothing personal, but nobody upstages me."

Jack was slow to get up. The audience was jeering him to exact retribution.

Austin ran up hard against the ropes. He turned his back into the hemp retaining cords and was repelled even more forcefully back. No sooner was Jack standing than Austin knocked him to the mat again.

BOOM!

Apparently, any thoughts of letting Jack win the bout were on hold. Austin unleashed an arsenal of maneuvers. Jack fell victim to the big splash, the body avalanche, the vertical press, even the tilt-a-whirl crossbody. He endured a broncobuster and an overhead chop as well as Austin's signature crooked-arm lariat. The action was punctuated by another BOOM! each time Jack was pummeled to the mat.

Jack was on his knees. His headdress felt more and more like a crown of thorns. He gave Kayla an anguished look.

✦

Austin turned to see who Jack was looking at and saw the expression on Kayla's face. Kayla's eyes met his and his resolve to humiliate Jack faltered. He'd taken this retribution business a bit too far. Having the crowd against him was part of the show. He was resigned to his heel status. But to be seen as a bully in the eyes of Kayla was something else entirely.

"Had enough?" Austin asked Jack. He stood before his crouching opponent and offered the lad a hand up. Jack was slow to accept. When he did, he did so cautiously. Jack took Austin's hand and pounced. His tights were like a secret weapon. They thrust him upward with a force that caught Austin by surprise and overcame him. Jack yanked Austin's arm behind his back. He twisted it around as far as it would go and then twisted it a little bit farther.

"Ow!"

"Had enough?" Jack asked. Then he flipped Austin on his back. "Boom!"

Jack ran up hard against the ropes and they sent him flying back at Austin, flattening the wrestler before he could defend himself.

"Boom!"

The amplified sound from the mic went a long way toward firing up the crowd and that energy galvanized Jack. He unleashed his own arsenal of attacks. The momentum of the bout had turned in his favor, and he didn't let up.

Now it was Austin's turn to feel like he'd had enough. His aching neck was screaming at him. Austin hadn't been in a real match in years, and he'd forgotten something fundamental about real hand-to-hand combat. Whether it was a charging bull or an irate wrestler, at any time in life the stakes could suddenly become high.

He also knew that high up above the bleachers, Vic was watching.

＋

Vic made his living promoting gimmicks. No matter how successful he was over the years, he knew that show business was a fickle enterprise; success was hit or miss. Every baby-faced wrestler who faced a heel in the ring was essentially just another a rodeo clown facing down a bull. The art of Vic was to present to the audience a clown that they could get behind and a bull that they respected. It wasn't always easy and it wasn't always successful. In show business, the rule of thumb was that good must ultimately triumph over evil. That's what kept the marks tuning in and coming back.

It was Vic's job to create a scenario of ill will between Chief Tenaya and Austin Sway, between the Native American Indian and the American Cowboy. So far he hadn't come up with much. Their storyline was weak; basically the two wrestlers didn't like each other. They were reported to be mortal enemies, but nobody ever said why.

In the nine months since Vic introduced their rivalry, there had been something lackluster about the matchup. Even as recently as last night, the audience in Vegas was ambivalent. Some were ardently rooting for the cowboy and others were squarely in the camp of the Indian, but the majority was on the fence. They didn't know who to root for.

"Hey, redskin!" Vic heard someone yell.

High up in the booth, the implacable face of Vic came to life. His eyebrows tightened and he listened. Verbal arguments were breaking out between factions in the bleachers below him, and Vic strained to parse their meaning. Any number of folks in Mariposa could have filled him in on animosity between Chief Tenaya and the White man. Now it was manifest before his eyes.

Vic sensed something new. He hadn't gotten to where he was today without taking certain risks. It was at times like these, when the audience was at odds with itself, that the wrestling business got dicey. It flew in the face of formula, but wherever emotions got hot there was an issue to uncover and exploit.

The plight of the Indian had for many years supplanted the earlier celebration of the cowboy settlers who supplanted them. These days, schools across the continent taught the injustice wrought upon the Native American and scant praise was given to the bravery and guile it took to wipe them out. A museum of the Forty-Niners in downtown Mariposa preserved much of the detritus of that bygone era. Few world travelers paid the entrance fee.

Vic sensed that things were changing. There was a cultural clash of ideology afoot, a war of civil mistrust. Like a house divided, two conflicting scenarios could not stand without a fight. Presumably the two sides would inevitably merge. In the interim, there was strife. He could hear it in the stands as each camp claimed the other was touting alternate truths. Vic was more than happy to personify both sides in the likes of a cowboy and an Indian sporting multicolored spandex tights head-locked in the debate. The ever-evolving goal was to create a more perfect union. In the short term, where there was adversity, Vic knew there was money to be made. He was a provocateur.

✦

Austin lay on the mat, dazed. Big Eddie reached for the microphone, ready to broadcast the fateful words that would end the match. Austin wasn't too sure he wanted it to end.

This evening's bout had turned real. It awakened in him the long dormant joy of battle. And with that feeling came an epiphany: what took the life out of his life's work was the numbing reality that the outcomes of all his wrestling matches were predetermined. When it came to pro wrestling, there was no free will. There was no battle, no strategy, only pratfalls. Physical prowess in this profession was merely a physical affectation. There was no reward for hard work. By taking steroids, Austin wasn't cheating. The game was already fixed by Vic, the big guy in the booth upstairs, this flim-flam man, this despot of an authoritarian ruler whose brand was built at the expense of other people's decline. Back in the day when Austin and Laredo were barrel men, danger was true danger. They didn't have some puppeteer like Vic up there, script in his hand, pulling the strings and calling the shots. Their fates were true Fates cast at the whim of an irrational, irate bull.

Maybe it was the venue and the warm homecoming he had received. He just didn't feel like losing. Or maybe it was having his father in the audience for the first time. To a large extent it was probably because he was sick of being told what to do. Whatever the reason, Austin wasn't in the mood to resign. If Jack wanted to win this bout, he would have to do it fair and square.

From his days as a rodeo clown, Austin knew that pure athleticism was not enough to empower a man to outrun a bull. Twelve hundred pounds of muscle and mass punctuated by sharp, unforgiving horns was a force of nature. It took agility to sidestep and caginess to outmaneuver the brutishness that life dished out. At times, only a barrel stood between him and the Angel of Death. This was the drama that people paid to see.

A sculpture from one of the world's earliest theatrical events survived from the Bronze Age. It depicted a Minoan man doing a backflip over the horns of a charging bull. The figurine was a metaphor of the human struggle against the forces of destruction that haunt our sleep and compel us to get up every day to fight the good fight, to dodge and duel the muddled obstacles that confront and confound us throughout the day and over the course of our lifetime. There were bulls in everyone's life that they could not outrun, bulls that they must turn to face with enough poise to dodge and outmaneuver.

Austin resolved then and there to take control of his life. If he fell on his face, he had only himself to blame. He needed to pick himself back up, dust the dirt off with his hat and move on, knowing that in no small way his fate was in his own hands. He saw now what had been clear to his twin brother all along. *Amor fati* didn't mean to embrace one's predetermined fate. It meant to live freely within the constraints of our world. This was the truth he wanted to convey to the crowd. We were all in a dance with death. It was the dance that mattered.

✦

"Had enough?" Jack asked, again.

This was an 'I Quit!' match. Jack needed to do more than pin his opponent. He had to wear him down to the point of submission.

Jack did his grizzly bear imitation just like Kayla taught him and he got a laugh. He was Chief Tenaya to them. When Austin stood up, Jack wrapped him in a bear hug, the most arcane of wresting moves. It was the only thing Jack could think of to do. He locked his hands around his opponent and squeezed. Then he lifted the cowboy off the ground and shook him from side to side. Truth be told, this move only worked when the wrestler using it was substantially larger than his opponent. Jack's action produced some pain, but its chiropractic results could not be overstated. Jack felt a series of pings and pops go up Austin's back as his opponent's spine came back into alignment. He released his hold, immediately fearing that he had injured the man.

Austin stumbled back. He rolled his neck around and his range of motion seemed to be greatly restored.

"Thanks, pardner," Austin said.

✦

Austin ran to the far ropes and climbed to the second level. Then he froze. He had thought about doing this move last night during the Pay-Per-View in Vegas, then thought the better of it. He had been in a similar position earlier in the day, balanced precariously on the handrail overlooking the parking lot of the Best Western Hotel in Bakersfield. Only this time, instead of looking down on his car, he looked down into the rodeo ring and saw a hooded figure standing up from behind a rodeo barrel. The shadow-faced figure was shaking a wooden staff at him.

"No way!" Austin yelled at the Angel of Death.

He looked back. Jack was closing in fast. There was only one way out.

We are all going to die, Austin told himself, but he was damned if he was going to do it passively. In one fluid motion, he stepped up to the third level and launched himself into an aerial back flip over his advancing opponent. Half way around, Austin's hands landed squarely on Jack's shoulders, forcing Jack down into a crouching position while Austin sailed overhead. He landed squarely on his feet. The crowd went wild.

Jack clambered to his feet to face Austin. Unfortunately, his tights declined the mission.

To be fair, the material was old. It had seen better days. These were a Little Person's tights, and Big Eddie hadn't wrestled in years. But even still, what was it with today's modern materials? Spandex was a miracle of modern technology. Yet, not unlike Buck LeGrande's double-faced toupee tape, when Jack's elastane tights surrendered, they surrendered unequivocally. They gave up the ghost, admitted defeat, capitulated to the stresses of old age and remained a clump around Jack's ankles. If the tights could talk, they would have yelled "I quit!," so broken was their spirit.

The tone of the evening shifted dramatically. Animosity and anger gave way to laughter. Jack stood naked for the second time tonight, this time for all to see. The cameraman captured his posterior for posterity. Jack pulled the feather headdress from his head and covered himself.

Big Eddie stepped up quickly, microphone in hand, its audio cable snaking across the ring, ready to officiate over Jack's resignation.

CHAPTER 27

SHOW BUSINESS WAS never a precise undertaking. No matter how buttoned-up the production company, there were always unforeseen events. On any given night any number of things could go wrong. Jack was not the first person in the world to find himself the victim of a wardrobe failure. He tried to gather the material in his fist and lift it up while still covering himself with the feather headdress. Admitting defeat was just a formality.

As Big Eddie approached, a new contestant climbed to the third rope of the ring.

BunnyLee yelled, "Austin, look out!"

Puddles jumped from BunnyLee's arms and ran to the edge of the ring, barking wildly.

Austin turned and saw the hooded figure towering above him. The figure took a swipe at Austin with the prayer stick and missed. His hood fell back.

"Buck!" BunnyLee yelled.

Buck lost his balance and fell onto the road-weary wrestler. He grabbed his nemesis around the neck and held on.

"Ow! What the...?"

"Buck!" BunnyLee yelled again. "Stop! You've got it all wrong!"

Austin grabbed hold of Big Eddie's shoulder for support and Big Eddie grabbed Jack's arm. The mass of flailing arms spun around in circles, wrapping itself in audio cable.

"Buck! It's not what you think!"

BunnyLee climbed into the ring.

✦

Frankie saw the cameraman unclip the camera from its tripod and hoist it onto his shoulder with the clear intention of going run-and-gun. The former linebacker stepped in front of the lens to block his shot. Frankie knew first-hand the damage caused by Buck's *Sesame Street* outtake and he wasn't about to let history repeat. "Where do you think you're going?" he asked the man.

"Hey, let him go!" Rebekah said, "We're with the press!"

As the cameraman attempted to slip around, Frankie tripped him and the portly man fell with his camera to the dirt.

✦

Jimmy Chan stood behind the elevated wrestling ring and covered Buck with his gun. He loved holding this gun, this symbol of American freedom and individualism. He twirled it on his trigger finger like a gunslinger.

He shouted, "Ladies and Gentle Men. At no time in history of professional sport is such important fight. At one corner, Austin Sway, the Dust Devil! And fight him, first time in ring, Nick Derringer, aka Top Dog!"

Chan feigned shooting his gun, "Pow! Pow!" He blew virtual smoke from the barrel then aimed the gun again. "Go ahead, make my day!"

Buck rode Austin's shoulders in a move that the wrestling aficionado might call a cross between the "helicopter" and the "bucking bronco." Austin spun his sneak attacker around in circles. Buck held on tight.

✦

Austin stopped himself from tossing his assailant over the ropes when he caught sight of BunnyLee. Best to just ride this out, he told himself.

✦

Clinging to Austin's neck with one arm, Buck swung his prayer stick wildly. He wasn't trying to hit anybody, only trying to regain his balance, but the effect was the same.

BunnyLee stood before the swarming mass of men.

"Jack!" She yelled, "Jack, do something!"

There wasn't much Jack could do. In one hand he covered his crotch with the feather headdress, with the other he pulled up at the clump of tights around his ankles.

BunnyLee ducked to avoid being hit by Buck's flailing prayer stick as the mass of four men rotated in front of her. Coming around behind, the tail end of it clipped her between the shoulder blades. She went plummeting into the ropes. The ropes relented and then rejected her just as willfully. She came careening back into the thick of it. The second time in she got whacked in the stomach and the force brought her to the mat. "Boom!" was the sound from the microphone underneath.

Puddles was beside herself. A mere pup, she was not able to jump into the ring. She ran under the platform and began to howl. She raised her head high and opened her throat full. Her young voice was loud, deafeningly loud as it was made ever so much louder by the specialty mic aimed up at the mat. Through the wonder of amplification, Puddles' voice reverberated across the valley.

"BunnyLee!" Buck yelled as he caught sight of BunnyLee sprawled out on the mat.

Chan moved closer and followed the action with the barrel of his gun.

The tangle of audio cable was tightening. Austin couldn't move either of his feet.

"Get this guy off me!"

✦

Jack tried to grab Buck, but the only thing he came up with was his hair. Buck's new roll of name brand double-faced tape held much better than the generic variety from the night before. But Jack's grasp was firm. He yanked and the hairpiece popped off. Jack held it up to see what it was before tossing it away.

If there was ever any doubt among the general public whether Buck LeGrande's hair was his own, irrefutable evidence to the contrary was now on full display. Hollywood's best-kept secret was now unmasked. That area of his body that never saw the light of day now glowed under the harsh theatrical Fresnels. It looked as if Buck had gone to The Final Frontier spa and gotten one of their trademark bleaching treatments.

✦

Frankie winced at the sight of Buck onstage without his hair for the whole world to see. There was little he could do to protect Buck from humiliation. Among those in the crowd who were whooping it up, and there were many, those on the Native American side were hooting loudest. They were getting their money's worth watching the White man get scalped. They hadn't seen that one coming.

✦

Chan struck a series of poses from vintage Hollywood movies. He followed the action in the ring with his gun, saying with an English accent, "The name is Chan. James Chan."

Running full stride, Kayla yelled, "Don't shoot!" She blindsided the Cantonese cook. She knocked the pistol out of his hand, but not before it went off. On stage, the wrestlers all fell to the mat in a clump. The gun flew under the stage and out the side where it came to rest at Brokenclaw's feet. The off-duty game warden stooped to pick it up.

✦

BunnyLee was dazed. She saw stars. Literally. The clear mountain sky was awash in them. She leaned her head against the corner turnbuckle of the lowest rope.

Austin and Jack were hogtied by the audio cable and Jack, doubly so, by the tights. Neither could get up. Big Eddie wiggled free. He captured the official words from Austin and Jack as together they said "I quit!" into the microphone. Big Eddie grabbed Buck's arm, raised it over his head, and declared Buck the winner.

Kayla climbed in under the ropes and helped set Jack and Austin free.

Buck rushed to BunnyLee.

CHAPTER 28

BUNNYLEE LAY BY the corner stanchion and looked up at the heavens.

"You okay?" Buck asked.

"It was Puddles you saw in the cabana last night. I wasn't with anyone."

"That's not what I saw."

"Puddles was the man in the Stetson hat."

"Then who the hell is that?" Buck asked. He pointed at Austin. Austin, Jack and Big Eddie were unwinding themselves from the audio cable.

"He's someone I met who helped me out. I only met him today."

"Today? You signed the guest register together!"

"Because somebody cancelled my credit cards!"

"I saw you kiss him! And you ate an Acorn Dog! Which, by the way, contains meat!"

"You crossed a picket line to buy a dog!"

"Who told you that?"

"My friend Rebekah. She was there. She's the reporter who interviewed you at the pet store."

"I wanted to get you something nice."

"And you did. Puddles is the nicest gift. Then you slept with Jadé!"

"Is that why you left?"

"I didn't leave!"

"Then what are we doing way out here?"

"I came to cure Puddles. I would never have left without saying goodbye. You were mad at me because I laughed this morning, but I didn't mean it to sound like that. This whole thing about your hair... I wanted you to know that it didn't matter. But I should never have laughed. And I shouldn't have taken your car."

"I don't care about the car. By the way, here's your phone and your change purse. You left them in the Bentley."

"Thanks."

"I didn't want you to leave."

"You wanted me to stay?"

"Wait a minute! Not so fast! You crashed my tennis party! There is no way you could have known who the Klingons were because they only appear in costume!"

"You're right."

"I am? You did? Really? Why?"

"I got the directions wrong. I went to the wrong address. I was supposed to be in the game across the street at the Shpielman's house. I stood them up."

"You were subbing at Evan Shpielman's? I've been trying to get into that game for twenty years! Wow, you really missed out!"

"That's what Rebekah said, too. But then I would never have met you."

"Does that mean you'll reconsider falling in love with me?"

"Oh, gosh. I have so many doubts, so many unanswered questions."

"Like what?"

"Well, we never talked about it, but everybody asks..."

"What?"

"...about Kermit the Frog."

"Oh. That. What do you want to know?"

"I didn't have the heart to look it up online. You've been so kind and generous. But from what everybody tells me, you strangled him. People ask and I guess I just need to know, what happened between you and Kermit the Frog?"

"It was just a reaction, BunnyLee. He was messing with my hair and I was afraid he'd pull my hairpiece off. BunnyLee, anyone would have done the same. I couldn't lose my hair. Not on camera."

"And that's when you decided to murder Kermit?" Tammy asked through a mouthful of popcorn.

"Huh?"

A group of people was forming around Buck and BunnyLee. They were standing on the ground outside the ropes. Rebekah was plugging in her microphone to catch what Buck and BunnyLee were saying. Her cameraman stood behind her, capturing the event on digital.

"Kermit the Frog is a puppet, for Godsakes! All I did was grab the puppeteer's wrist! He wasn't even the guy who normally did Kermit. I'll admit that when they played the clip back in slo-mo it looked pretty violent, but I have an image to protect, BunnyLee."

"Mr. LeGrande, have you been shot?" Rebekah asked. She was referring to a spot on his backside that looked like a wound oozing red through his trousers.

"I would never hurt anyone. BunnyLee, you need to know that!"

"Yeah, right!" Tammy said.

"Excuse me, but I'm having a private conversation here!" Buck said.

"I'm just calling it the way I see it." Tammy said.

"This is none of your business," BunnyLee said.

"Of course it's my business!" Tammy shouted. "You're stars. Everything you do is my business."

"No, it's not!" BunnyLee said, "Go away!"

"I'm not going anywhere. It's is a free country."

"Don't pay any attention to her," Buck said. "Listen, I just need to know, was it Archie?"

"What are you talking about?"

"I know you took Puddles to see him about her teeth."

"That's no secret."

"So it was Archie in your room last night?"

"Yuck! No! I told you! It was Puddles! Don't you get it? I was taking a picture of her in her sheriff costume to email to her agent last night. The lamp was on the floor. When Poodles stood on her hind legs, the shadow on the wall of her in her Stetson made her look ten feet tall!"

"Puddles has an agent?"

"Of course she does. But you have to know! I would never have done that. I would never have had a man over like that."

"It's not like I have the right to ask you not to."

"I would never have."

Rebekah tapped Buck with her microphone. "No, seriously, Mr. LeGrande. I think you've been shot."

"What's she talking about?" BunnyLee asked, sitting forward. "Rebekah, what are you talking about?"

"It looks to me like he's been shot, BunnyLee. I heard a gun go off."

"There was a Chinese man with a gun..." Kayla said.

"It's only a scratch," Buck assured everyone.

"No, it's not," Rebekah said.

"Show me where!" BunnyLee said.

Rebekah pointed to what looked very much like a bullet hole in his pant leg.

"Buck! You've got to get help! Somebody get help!"

"The ambulance crew is all on the Tilt-a-Whirl," Jack said.

"Jack, could you go?"

"O.K," he said without hesitation, but then thought about the logistics. "Gosh, I wish I had my clothes."

"Go! Hurry! Please hurry!"

Jack climbed out of the ring. He gathered the waistband of his tights up around his stomach with both hands and ran.

"I'm okay, really," Buck said. "Although I do feel a bit lightheaded."

"Oh, Buck, I've really made a mess of things."

"I'm sorry, BunnyLee," Rebekah interrupted, "but you're part of the story now."

"What do you mean? Rebekah, are you outing me?"

"I think everybody should just relax while I take a nap here," Buck said.

"Look, he's passing out!" Tammy said, between mouthfuls. "He was aimin' at whackin' BunnyLee and turns out he's the one got whacked!"

Frankie lifted Puddles up onto the mat. She was still wearing her Stetson and sheriff's badge and she carried Buck's toupee in her mouth. Puddles dropped Buck's hairpiece by his side and nudged him to pick it up. Then the dog sneezed.

"I came all the way up here to try to get Puddles some help and everything has gone wrong. Meanwhile, I never found the Native American dog whisperer."

"That would be me."

Officer Brokenclaw stood outside their corner and looked in.

"Oh, please, not you again!" Buck groaned.

"You're the dog whisperer?" BunnyLee asked.

"If you believe what they say in the brochure."

"Then can you tell me why my dog has been having these sneezing fits?"

"We see a lot of that with certain breeds. It's more of a problem in the country, of course. Now my friend Jack there, who went for help? He raises dogs on his ranch."

"Jack raises dogs?" Kayla asked.

"You see it more with the pedigrees. They're allergic to his cows."

"I don't think Puddles has ever even seen a cow before tonight."

"Oh, yes, every day! Mr. Buck wear bovine cow on head!" Chan said.

"What?"

"Hairpiece fashion from baby yak hair. Fashion from wild Himalaya Mountain longhair bovine cow."

"Hey, I pay a lot for those things," Buck said.

"Very nice, baby yak hair. Very fine. Eighteen micron!"

"So you're saying I'm the cause of Puddles' sneezing?" Buck asked.

"Not you. Hair on head."

"Buck, you don't need that thing," BunnyLee added gently.

"I can't afford to look old. When you met me, you thought I was in prime time. But I'm in re-runs, BunnyLee." He was clearly having trouble keeping his eyes open.

"Like I'm getting any younger?"

"I love you, BunnyLee," he said, "I want you to marry me. Will you do that for me?"

"Are you proposing to her?" Tammy asked.

Buck nodded.

"You're asking me to marry you?"

It was incomprehensible that her chance encounter with Buck would lead to this. The question itself seemed impertinent. And BunnyLee was a firm believer that proposals like this should be posed in private. Feelings were a private matter. Intimacy was a private matter. How else could one be sure that one's heart was true?

She was wary of Buck's stardom, and she was wary of her own modest renown. Celebrity trampled privacy these days; now everybody's personal business seemed to be everybody else's business, too. When had the line between privacy and publicity become so blurred? Nowadays, inner life was a liability. The whole world seemed willing to make the trade for fame, but she knew deep down that such a deal was risky: kind of like selling your soul or a piece of your heart. Could you ever buy it back?

BunnyLee looked from face to face. Buck's recovery seemed to hang on her reply. Austin nodded. Chan bounced up and down. Frankie looked away. She wanted to say what she felt, but ambivalence was out of the question. If he were to die in her arms, she would never forgive herself for dithering.

"How could I say no?" BunnyLee asked, forcing a smile.

"I'll take that as a yes," Buck said.

"I knew it!" Tammy exclaimed.

Buck sang in a fading voice, "Could she woo… could she coo… could she, could she, could she coo…"

His voice trailed away.

"Does it hurt?" BunnyLee asked.

"I don't feel any pain," Buck answered. "It's right, what you said about despair. I was desperate without you and now I'm on the other side of despair. I feel free. But that whole thing with the poem, *Be Drunk!*, that you recited from heart? Be drunk, on wine, poetry or virtue? it didn't work for me. Drinking only made me carsick. And virtue? Forget about that. I'm no monk."

"So I guess that leaves poetry."

"I'm no poet, BunnyLee."

"Poetry is art. That's what I take it to mean. 'Be drunk on art!' Then you don't have time to contemplate mortality. Be drunk on your work!"

"I haven't been working."

"You need to be. Not just for the money."

"I wonder when that kid is coming back. I'm afraid I'm not going to make it."

"No, Buck, hold on! Help is on the way."

"Funny thing, when you're an actor, you always think that your best roles are ahead of you. I always thought I'd take a stab at Shakespeare before I died." With a tinge of irony, Buck recited, "A hit, a palpable hit!"

"Lear?" Brokenclaw asked.

"No! Hamlet, smartass. I was looking forward to doing that new series."

"The Return of Malibu Man?" Frankie asked.

"It's a good part for you, Buck. You could play it for years.

But you'll need to sink your teeth into it and play it to the hilt!"
BunnyLee said. She looked at Frankie who silently thanked her.

"No, this is something brand new. Tell them Chan!"

"Mr. William Morris Agency call. Cast leading role. Top Dog."

"They left a message this morning." Buck pulled the phone
message from his back pocket and handed it to BunnyLee to read.
"They want me," he said.

"Top Dog is a reality show about dogs, Buck," BunnyLee said.
"There aren't any actors in it, just owners with their dogs working
as runway models. They've cast every part except Top Dog.
Puddles auditioned for that role. That's what the callback was for.
When I lost my phone, I gave them your home number."

"The agent call was for Puddles? Not Mr. B?" Frankie asked.
"Then you can do *The Return of Malibu Man*, Boss!"

"I am dead!"

Buck closed his eyes and went limp.

Puddles whimpered and licked Buck's scalp.

BunnyLee started to cry.

Rebekah finished sending a text and pulled out her makeup kit
for some quick touch-up.

With one free hand, Jack led the first aid technician through
the crowd. It was Shirley, the desk clerk from The Reservation. She
was staggering, and it was all that Jack could do to steady her and
keep his tights up, too.

"Mariposa just set the Tilt-A-Whirl world record!" Jack
exclaimed.

"One thousand, three hundred forty-seven revolutions!" the
first responder bragged. She was woozy. She covered her mouth.
"I'm not feeling too good," she said as she took off in search of
some open turf.

"Shirley was the only one still standing," Jack said. "The others
were too dizzy to walk. Oh, golly, did he... die?"

"Is he dead?" Rebekah asked. She was hurriedly brushing her
hair, refreshing her lipstick, applying eyeliner.

"Rebekah, we're on in ten!" her cameraman alerted her.
He switched on a light mounted directly over his lens and it
illuminated Rebekah's face.

Rebekah lifted her microphone and held her expression until
she received her cue. The live feed from the anchor in L.A. on the
monitor broke the silence.

"Five...four...three..." the cameraman counted down. He signaled the last two seconds with his fingers, and then gave her the prompt that she was on.

The voice of the news L.A. anchor said, "For this late-breaking story, we take you live to Mariposa where our own Eyewitness News reporter, Rebekah Brinkley, is standing by. Hello, Rebekah, this is a big story. You're on with our affiliate stations coast to coast. Is it true that Buck LeGrande has been shot?"

"Yes, Alex. The events leading up to this heartrending story are sketchy, but it seems that the famous actor was hit while appearing in a celebrity tag-team wrestling match with his female partner, BunnyLee Welles. His guest appearance was not on the program so it has taken us all by surprise. In what was shaping up to be the feel-good story of the night, with all these celebrities coming out for a good cause, the icing on the cake was this unlikely duo beating both Austin Sway and Chief Tenaya. Then things turned tragic. A gunman stepped out of the shadows and shot the star for no apparent reason."

"Okay, Rebekah, stay with the story," said the anchor in the newsroom. "We're going to be coming back to you again live right after this from our sponsor." On the monitor, anyone who cared to listen heard the distinctive voice of BunnyLee Wells pitching Dial-a-Denture.

The real-life BunnyLee sat with Buck. Puddles nestled in between. She heard herself delivering her famous lines during the commercial break and she buried her head in Buck's chest. She couldn't bear to even look up and allow her tear-streaked face to become the news-cycle image of tragedy.

Jimmy Chan tugged at the news reporter's sleeve and whispered, "He not dead. He sleeping."

"This is real, Chan!" Frankie chided the cook. "Not make-believe." Frankie's screenwriting hopes were clearly dashed at this unforeseen turn of events. "Don't come actin' like you don't know what happen and you start the whole thing!"

"Not real. Pop gun!"

"The cook is right," the fish and game warden said. "It was a tranquilizing gun. There was enough sedative in there to take down a wild buck, and I don't mean the human kind."

"What?" BunnyLee asked, raising her head at this glimmer of hope.

"So who shot him?" Rebekah asked.

"The shot went off by accident," Kayla said. "I…"

"Unlike other guns of this type, the bullet collapses when it strikes the fur…or skin in this case. The sedative is drawn immediately into the bloodstream. There will be some bleeding, but minimal penetration."

"So he's not dead?" Rebekah asked.

"How long'll he sleep?" Frankie asked.

"Normally I would say ten to twelve hours. Unless he's had something to drink today."

"Oh, yes, starting with breakfast," Chan said.

"In that case, it could be a lot longer."

"He be awake by Monday?" Frankie asked.

"Yeah, I'd say by Monday morning, sure. They're very docile, for starters. Before the hangover sets in."

"Awake enough to sign his name?"

"I expect he'd sign anything you put in front of him."

"That's good enough for me!" Frankie said.

"So, he's alive?" Rebekah asked.

Buck lifted his head and began mumbling something. BunnyLee bent her head to listen.

"He's says he's not signing anything unless there's a part in it for Rex West. What's that…? A recurring part, not some secondary part, either. He says Rex gets to play the villain."

Buck's head dropped back into BunnyLee's lap.

"I can work with that," Frankie said.

The cameraman flipped on the obie light and was again counting down from five. Rebekah lifted her mic and held for her cue.

"Events are changing rapidly here in Mariposa, Alex," she reported. "It would appear that news of Buck LeGrande's death is premature. Although his condition is grave, by all accounts he will live to ride again. So we can all breathe a collective sigh of relief. And we can look forward to him appearing in a brand-new series called *The Return of Malibu Man*. We also have some exclusive footage, and this is going to come as a shock to many of our female audience. Buck LeGrande, the infamous Hollywood heartthrob, our town's most eligible bachelor, has gotten engaged. He drove all the way up here today just to pop the question." The cameraman panned to a two-shot of BunnyLee cradling Buck's head in her arms. "We have the whole proposal on tape. I think it's cued up. Can we cut to that now, Alex?"

BunnyLee felt she had no choice but to look squarely into the lens and say the words, "Hi Mom, hi Dad" before the cue light went out and they went to the videotape.

CHAPTER 29

THE STAGEHANDS HEFTED road boxes into the equipment truck. Frankie went for the Bentley. Rebekah and her cameraman wrapped things up in their production van. Tammy hung around the news crew demanding an account of all the famous people they had ever met.

✦

"Is this yer dad?" Kayla asked Austin. He was standing off to the side talking with an older man. She held her hand out for the elder Mr. Sway to shake. "Hi, I'm Kayla."

"Always happy to meet a pretty girl."

"I am pleased to meet you, too." She turned to Austin. "I come to say that if I was to ever get a ranch, however big or small, you will always be welcome there. That goes for you, too, Grandpa."

"Grandpa?" the elder man repeated. "Whoa! I don' think that honor's in the cards for me."

"I'm afraid you're missing the point here, Pop," Austin said. "She means for real."

"Huh?"

"Whereas it was never clear who my own pa is," Kayla said, "who my grandpa is was never in doubt."

"What's going on here, Austin?"

"By the looks of things, and if we are to believe her mother over there, there is a distinct possibility that you have a granddaughter.

I only met her tonight. But check out those eyes. Don't they look like Mama's?"

"So you're sayin' she's your daughter?"

"Or otherwise his niece. It's even money," Kayla said, "Though if you look here on the top of my head, my hair parts the same side as his, so that tips the scale in Austin's favor for bein' my dad. Either way you're definitely my grandpa. I suppose yer as proud of bein' his relation as I am."

"I've had a lot to prove in life to live up to this man," Austin said. He studied his father for a trace of atonement.

"I expect you've proven a lot, son. Though there's much to your story that I'm just as happy not knowing."

Austin thought he saw a crinkle of forgiveness around the eyes of that otherwise fearsome face. There was more than an ounce of irony to the fact that, the very night at the Golden Nugget that he and Laredo had broken with their dad, Kayla was conceived. And now, almost two decades since, she stood to bridge the schism that had formed between them. *Amor fati.*

"Kayla was asking me earlier about getting into show business. I guess it's in her genes," Austin said, turning to answer Kayla. "If that's what you want, you can come along. You can get your Uncle Eddie to book you your itinerary."

Kayla's attention was divided. She had her eye on the back of the equipment truck. She watched Jack hop down to the ground with his street clothes on. "That will be amazing. My mom has a dealing job lined up in Tahoe, so she's gonna follow along. But I'm gonna ride with you."

Austin watched Kayla looking at Jack. "I'm not in a position to dole out advice, but if there is one thing I have learned along the way it is that love is a commodity that's in short supply. It's not something to casually turn your back on. I have half a mind to retrace my steps to a woman named Kat I met today."

"Thanks," Kayla said. She jogged over to catch Jack before he left. "You were right about those bein' my Uncle Eddie's pants," she said to him.

"That's O.K. It all worked out, I guess."

"And I am truly sorry I bit your tongue. That was just me pretendin' to be a grizzly."

"It didn't hurt too bad."

"You sure looked swell up there. Shame none of these folks

here knew it was you."

"There's a not a soul in Mariposa who doesn't know that it was me up there on stage tonight," Jack said. "It's not somethin' I'm gonna live down any time soon."

"Well, okay then. This is a recognition that you deserve, because folks should know that you saved the day."

"And made an ass of myself to boot."

"I think you are somethin' else! I think maybe you have a future in show business. I could ask my dad to ask Vic."

"I don't think so."

"You sure?" Kayla asked. "Because I think I'm gonna ride along with him for a spell."

"If that's what you want."

"It's what I set out to do."

"Then you should."

"I was hoping maybe you wanted to come along, too."

"Me? Nah. Afraid I've had my fill of show business."

"It would only be for a while because, like I said, it's what I set out to do."

"You've got to do what you've got to do."

"That's what I'm tryin' to sort out. Followin' my heart is not that easy when it's split. It all depends."

"Depends on what?"

"Okay, here goes. It depends on what my feelings mean. I guess what I'm askin' is, because there ain't a lot of time to be beatin' around the sagebrush here, I guess what I mean is, I want to know how much business there was between you and me that we left unfinished back here in this equipment truck. Because once I leave, I don't suppose either one of us is ever gonna know."

"A fair amount, I expect."

"I was thinkin' the same. I am only fixin' to be gone a spell. I just want to get to know the man. I am gonna write you."

Jack shrugged.

"And I want you to know that yer havin' a ranch and all, and the fact that you raise dogs, I just want you to know that it's just you that's got my heart all tied up in a knot. That other stuff is just extra special. There, I said it."

"I'm glad you did."

"So, now I want to kiss you for real."

✦

"Hamburger, hotdog. All yang, no yin. How you win like that?" Jimmy Chan asked as he jabbed his forefinger into Austin's stiff joints.

"Ouch! Hey, cut it out! Who are you?"

Chan saluted the famous wrestler, "Jimmy Chan, Chinese Cook, at your service. Mr. Austin much like famous Chinese wrestler Gorilla Monsoon. Gorilla Monsoon insisted everything. Very hard to listen to other. He insisted oxtail spicy noodle. During year of dog, every time big match begin, Gorilla Monsoon shout, 'Give me bowl oxtail spicy noodle, Chan!' After match, Gorilla Monsoon always excited to say, 'I win because I eat oxtail spicy noodle. Give me oxtail spicy noodle every day, I win every day.' This A-number one dish Gorilla Monsoon love."

"You cooked for Gorilla Monsoon?" Austin asked.

"No." Jimmy Chan laughed, and then continued in earnest, "Great Uncle Chan. Long time ago in Manchuria Province."

"Manchurian Province?"

"Mr. Austin famous like Gorilla Monsoon. A-number-one wrestler. You need Jimmy Chan play supporting role on great America road adventure, ride shotgun, cook differing food group, win every day."

Officer Brokenclaw came up from behind and put his arm around the cook's shoulder. He spoke with the authority of a western sheriff. "In my report I'm going to write that you sedated a wild buck during rutting season, which if you think about it, is essentially what happened. I would choose to omit the part about your having stolen government property. No need to bring inquiry to the fact that I left the squad car unlocked. Meanwhile, I would suggest that you get out of Dodge before that news reporter starts sniffing around."

Jimmy Chan saluted the fish and wildlife warden and thanked him for the largess of Western justice. "Whack whack, every day! Jimmy Chan ride shotgun with Austin Sway. Cook every day. We leave right away, okay?"

"So you need a ride out of town, do you?" Austin said to Chan. "My Pappy and I will be leaving soon enough, along with his granddaughter. I guess we could use a cook. But let's get one thing straight. Gorilla Monsoon was from New York, not Manchuria."

"New York?" Jimmy Chan asked. "Could be. Great Uncle Chan always say, 'Never let truth get in way of good story!'"

✦

With Puddles in her arms, BunnyLee scrolled through her texts.

Frankie arrived with the Bentley and carried Buck to the backseat. Rebekah wrapped her sound cables into a case with her mic.

"I've got three OMG's, two WTF's, eight people wondering whether that was really me, and I haven't even gotten through my email. My whole life is thrown out of whack."

"You're welcome!" Rebekah said.

"For what?"

"For making you famous, this time for real."

"More like a fool for all to see. I really let my emotions get the better of me."

"You love him?"

"Wait a minute! Am I talking to Rebekah my friend or Rebekah the television reporter?"

"Friend."

"Well, friend…Monday, when Buck wakes up, he's going to have forgotten all about this proposal of marriage thing."

"Earth to BunnyLee! Buck LeGrande didn't buy you that dog for nothing. He didn't follow you up here for nothing."

"You don't know the whole story. Buck is a man of the world."

"Would you stop?"

"All his life, women have been tripping over each other for his attention."

"Exactly. But that's not the story. The story here is that he has not pursued any one of those women. Until now. That's the story!"

"I don't know."

"He's the one who jumped in the ring. He took a big risk. He just proposed to you. What more could you ask for? What's in your way? What do you have to lose?"

"My privacy? My pride? My sense of self? My way in the world?"

"None of the above."

"My freedom?"

"The question is, do *you* love *him?*" Rebekah said.

"I don't know. I guess. I mean maybe." BunnyLee started to smile. "I mean, yeah, I know I like him a lot, but..."

"But yeah means yeah," Austin said. He had overheard BunnyLee and Rebekah talking.

"What? Oh, hey, Austin," BunnyLee said. "I thought you'd left already."

Austin tipped his hat to Rebekah, "Ma'am." And then to BunnyLee. "I promised you a ride back to The Reservation, if you're still going that way."

"Thanks. You're the best! I'm gonna ride home with Frankie and Buck. Oh, and here's the money I owe you."

BunnyLee pulled her change purse from her front pocket.

"No," Austin said, "that was on me. So, you're going home?"

"Did I just say that?"

"You did."

"Right. I did. Home. I guess I'll find out soon enough. I'm either the gal who's five times lucky or just a fool for love."

"Or both," Rebekah said.

What others are saying about Five Times Lucky

David Temple's tour de force, Five Times Lucky, is a delicious comic odyssey through the underside of Hollywood's fame game. With a sure hand for deft, cinematic prose and a remarkable ear for dialogue, Temple has crafted vivid characters that are sometimes seedy and always hilarious.
—Jerelle Kraus, *The New York Times*, Art Director

The biggest take-away for the editorial reader is simply how very timely this story is. On the nose, up to the very second of a part of the culture that is being played to perfection in this story. BunnyLee engages the reader from the first sentence. Wonderful story, well told.
—Scott Wolven, *The Writer's Hotel*

ABOUT THE AUTHOR

 P. David Temple was an award-winning commercial Director and Cinematographer in New York and Los Angeles and was a judge in Cinematography for the Emmys. He traveled as a cameraman with the World Wrestling Federation during the heyday of Andre the Giant and Hulk Hogan, video-taping post-match interviews six weeks in advance of the bouts. He is a graduate in Philosophy from The University of Michigan. Other writing credits include *Trade Secrets*, published in <u>The Best Ten-Minute Plays of 2019</u>, by Smith and Kraus, NY. His full-length play The Purple House on Page Street was a finalist in the Eugene O'Neill National Playwrights Conference.

Made in the USA
Middletown, DE
03 December 2020